D1519762

Youthful Preaching

LLOYD JOHN OGILVIE INSTITUTE
OF PREACHING SERIES

SERIES EDITORS:

Mark Labberton
Clayton J. Schmit

The vision of the Lloyd John Ogilvie Institute of Preaching is to proclaim Jesus Christ and to catalyze a movement of empowered, wise preachers who seek justice, love mercy, and walk humbly with God, leading others to join in God's mission in the world. The books in this series are selected to contribute to the development of such wise and humble preachers. The authors represent both scholars of preaching as well as pastors and preachers whose experiences and insights can contribute to passionate and excellent preaching.

OTHER VOLUMES IN THIS SERIES:

The Eloquence of Grace: Joseph Sittler and the Preaching Life edited by James M. Childs Jr. and Richard Lischer

The Preacher as Liturgical Artist: Metaphor, Idenitity, and the Vicarious Humanity of Christ by Trygve David Johnson

Ordinary Preacher, Extraordinary Gospel: A Daily Guide for Wise, Empowered Preachers by Chris Neufeld-Erdman

Decolonizing Preaching: The Pulpit as Postcolonial Space by Sarah A. N. Travis

Bringing Home the Message: How Community Can Multiply the Power of the Preached Word by Robert K. Perkins

Blessed and Beautiful: Multiethnic Churches and the Preaching that Sustains Them by Lisa Washington Lamb

Youthful Preaching

Strengthening the Relationship between
Youth, Adults, and Preaching

Richard W. Voelz

 CASCADE *Books* · Eugene, Oregon

YOUTHFUL PREACHING
Strengthening the Relationship between Youth, Adults, and Preaching

Lloyd John Ogilvie Institute of Preaching Series 7

Cascade Books
An Imprint of Wipf and Stock Publishers
199 W. 8th Ave., Suite 3
Eugene, OR 97401

www.wipfandstock.com

PAPERBACK ISBN: 978-1-62564-533-3
HARDCOVER ISBN: 978-1-4982-8875-0

Cataloging-in-Publication data:

Voelz, Richard W.

Youthful preaching : strengthening the relationship between youth, adults, and preaching / Richard W. Voelz.

x + 214 p. ; 23 cm. —Includes bibliographical references and index(es).

Lloyd John Ogilvie Institute of Preaching Series 7

ISBN 978-1-62564-533-3 (paperback) | ISBN 978-1-4982-8875-0 (hardback)

1. Youth. 2. Preaching to Youth. 3. Youth sermons. 4. Preaching. 5. Pastoral Theology. I. Title. II. Series.

BV4010 V67 2016

Manufactured in the U.S.A.

For Meredith and Elly

Oh! That Good Things might be Produced among our Young People, by our Discourses on them!

—Cotton Mather
The Best Ornaments of Youth
Delivered on September 3, 1706

Contents

Acknowledgments

This book began as my doctoral dissertation as a student in the Graduate Department of Religion at Vanderbilt University. It was not what I had intended to write upon my entrance into the program, but during one of my first-year seminars, I related some of my preaching experiences that centered on young people. Upon the conclusion of my presentation, Professor Brad Braxton exclaimed to me, "That's the book we need!" I admit that I wrestled with what this might mean. As I will show, preaching and youth have not proven to be the coziest partners in contemporary times, nor has there been much, if any, mutual academic interest between the subjects. There is a gap in the literature writ-large concerning these topics and I was concerned with the reception of this material as a topic worthy of ongoing attention. Much to my delight, Professors John S. McClure, Ted A. Smith, Robin M. Jensen, Brad R. Braxton, and Bonnie Miller-McLemore all displayed tremendous enthusiasm for this project, which only served to confirm my "call" (if one can speak of such a thing in the academy—and I think one can) to think and write in this area. Dale P. Andrews came to Vanderbilt at a late stage, rounded out my dissertation committee, and offered his support. Members of the Academy of Homiletics have encouraged me as I engaged them in conversation and presented portions of this material, for which I am thankful.

The Academy of Preachers, led by Dwight A. Moody, came into existence just as I was beginning to write this in its dissertation form. My contact with the Academy, and the young preachers it serves to identify, network, and inspire have served to validate the voice of young preachers for me. A generous scholarship from the Higher Education and Leadership Ministries of the Christian Church (Disciples of Christ) supported the later stages of this work in the dissertation stage.

My fellow students in the Homiletics and Liturgics program at Vanderbilt University functioned as a primary community for these ideas as they formed. Amy Peed McCullough, Katy Rigler, Noel Schoonmaker, Alex Tracy, and Joshua Villines were all invaluable as initial conversation partners. Mark Shivers walked lock-step with me through the program, held me accountable for our mutual progress, and critiqued drafts of the dissertation and this revised project. Gerald Liu, Brandon McCormack, Donna Giver Johnston, and Lisa Thompson provided encouragement as they entered the program. I also owe thanks to the short-lived Atlanta Homiletics Colloquy for reading and offering commentary on chapter one.

The people of Johns Creek Christian Church (Disciples of Christ) encourage their pastor by allowing me to nurture this area of my vocation, for which I am grateful. My wife Meredith has granted me patience, levity, and unwavering support. She continually confirms my call and as an educator she believes in the capacity for young people to do great things. She has provided the assurance that there is wisdom in listening to young people. Thank you.

Finally, I must thank the young people, many of whom I will never meet, who find it compelling to take up Christian and homiletic identities, and who add their voice to the chorus of witnesses to God's good news. I am hopeful that this work will help us to listen to them in ways that serve the ongoing work of proclamation.

Introduction

Commentary about young people rarely exists in short supply and in particular, we need not look far to find plenty of hand-wringing over the future of their faith. Every so often the news cycle witnesses an outpouring of writing on this subject. Within a span of four days in August 2010, three national news items emerged that explored the relationship between youth and adults, and on the relationship between youth, adults, and religion.[1]

The most significant of these reported on the findings of a book about Christian faith among North American adolescents by Kenda Creasy Dean, a well-known scholar on youth and Christianity and professor at Princeton Theological Seminary. In the article, John Blake summarizes Dean's study: "Some critics told Dean that most teenagers can't talk coherently about any deep subject, but Dean says abundant research shows that's not true. 'They have a lot to say,' Dean says. 'They can talk about money, sex and their family relationships with nuance. Most people who work with teenagers know that they are not naturally inarticulate.'"[2] Dean and Blake are referring to the research of Christian Smith and Linda Lundquist Denton, funded by the National Study of Youth and Religion (NSYR). In the study Smith and Denton conclude that young people in America are inarticulate about their faith, characterizing it as innocuous "moral therapeutic deism."[3] Dean acknowledges that the value judgments about young people's faith are

---

1. Blake, "Author: More Teens Becoming 'Fake' Christians," Debusmann, "Older People Enjoy Reading Negative Stories About Young," Betty Rollin, "Interfaith Divorce." See also Kenda Creasy Dean, *Almost Christian*.

2. Blake, "Author," lines 40–42.

3. Smith and Denton, *Soul Searching*.

deeply tied to the way that adults and communities of faith talk about faith with young people. Many young people are, according to Dean, becoming "fake Christians" as a direct result of the character of faith found among their parents and presented by their churches. But she also notes that it is an inappropriate generalization to label young people on the whole as inarticulate about their faith, or as possessing a faith that cannot stand up to the challenges of life. According to Dean, the relationship of youth, adults, and religion in contemporary North American culture is much more complex than it may appear.

This kind of story represents only a very small slice of the representations of youth found in media, culture, and academia. While young people enjoy positive depictions in some representations, others present a more dubious view. There is a palpable ambivalence concerning young people. Despite the characterization of "moral therapeutic deism," Smith and Lundquist Denton's summary of their research into the religious lives of teenagers reveals this kind of ambivalence:

> American teenagers can embody adults' highest hopes and most gripping fears. They represent a radiant energy that opens doors to the future for families, communities, and society. But they also evoke deep adult anxieties about teen rebellion, trouble, and broken and compromised lives. Parents, teachers, and youth workers behold their teenagers with pride, hope, and enjoyment, but also often worry, distress, and frustration. . . . So, many adults worry deeply that, whatever good there is, something may also be profoundly wrong about the lives of American teenagers.[4]

At the heart of their last sentence is a deeply seated fear: fear that adults are doing something wrong, that so-called "secular culture" is a monstrous force bound to consume the goodness of young people, or that perceived goodness is merely a ruse. In today's climate it can be difficult to gain a nuanced understanding of young people and easy to let media-driven representations rule the day.

It does not take long to recognize that the larger cultural discourse surrounding young people and faith most often does little justice to them, increasingly painting them with broad and antagonistic strokes. With the overwhelming presence of ambivalent representations and confusion about young people, how are we to understand, interact, and advocate for them in a responsible way in the arena of religious and theological studies? Bonnie Miller-McLemore frames the issue well:

4. Ibid., 3.

Taking children seriously as a theological subject requires a movement across the conventionally separate disciplines in the study of religion. It requires a circular hermeneutical movement—from an exploration of dilemmas, to an investigation of religious resources, back to renewed practice. This movement includes moments of serious social scientific, historical, biblical, and constructive religious and theological exploration as part of a larger practical theological effort in the public arena. In short, the best way to study moral and religious dilemmas of children and child rearing is from the perspective of practical theology fundamentally refined.[5]

Religious and theological studies possess the critical tools to explore those religious dilemmas concerning children in ways that can make an impact on wider arenas.

Miller-McLemore writes about a burgeoning movement in religious and theological studies that takes children and youth seriously. But in all of these discussions on adolescents and religion, the voices of those who work in preaching are silent. What can account for this? Adolescents act as listeners and preachers each week in Christian congregations across North America. Yet adolescent youth are conspicuously absent as major subjects of homiletic reflection. Unfortunately, this is an area of great neglect, a dilemma that requires investigation and renewed practice. This book is situated precisely in that gap, and strives to be an example of the kind of practical theological study Miller-McLemore describes.

Some of the resources for this practical theological work are already in place, as we will see. Homiletics as an academic discipline has made a concerted effort over the past generation to address and be addressed by underrepresented groups. No longer is the adult, white, middle-class male the sole voice in preaching and developing homiletic theory. Instead, homiletics has followed a similar, if delayed, trajectory as American theology, which has been informed by African-American liberation theology movements, feminist and womanist theologies, Latin American liberation theologies, Asian and Asian-American theologies, multiculturalism and pluralism, disability studies, postcolonialism, and other intellectual movements and perspectives that celebrate the contributions diverse voices make to preaching. But to date there is no focus on adolescent youth. In a sense, this book seeks to test the limits of homiletics done "from the margins."

Within the broad field of practical theology, I believe homiletics has been content to allow the fields of religious education and professionalized

5. Miller-McLemore, "Children and Religion," 41.

youth ministry to speak about religion and young people in contemporary times. Those who theorize preaching typically concede to stereotypes that young people do not listen to sermons or are deficient listeners (or are similarly deficient and trivial speakers), and thus do not necessitate homiletic reflection. This book seeks to reverse both of those trends by articulating a specifically homiletic view of adolescents as well as an adolescent view of preaching.

To do so, we must bring into focus three important methodological concepts. First, talking about adolescents in an area where they are neglected is not simply adding another "other" to a discussion currently enjoying discussions about the "other." That is to say, we are not just pitting "youth" or "adolescent" theories and practices of preaching against "adult" theories and practices of preaching. Operating in this manner would create a center-margin dynamic that does not give helpful resolution of the situation.[6] The social grouping of "youth" presents a different kind of "otherness"—a temporary identity marker, rather than a permanent one. As such, I do not seek to add another "other" to homiletic discourse, or engage in a discourse of competing otherness (indeed it is fruitless to ask, "Who is the *most* 'other' to preaching?"). Rather, I suggest the notion of adolescents as entirely other to preaching can be avoided through careful attention to the various ways adolescents have engaged and are engaging preaching in the North American context.

Second, without the abilities to speak and write in academic discourse, we are necessarily engaging in a different type of writing about the experiences of those who are marginalized. I believe the type of homiletic work I am doing engages in what is variously known as "advocacy theology." David Jensen defines advocacy theology in his writing on children when he says, "an advocacy theology seeks to speak with those whose voices are often not heard. Children's voices often drown in the cacophony of commercialization and violence that characterize the (post)modern world. Attempting to hear them is fraught with peril: often we think we hear their voices when we really are hearing only ourselves and our intentions for children."[7] In this project, I am making theologically-informed arguments for those who are

---

6. Nancy Fraser describes this scenario as a "subaltern counterpublic" formed in contradistinction to a "dominant public" that controls the public sphere, with the intention of "formulat[ing] oppositional interpretations of their identities, interests, and needs." See Fraser, *Justice Interruptus*, 80–85. In the case of homiletics, there is no recognizable counterpublic consisting of younger preachers engaged in the work of creating a counter-discourse. We will, however, seek to construct a kind of non-adversarial/non-oppositional kind of counterpublic in the latter chapters. In this sense, there is no center-margin tension, nor should we seek to create one where it does not exist.

7. Jensen, *Graced Vulnerability*, xiii.

not able to advocate on their own behalf within the confines of academic theology, being careful not to mistake my own voice for the voices of the young people to whom we will listen.

This leads to the third, and perhaps most important, methodological commitment. We must decide how we are going to talk about the period of life known as "adolescence" and the group we call "adolescents" or "youth." As discussed earlier, conversations about the traits associated with those known as "adolescents," "youth," "young people," and/or "teenagers" are defined by a number of different viewpoints including, but not limited to: commercial marketing, media depictions and popular culture, developmental psychology models, educational structures, and combinations of all these.[8]

One way of framing the popular definitions that pervade American culture is through what I will call "ontological adolescence." This is a concept that is borrowed and re-shaped from Victor Anderson's concept of "ontological blackness," a way of describing how race for African Americans is constructed and re-constructed into a deterministic function of identity formation apart from the varieties of African American experience.[9] Anderson defines his term as "a covering term that connotes categorical, essentialist, and representational languages depicting black life and experience" and his work "examines the ways that racial discourse operates rhetorically in African American cultural and religious thought."[10] Anderson conceives of racial discourse in contemporary America as a function of rhetoric with implications not only for discourse, but also for cultural and economic systems and social structures, as they relate to (and shape) the experiences of African Americans.

I argue that much the same is true of how adolescents are defined in the contemporary cultural imaginary, such that we can borrow Anderson's terminology. For the present situation, I name the problem "ontological

8. I will use the terms *adolescent, adolescence, youth*, and *young people* interchangeably. I do not use the word *teenage* or *teenager* because of the negative cultural images attached to these terms.

9. Anderson, *Beyond Ontological Blackness*, 11.

10. Anderson, 11. There are two main differences, however, in the ways that I appropriate Anderson through ontological adolescence. First, although the concept is reified in language and culture, ontological adolescence does not take on the same type of binary polarities that cannot be transcended for African Americans (14). Rather, these polarities (i.e., youth/adult) are not only open to transcendence, but that transcendence is encouraged in many ways. Second, ontological adolescence differs from Anderson's concept in that it does not make use of any "cult of heroic genius" whereby a devotion to the essentialized categories of youth as a group is appropriated as a celebrated point of reference for youth identity (13–14).

adolescence," which, like Anderson's term, is a term that connotes categorical, essentialist, and representational languages depicting the lives and experiences of young people in America. Depictions of young people have hardened into stereotypes that disregard historical factors and contemporary differences. Cultural and educational theorist Henry Giroux observes that

> The dominant media now habitually reinforce the public perception of young people as variously lazy, stupid, self-indulgent, volatile, dangerous, and manipulative. . . . The American public is relentlessly treated to stories about how American children don't have a grasp of basic modes of history, language, and mathematics, and yet there is a deafening silence in most of the reports about how conservative policies have systematically disinvested in public schools, turning them largely into dull testing centers for middle-class students and warehousing units and surveillance centers for working-class and poor youth of color.[11]

Giroux implicates not only media and public policy, but the marketplace in how it "limit[s] the roles available for youth to those of consumer, object, or billboard to sell sexuality, beauty products, music, athletic gear, clothes, and a host of other products."[12] As a result, Giroux says that "while youth have been increasingly removed from the register of public concern, civic commitment, and ethical responsibility—viewed as a bad social investment—they linger in the public imagination as dim-witted, if not dangerous, ingrates, unworthy of compassion and so justifiably relegated to the civic rubbish pile."[13] Giroux's language here exhibits rhetorical flourish, but presents the "problem" of youth in stark relief. Contemporary representations of youth reify their roles as inconsequential, at best, and disposable at worst. This project seeks to account for the ways that the discourse surrounding preaching in particular has participated in the promotion of ontological adolescence, limiting young people's roles as they relate to preaching. In response I want to invite homiletic thinking, as part of the larger public arena of thought, to new imaginations of young people through listening and through renewing theories and practices of preaching for, to, and with youth.

---

11. Giroux, *Youth in a Suspect Society*, 14.
12. Ibid., 14.
13. Ibid., 16.

SCOPE

To my knowledge, this is the only book on preaching and adolescents in North America undertaken from the perspective of critical homiletics. I say this in order to point out at the outset that I will not be able to address every question or aspect of the relationship between preaching and youth. I am not writing a set of prescriptions or a how-to manual for preaching to youth in either intergenerational or youth-only settings. Those books do exist and I believe that their benefit is limited.[14] I do believe, however, that communal best-practices might arise from the kind of communicative practices I describe in chapters three through five.

I am also not using developmental psychology as a way to inform the relationship between preaching and adolescents. While developmental psychological models might help frame some general expectations of adolescents (cognitive, emotional, physical), using those models to prescribe universal homiletic practices does not necessarily promote the type of homiletic engagement I will advocate. By avoiding these approaches, I also hope to avoid at least one problem that sometimes accompanies developmental models: the problem of positioning the adult as the all-knowing observer and manager of adolescents.[15]

I do hope to accomplish a few goals as a result of this project. First, and most importantly, I hope to set a theologically and ethically grounded agenda for faith communities that take preaching and youth seriously. Rather than uncritically incorporating the representations and relationships of ontological adolescence into the preaching practices of a community, I hope that thorough examination of history, culture, and discourse, articulation of a theologically appropriate homiletic, and critical listening to youth sermons will lead toward new understandings of youth in both academic homiletics and communities of faith. As a byproduct, I believe that this project has implications for practical theology beyond preaching. That is to say, in describing a "disposition"[16] for adolescent-adult homiletic relationships, I hope to envision the kind of conditions that can permeate other adult-adolescent relationships. In doing so, rehabilitated representations and renewed relationships become a theologically-informed basis for public

14. Some of these will be examined in chapter two. I have written elsewhere about those works and make suggestions for the practice of preaching in youth-only settings. See Voelz, "Oh Be Careful."

15. In assuming a cautious stance about the rigid use of developmental models, I take some cues from "critical youth studies" and "critical psychology" in regard to developmental psychology. I will explore this further in chapter 3.

16. Use of this term is detailed in chapter 3.

life beyond the church and academy. In other words, I believe preaching can lead the way toward renewed and strengthened relationships between youth and adults.

OVERVIEW

In order to reach these goals, we will first seek to establish a specifically *homiletic* history of adolescence in North America in chapter one. As a way of narrating this history, I will summarize the substantial, but yet unwritten social history of American adolescents as listeners and preachers. A historical survey of the relationship between preaching and young people in North America will show that adolescents have not always displayed ossified social characteristics and that their relationship to preaching has not always been that of "other," as contemporary voices position them. Instead, the contemporary relationship between preaching and adolescents is one that has changed (in both positive and negative ways) over time due to shifts in social and religious life in North America, and due to changes in the roles of constituent disciplines within practical theology. Constructing this history also begins a preliminary practice of listening to adolescents, which I will advocate as a necessary condition of renewed relationships between preaching and young people later in the project.

Chapter 2 traces how the trajectory of preaching and adolescence exhibited in the late nineteenth and early twentieth century solidifies in contemporary literatures. In this period homiletics grows silent regarding young people, effectively ceding its voice to religious education. In contemporary mainline denominational, university-based homiletic theory, I identify an overwhelming silence toward adolescents, but I also point to places where ontological adolescence creeps in as a way of describing adolescents as deficient listeners. In contemporary youth ministry literature that discusses preaching, we will see how adolescents are portrayed as an undifferentiated audience with idiosyncratic needs/tendencies to which preaching practices should cater. Finally, I will explore how the contemporary literature of critical youth studies, childhood studies in religion, and religious education of youth helpfully frames adolescents and their religiosity, but ignores homiletic theory and practice. Each of these three types of discourse lack the ability to fund preaching theory and practice that adequately responds to adolescents, exposing the need for a homiletic discourse that honors the rich texture of adolescents' lives as well as renews the relationship between preaching and adolescents.

Chapter 3 presents a theological and ethical corrective to the problem I describe in chapter 2. If the discourses of ontological adolescence, silence, or false representation are the prevailing approaches to young people, then we must envision new ways to imagine the relationship between adults, youth, and preaching. As a way to strengthen this relationship, I will advocate new communicative practices among homiletic communities (that is, intergenerational communities not limited to congregations that care deeply about preaching) fueled by a normative disposition characterized by liberation and formation. In order to flesh out what I mean by liberation and formation, I describe these twin poles in terms of Christian theological ethics. This disposition provides a foundation for listening and speaking to one another that resists representations characteristic of ontological adolescence and opens up a new kind of public, homiletic sphere of interaction. In this new homiletic space, young people's homiletic voices can speak back to existing homiletic theories and practices, and speak back to Christian theology and practice, even as adults maintain a significant interest in their formation.

Guided by liberation and formation, homiletic communities are compelled to engage in in-depth, critical, and reflective listening to young people not simply as listeners to, but also as *producers of* preaching. In order to do so, chapters 4 and 5 will present a method for the kind of listening mandated in chapter 3 by incorporating the tools of rhetorical analysis. Since false representations are at the heart of both silence and ontological adolescence, we will formulate a constructive method that begins with listening to adolescents' sermons, then use methods of rhetorical criticism that are capable of interpreting the ways that adolescents construct two kinds of communicative identities: Christian identity and homiletic identity. In other words, we will seek to interpret the ways that young people self-identify as people of faith and as preachers. A final component of the rhetorical analysis posits a way for communities to evaluate these sermons in the modes of liberation and formation through the normative lens of their own theological and homiletical commitments. We will use thirteen sermons by young people as a way of bringing life to these theoretical commitments. A theologically-informed ethic of listening forms one of the main commitments of this project, so their sermons are provided in full transcripts in the Appendix. In these chapters, I hope to present a method that can be reproduced in communities committed to renewing homiletic relationships with young people.

My denomination, the Christian Church (Disciples of Christ), gives the following as a statement of identity: "We are Disciples of Christ, a movement for wholeness in a fragmented world. As part of the one body of

Christ, we welcome all to the Lord's Table as God has welcomed us."[17] Beyond revising preaching theories and practices, it is my hope that this book might help those of us who care about youth and preaching engage in a type of listening practice that moves communities of faith, young and old, away from fragmentation and toward wholeness—the kind of wholeness that we Disciples believe is characterized most clearly in our experiences at the Lord's Table. For Disciples, this is a table that acknowledges the agency of all (indeed, in the Disciples' tradition presiding at the table is not restricted to ordained clergy), while recognizing that plurality may open us all up to new insights and practices. As we engage young people through critical and reflective listening here, we open ourselves to the insights that they might bring regarding preaching and Christian faith, even as we pay close attention to the formative needs that young people present.

17. "About the Disciples." http://disciples.org/our-identity/.

1

Beautiful and Dangerous

Adolescents and Preaching in Historical Perspective

Contrary to the image of the bored teenager that often characterizes contemporary images of the relationship between adolescent youth and preaching, young people have been regularly and highly engaged with preaching through American history. In order to provide a context for contemporary preaching dispositions toward adolescents, this chapter will narrate the substantial history of North American adolescents as listeners and preachers through the eighteenth, nineteenth, and early twentieth centuries.

This kind of historical narrative functions in two distinct ways. First, the narrative breaks open assumptions about a passive relationship between adolescents and preaching. A preaching-centered history of adolescence in North America will show that adolescents have played various roles in faith communities, and they have not always been marginal to preaching. Second, this narrative initiates a preliminary practice of listening to adolescents about preaching, pushing toward transformed practices of listening and speaking for, to, and with youth.

PREACHING AND YOUNG PEOPLE IN EIGHTEENTH-CENTURY AMERICA[1]

Youth were often the focus of preaching when congregations gathered and young people's societies met in late seventeenth century and throughout eighteenth-century New England. Cotton Mather indicated that young people were a particular portion of preachers' audiences when he said,

> When the Word of God is Opened and Applied in the Sermons of His Ministers; young Persons make a part of our Auditory. Young Persons are to take their Portion in all the Sermons of the Evangelical Ministry, wherein Wisdom says unto them, 'Unto you, O Men, I Call, and my Voice is to the Sons of Men. Yea, the Prudent and Faithful Stewards in the House of God, will sometimes Carve out a Special Portion for the Young Persons in their Auditory.[2]

As subjects of preaching, young people were integral parts of how the Puritan sermon was "as important for social meaning as for spiritual enlightenment. It not only interpreted God's plan of redemption and told the people how they must live as a church but also defined and legitimated the meaning of their lives as citizen and magistrate, superior and inferior, soldier, parent, child, and laborer."[3] With "social meaning" and "spiritual enlightenment" in mind as distinct categories, a preaching-centered history of adolescence in this period begins to show how preaching helped situate "youth" in both social and theological categories.

Young People as a Social Category in Eighteenth-Century Preaching

How is "youth" defined? There seems to be no standard answer in Colonial preaching. Samuel Moodey distinguished groups of ages: "And as this Judgment shall be Universal with respect to Persons, viz. Youth as well as Children and Infants below them, and Middle, with Old Age above them; so shall it be Universal with respect to the Works done in the Body, Eccl.

---

1. In describing Puritan New England below, we are exposed to a significant thread of religious life in early America, but we should also recognize that Puritan preaching is not the only preaching available in this era, nor is the Puritan experience in New England representative of all early American experience.

2. Mather, *Young Man*, 10.

3. Stout, *New England Soul*, 23.

12.14."[4] Cotton Mather distinguished between "young men," "old men," and "children" as a result of the conflation of two Scripture texts: 1 John 2:14 (young men) and Ps 148:12 (old men and children).[5] Later Mather preached on the occasion of the death of two individuals, "a youth in the *Nineteenth* year of his Age" and "a *Child*, hardly more than seven years of Age."[6] Benjamin Colman preached upon the death of fourteen-year-old Elizabeth Wainwright, whom he called a child.[7] Likewise, Thomas Prince preached a sermon to "the youth of the town of Boston" upon the deaths of three young men aged twenty-two, thirty-two, and twenty.[8]

Jonathan Edwards "held special religious meetings for 'children' who were 'under the age of sixteen' as well as for 'young people' between the ages of sixteen and twenty-six.'"[9] Edwards also divided the ages by children (ages one to fourteen), young people (ages fifteen to twenty-five), middle-aged (ages twenty-six to fifty), and elderly (ages fifty and beyond).[10]

Colonial preachers do identify three interrelated factors in the life course that distinguish youth from adult members of the community. First among these is that youth are still under the leadership of their parents. Of the fifty plus sermons analyzed from this period, almost every sermon contains within it an instruction for young people to obey their parents and some with instructions to parents about their duties to young people. A second factor is work. Preaching to a society of young men, Colman stated that in the beginning of youth, young people choose their "trade" and their "Master."[11] Making a living by work, either by trade, inheritance of family farms, or business often led young people out of the family home and marked a transition to adulthood.[12] Youth as a precursor to marriage and child-bearing forms a third social indicator. Again, Colman observed,

4. Samuel Moodey, *Vain Youth*, 7.

5. Mather, *Youth in Its Brightest Glory*, 3–5.

6. Mather, *Vita Brevis*, 29–30, 33–34.

7. Colman, *Devout Contemplation*.

8. Prince and Byles, *Morning Health*, A3.

9. Brekus, "Children of Wrath," 302.

10. Stout et al., *Sermons and Discourses*, 156. For other ways that early American religious leaders made age distinctions through religious practices and otherwise, see Beales Jr., "In Search," 94–109.

11. Colman, *Early Piety*, 32–33.

12. Harvey Graff says that what is at stake for youth, is "competence, " or "the skills and abilities" that lead to independence from the family home, though the ability to achieve competence and independence lies mostly with white middle and upper-class males. Graff, *Conflicting Paths*, 27–28. One of the strengths of Graff's history is that he highlights the many paths on the journey to adulthood in American history that are complicated by race, gender, economic status, and geography.

there are other and Superiour Relations which the Young Person hopes in a few Years to come into, and this will make him a
blessing to his own Family when he comes to have one; a blessing to his Consort if he marries, a blessing to his Children if God
give him any, a blessing to his Servants when he has them under
him. And so the Young Woman becomes a blessing in the house
of her Husband, a blessing to her Children and Servants, if from
her early days she be truly Religious. . . . And now you dispose
of your self in Marriage ordinarily, place your Affections, give
away your hearts, look out for some Companion of life, whose
to be as long as you live. And is this indeed the work of your
Youth?[13]

Youth were either on the cusp of life with marriage and children or had
recently arrived. Colman's sermon, and others like it, served to reinforce the
social conventions surrounding the period of youth from the position that
Stout calls "authority incarnate."[14] While substantive, these social definitions do not help define childhood and youth *theologically*.

Young People as a Theological Category in Eighteenth-Century Preaching

Ministers in Colonial New England possessed a concordance-like knowledge of the Bible and imitated the sermons they heard, creating a reser-
voir for their preaching. Scripture texts that contained the words "youth,"
"young," or that publicized the youthful ages of biblical characters were fair
game. As a result "youth" becomes a theological category as well, defined in
preaching by the major biblical texts used and the use of those texts turned
toward major themes, doctrines, and methods of biblical interpretation.
And as we will see, this theological category is riddled with contradictions.

In the Wisdom literature and the Psalms, preachers found foundational texts presumably addressed to readers in all times and places, and
especially the young. Proverbs, Ecclesiastes, and the Psalms contain exhortations for wise living as well as instruction in how to conduct oneself and
were also believed to be written by those whose own youthful periods were
instructive. The admirable parts of David and Solomon's lives would lead
young people to pious living of their own.

Numerous sermons use the first part of Eccl 12:1: "Remember your
creator in the days of your youth" or Eccl 11:9: "Rejoice, young man, while

13. Colman, *Early Piety*, 31, 33.
14. Stout, *New England Soul*, 23.

you are young, and let your heart cheer you in the days of your youth. Follow the inclination of your heart and desire of your eyes, but know that for all these things God will bring you into judgment."[15] The beginning phrase of Ps 25:7 was a point of departure for talking about sin: "Do not remember the sins of my youth or my transgressions." Similarly, the instruction to young people against sin becomes a direct address from Prov 1:10: "My child, if sinners entice you, do not consent." Psalm 90:5–6 warned young people about the uncertainty of the number of their days of life, saying "like grass that is renewed in the morning; in the morning it flourishes and is renewed; in the evening it fades and withers." Likewise, Israel Holly used a single phrase from Job 1:19 pointing to the uncertainty of years of life: "and it fell on the young people and they are dead."[16]

Texts from other areas of the Bible appear as opening texts, but not in the same volume as that of the Wisdom literature and Psalms. Titus 2:6 was popular: "Likewise, urge the younger men to be self-controlled." Cotton Mather, in one of his many addresses to young people, took a cue for his ministry from Zech 2.4: "Run, say to that young man." He believed "To bring the Messages of Heaven to Young Men, is an Angelical Service."[17] Moses, Ruth, King Josiah, Obadiah, Samuel, Timothy, Mary the sister of Martha, and John the Disciple were all used as examples of faithfulness to God in the time of youth.

These texts led ministers to develop themes about the theological nature of young people. Most significant among these themes is "early piety." Young people were encouraged to commit themselves to "early piety" or "religion." In this, young people faced a double-bind. Young people were described as prone to indiscretions born of a sinful nature. Samuel Stillman directly addressed young people saying, "there is no period of life more dangerous than that of youth. Then the passions are strongest, and the temptations to indulge them are almost innumerable."[18]

The other half of the double bind appears even within the same sermons. Stillman declared "the youth [who] make a great part of our state worshipping assemblies, are the flower of the community, and on them we naturally place our expectations of future supplies in the Church and in the State."[19] Young people were not only dangerous but beautiful flowers in the

15. For clarity in this section, quotes from biblical texts are taken from the NRSV, unless otherwise noted.

16. Holly and Watts, *Youth Liable to Sudden Death.*

17. Mather, *Young Man*, 1.

18. Stillman, *Young People*, 7, 9.

19. Ibid., 5.

prime age to choose religion. They were moldable, the right time for the good impressions a life of religion can leave. Israel Loring remarked,

> It remains therefore that Youth, which is the morning of our day, the flower of our time, is the fittest season of all others to Remember God in. Our Understandings, Memories, Affections and Strength are then in their vigour, and don't fail us; besides Young Persons are not yet plunged so deep into worldly incumbrances and cares, as in all likelihood they will be afterwards; and therefore this golden opportunity of life should be laid hold of, and improved to the best purposes.[20]

The time of youth was also the time of more powerful activity of the Holy Spirit, according to Josiah Stearns.[21] Youth were warned of the difficulty of turning to God later in life from Jer 1:23: "Can Ethiopians change their skin or leopards their spots?"[22] The best choice was to ratify their faith by devoting themselves to "the religion of the closet," earnestly seeking after God.[23] They were urged over and over to "remember your Creator in the days of your youth."[24]

The concern for early piety came as much out of concern for individual salvation as it did for the fate of the young nation. To establish America as a city on a hill, older generations needed younger generations to take faith seriously.[25] Each succeeding generation hoped that America would become the place the first settlers had dreamed. To accomplish this, young Americans would have to eradicate the bad behaviors toward which they were inclined. This second great theme, morality, played a large role in preaching to the youth of Colonial America. Sermonic lists of moral and ethical instruction defined acceptable behavior for young people. In order to protect a young person's sinful lifestyle from hardening in old age, ministers encouraged youth to obey their parents, and to attend to sobriety, chastity, modesty, keep good company, not swear, and refrain from particular types of entertainment.[26]

The possibility of early death also stimulated young people's piety. While it might be easy to consign this practice as a rhetorical scare tactic,

20. Loring, *Duty and Interest*, 11–12.

21. Stearns and Peirce, *Sermon, Preached at Epping*, 21.

22. See, for instance, Barnard, *Two Discourses*, 15.

23. See, for instance, Mather, *Young Man*.

24. See again, Barnard, *Two Discourses*, 18.

25. Stout, *New England Soul*, 54.

26. For example, see Stillman, *Young People*. His sermon proceeds by outlining a list of this type.

that would ignore the realities of Colonial life. Deaths among young people were all too common and a pious life assured eternal rewards should one die early.[27] Preachers did not shy away from this reality. Edwards preached a sermon entitled "Youth is Like a Flower that is Cut Down" from Job 14:2, "He cometh forth like a flower, and is cut down." After addressing the hopefulness of young people, Edwards' notes say,

> When young people die, then the flower is cut down. A flower is a part of the plant that appears furthest from death and yet is nearest to it. . . . So it [is] as it were oftentimes with young people. How often do they die without many days' warning. [It is] unexpected. [They have] little time to think of death. Disease seizes 'em strongly, baffles all medicines, and hastens 'em out of the world.[28]

In extremely frank language, Edwards and others warn of the reality of young peoples' untimely deaths.

A final theme revolves around the authority of the minister. If cultural norms had not secured enough authority to the preacher, then the preacher could certainly make his own authority clear. Israel Loring imagined the scene of those youth who "come short of heaven" because they did not listen to the pleading of "Christ's ministers."[29] Cotton Mather warned young people: "Children, When sermons are Preaching, you have the Great GOD speaking to you in them. Instead of Sporting, or Sleeping, or any Irreverent Carriage here, Oh, with what Reverence and Godly Fear ought you to behave yourselves. . . . Tis not a weak Man, but the Great GOD, who is now speaking to me! . . . You are Deaf to GOD, if you hear us not!"[30] Youth were subject to the authority of the preacher's word, preached in the place of God.

The preacher also employed methods of biblical interpretation that framed the ideal life. Typology provided examples for Christian piety. David, Solomon, Moses, Ruth, King Josiah, Obadiah, Samuel, Timothy, Mary the sister of Martha, and John the Disciple all serve as types of faithfulness in youth. Reaching beyond character typologies, Cotton Mather used the doves of Isa 60:8, "who are these that fly like a cloud, and like doves to their windows?" and the doves in the Noah story as a type of the ideal Christian young person.[31] As the doves fly to windows for protection, and returned to Noah, so should young people's souls return to God.

27. Graff, *Conflicting Paths*, 28.

28. Stout et al., *Sermons and Discourses*, 325.

29. Loring, *Duty and Interest*, 30–32.

30. Mather, *Young Man*, 10–11.

31. Mather, *Columbanus*.

Signs of Youthful Agency

At first glance, the way these sermons address youth and describe them seem to obscure their voices. Upon closer inspection however, young people were more both directly and indirectly active in the preaching process than a surface reading might suggest. Inasmuch as live preaching in Colonial America was authoritative, the published sermon continued the life of the sermon. Many of these sermons seem to have been printed at the bequest of young people. Of the sermons analyzed from this period, sixteen state in their preface that they were published at the request of young people, by a young people's society, or were actually published by young people. One was published at the request of the parents to whom the sermon was directed. Four were published at the desire of "many hearers."

A skeptical view would see the requests for sermons as placating preachers, an attempt to garner social standing. Such subversion would still have shaped what constituted "successful" preaching among young people in the Colonial period. Still, religious fervor took root among young people, especially in the Great Awakening as those below age twenty filled church membership lists.[32] Recently converted or discerning young people may have found value in sermons and requested their publication. In this case, preachers would have been attentive to these requests, contemplating their own preaching to young people accordingly.

Closely related is the setting of these sermons. Voluntary associations like young people's societies were "intended to harness youthful energies. . . . Ministers encouraged the formation of young men's societies, where youth could meet regularly to pray, sing psalms, hear sermons, and discuss religious subjects."[33] These meetings constituted special occasions for preaching. Samuel Stillman commented at the end of a sermon: "I shall conclude with an address to the young men, at whose request we now appear in the house of God."[34] It is evident that the meetings influenced preaching to some degree.

Young people were heard more directly in other ways. In sermons for deceased young people, preachers ventriloquized them, giving the voice of the deceased a role in the sermon. In this way, though young people were not occupying the physical spaces of preaching, their voices were incorporated as proclamation and as examples of faith. Preachers who found

32. Stout, *New England Soul*, 197. For more on specific numbers and ages of conversion, follow Stout's notes in this section. See also Willingham, "Religious Conversion"; Greven, "Youth, Maturity, and Religious Conversion," 144–55.

33. Steven Mintz, *Huck's Raft*, 29.

34. Stillman, *Young People*, 29.

faithful speech among the recently deceased incorporated it into pleas for youthful piety.

John Rogers printed a collection of three sermons for young people "occasioned by the imprisonment, condemnation, and execution of a Young Woman who was guilty of Murdering her Infant begotten in Whoredom— To which is added, an account of her manner of Life and Death in which the Glory of free Grace is displayed."[35] As the quotation from the title page indicates, Rogers appends the testimony of Esther Rogers to his sermons. Similarly, Josiah Stearns included a few opening remarks in his funeral sermon about the piety of a recently deceased young man. As a postscript, he includes the ecstatic death-bed speech of Samuel Lawrence.[36]

Cotton Mather preached upon the death of a young man and a child, and said of the young man, "behold, I am the Instrument now to bring his Testimony."[37] Mather went on to describe the young man's wishes, but only summarizing his thoughts. Benjamin Colman declared

> GOD can make the Death of your Companions a most awaken-
> ing and effectual Sermon to you: and it may be worth anoth-
> ers dying to do thy Soul good, and bring thee home to Christ:
> It preaches to thee in a more affecting manner than any meer
> words can, and in the happy [unreadable] to Relatives, when
> their affections are stirred, and their Souls the more easily come
> at. And O that our Young people wou'd but hear the good Coun-
> sels from the Funerals of their pious Friends that die young![38]

The dead bodies of faithful young people functioned as a type of non-verbal sermon.

If the preacher's own words were insufficient, the episodes of dying and death-bed speech could be relayed in moving fashion. Cotton Mather spoke of a recently deceased congregant: "Finally; ABIEL GOODWIN, shall without any Disorder now Speak in the Church! And . . . shall call upon our Young People to bear the Yoke in their Youth."[39] Mather continued by narrating her life and the course of her death, including lengthy quotations of her speech.

Though young people were not regular preachers in the pulpits of early America, they did speak in their own voices. Many young people participated in lay exhortation during the first Great Awakening. Elias Haven,

---

35. Rogers et al., *Death the Certain Wages.*

36. Stearns and Peirce, *Sermon, Preached at Epping,* 37–40.

37. Mather, *Vita Brevis,* 32.

38. Colman, *Devout Contemplation,* 23–24.

39. Mather, *Juga Jucunda,* 21.

commenting on the extent of the revival that led many young people to account their "humiliation and repentance," declared "there are many young People in this Congregation that are ready to witness for this."[40] Haven's statement expressed an ease with young people speaking about their faith experiences.

But not everyone was happy with the opportunities afforded young people in this time of religious enthusiasm. Charles Chauncy opposed the revivals that came to characterize the Great Awakening. Lay exhorters "worked to upset godly order in the churches [and] society. . . . Besides disrupting the settled churches, they upset social order by encouraging laborers to 'continue abroad 'till late in the Night, and so as to unfit themselves for the Services of the following day.'" They also upset the ordered ministry.[41] Chauncy opined:

> Another Thing that very much tends, as I apprehend, to do Hurt to the Interest of Religion, is the Rise of so many Exhorters. A Stranger to the Land, and the present Appearance in it, may be at a Loss to know, who are meant by these Exhorters: . . . there are among these Exhorters, Babes in Age, as well as Understanding. They are chiefly indeed young Persons, sometimes Lads, or rather Boys: Nay, Women and Girls; yea, Negroes, have taken upon them to do the Business of Preachers. Nor has this been accidental only, or in a single Place, or at a private House; but there is scarce a Town in all the Provinces, where this Appearance has been, but there have been also these Exhorters, in smaller or greater numbers: Neither have they contented themselves to speak in the more private Meetings of Christians, but have held forth in the publick Congregations.[42]

And while Chauncy condemned this, he noted that some encourage the practice.[43]

Preaching to young people was a staple in early American preaching and would continue, though not in the same volume or form. Much of the preaching proceeded in an authoritative manner, resulting in the construction of the ideal young person of Colonial America. Even so, young people managed to insert their voices into the preaching life of their communities. Through sermon requests, meetings, incorporated speeches, and exhortation, young people acted to exercise forms of preaching agency.

40. Haven, *Youthful Pleasures*, 24.

41. Stout, *New England Soul*, 204.

42. Chauncy, *Seasonable Thoughts*, 226.

43. Ibid.

BEAUTIFUL AND DANGEROUS 21

CONTINUITY AND CHANGE
IN THE NINETEENTH CENTURY

As North America entered the nineteenth century, recovery from the Revolutionary War meant social changes swept the young nation. Industrialization, urbanization, and pushes to the frontier rearranged the dynamics of families, economic life, and the roles of churches. Later on, the Civil War would test the nation's ability to sustain its ideals. These broad-stroke social changes were accompanied by religious changes as well. The Second Great Awakening fueled more religious revival. Many denominations and churches created institutions that championed their causes and an increasing theological diversity resulted from the freedoms Americans enjoyed.

All of these changes touched the nature of adolescence and so too changed relationships with preaching. Harvey Graff's categorization of "paths" of growing up in America provides a model useful for categorizing the relationships between adolescents and preaching in this era forward. These relationships can be categorized in terms of three paths: *traditional, transitional,* and *emergent.*[44] Features of each path include continuity and change in the style and substance of preaching, characterizations of young people found in preaching, the relationship between preacher and young people, as well as the roles of young people as preacher.

Traditional Paths and Continuity with the Eighteenth Century

Graff defines the traditional path as "the normative path for the time.... Sons followed in the footsteps of their fathers, within the bonds and bounds of family.... In a word, notions of stability and continuity define, if sometimes misleadingly, the traditional path."[45] Similarly, "stability" and "continuity" with earlier preaching traditions characterize the traditional path for young people. Much like the collection of sermons Increase Mather edited on early piety in 1721, the tradition of collected sermons continued.[46] Perhaps most significant were Phillip Doddridge's sermons, originally published in 1734 and reprinted through multiple editions in both England and America.[47]

44. Graff, *Conflicting Paths,* 29. Although Graff separates out female voices into a distinct category, I will integrate women throughout each of these categories. One note on historiography: The voices of servants, the poor and working classes, as well as African American, Asian American, and native peoples are difficult to track since primary materials are printed sermons.

45. Ibid., 20–30.

46. Colman et al., *Course of Sermons.*

47. Doddridge, *Sermons to Young Persons.*

It may be that when Mrs. Harriet Newell, at the age of thirteen (b. 1793), wrote of Doddridge's sermons in a letter to a friend (1806), she possessed the seventh edition of the collection, published in 1803. These sermons demanded reflection, as she recommended them to a friend, saying

> They are very beautiful sermons. It appears strange to me, why I am not more interested in the cause of Christ, when he has done so much for us! But I will form a resolution that I will give myself up entirely to him. Pray for me that my heart may be changed. I long for the happy hour when we shall be free from all sin, and enjoy God in heaven. But if it would be for his glory, I should be willing to live my threescore years and ten. My heart bleeds for our companions, who are on the brink of destruction. In what manner shall I speak to them?[48]

For Newell, Doddridge's sermons struck her as "beautiful" and as a collection that encouraged her devotion to Christ, disposing her to speak to her friends about the importance of faith. Printed sermons continued to be integrated into the popular religiosity of nineteenth century America. Samuel Kendal's *Seven Sermons to Young Persons* received printings in both 1809 and 1814.[49] This practice also occurred in places outside of New England when ministers like James Muir of Virginia published a general collection of occasional sermons entitled *Ten Sermons*, in which two of the sermons were directed to young people.[50]

Through the first two decades of the new century, the conventions of preaching to young people remain largely the same. Major texts, themes, and occasions for preaching do not change, nor does the ambivalence toward young people as simultaneously dangerous and holy. The voices of young people, particularly the deceased, still appear as persuasive voices.[51] The discussion of how to view young people in light of the new revivals continued. Although the format of the argument changed from sermons to essays in popular periodicals, the double-bind about the religious nature of young people continued. In the *Western Missionary Magazine* in 1804 (reprinted from *The Connecticut Evangelical Magazine*), two pseudonymous writers named Eubulus and Zepho exchange arguments about young people's religious nature, arguing both sides of the double-bind.[52] Young people

48. Newell, *Memoirs*, 6.

49. Kendal, *Seven Sermons*.

50. Muir, *Ten Sermons*.

51. Brownson, *Memento to Youth*, 21.

52. Eubulus, "On the Imperfect State." These essays are reprinted in a number of contemporaneous journals. Zepho, "Days of Youth," 147.

remained wedged between two differing views concerning their religious capacities. There are, however, changes that mark a transitional relationship between preaching and young people in the nineteenth century.

Transitional Paths in the Nineteenth Century

Graff defines the transitional path of growing up by "discontinuity, uncertainty, shifting expectations, and shifting locations . . . between apparent stability and continuity on the one hand and manifest opportunities and new rhythms or schedules on the other."[53] As the nineteenth century progressed, changes occurred in the relationship between preaching and young people that preserve tradition and suggest but do not fully embody emergent paths.

Perhaps the largest indicator of transition is the severe decline in the number of sermons available as the century progresses.[54] The question is how to account for this significant shift. It is reasonable to suggest that the kind of preaching that occurred on the frontier changed as American Christianity pushed westward. Much of this preaching was unrecorded and delivered for broad audiences outside urban areas. That does not answer for the decrease of these sermons in New England, however, with its established tradition of publishing sermons to young people. So another way to account for this shift is the rise of sensationalist morality tales that competed for time and interest of readers.[55]

The most significant explanation for the decrease is found in one of American Christianity's most durable institutions: Sunday Schools, which emerged as a powerful force in the 1820s and 1830s.[56] Initially conceived as instruction for the poor, Sunday Schools grew diverse in target audience, becoming one of the most influential tools by which young people were introduced to Christianity and exercised their religious voices. Horace Bushnell's ideas of childhood religious experience, described in *Christian Nurture* (1847) influenced the growth of Sunday Schools and changes in church architecture mark a shift from the centrality of the pulpit to the Sunday School classroom.[57]

53. Graff, *Conflicting Paths*, 30.
54. Thorough searches of research databases/catalogues such as ATLA and ProQuest, as well as the holdings of both the libraries of Vanderbilt University and Emory University, show a marked decline in sermon publications.
55. Moore, *Selling God*, 19.
56. See Boylan, *Sunday School*; Laqueur, *Religion and Respectability*. For resources on Sunday School literature, see "Shaping the Values of Youth: Sunday School Books in 19th Century America." http://digital.lib.msu.edu/projects/ssb/index.cfm.
57. Bendroth, "Horace Bushnell's Christian Nurture," 350. See Loveland and

Sunday School literature was used for instruction and given out as rewards for young "scholars." In many of the primers and tracts, publishers abbreviated sermons and placed them among other genres of literature. *Youth's Guide to Happiness* contained "poems, essays, and sermons. . . . Particularly calculated for the PIOUS INSTRUCTION of THE RISING GENERATION."[58] Unlike prior collections of material, preaching no longer dominated. *Youth's Guide* reflected changes in young people's reading habits. The title to the section of sermons reads: "Short SERMONS, designed for the use of those who have little time to read longer discourses."[59] Each sermon takes up no more than two full printed pages each and no full-length sermons are included.

A familiar sermonic device from longer sermons of the previous era appeared in *Youth's Guide*: death-bed speeches. No longer surrounded by lengthy sermons on the benefits of early piety, the death bed speech now stood alone as "obituary." *Youth's Guide* contained two such narratives, one of which was the "account of the happy death of Edwin Tapper, aged [fifteen] years."[60] The editor provided an account of Edwin's last days as he bore witness to his friends about the love of God.[61] The account of Edwin's ecstatic death-bed speech took up fourteen pages of the 105-page volume. The traditional sermon no longer sufficed for the formation of young people.

Another literary device included in *Youth's Guide* is the extended dialogue, which served as a type of question and answer on doctrine and morality. For nearly twenty pages, the fictional characters Charles and Henry exchange ideas on the truthfulness of the Bible, the nature of baptism and regeneration, sin and salvation, and ends with the encouragement to "Read your Bible with prayer: frequent those places where Christ is preached."[62] This kind of literature embodies the transitional path, simultaneously displacing printed preaching while encouraging the reader to seek out places where preaching could be seen and heard.

In other literature young people were able to express themselves beyond death-bed speeches. *The Guardian and Monitor,* a joint monthly periodical for youth, provided a variety of literature.[63] Among the poetry, commen-

---

Wheeler, *From Meetinghouse to Megachurch*; Kett, *Rites of Passage*, 120.

58. *Youth's Guide to Happiness.*

59. Ibid., 8.

60. Ibid., 57. Edwin's account is also reprinted in tracts from the Philadelphia Female Tract Society (1805), among others.

61. For an excellent account of the rise of narrative in nineteenth century preaching at large, see Reynolds, "From Doctrine to Narrative."

62. *Youth's Guide to Happiness Consisting of Poems, Essays, & Sermons*, 57.

63. For more on *The Guardian* and *The Monitor*, see the summaries provided on

tary on *The Pilgrim's Progress*, reports of revivals and deaths, excerpts from letters and memoirs, dialogues, short stories, and Sunday School anecdotes, young people's voices also appear. Upon the first issue, "a youth" leads the issue with an essay on the new year.[64] The young person makes observations about the progress of the world and extols the Sunday School.[65]

The transitional element can also be found in the report literature of nineteenth century religious organizations. For instance, the Providence Female Tract Society's annual report in 1817 observed that the religious tracts they distributed were "powerful, pungent, melting preachers of righteousness" in their own right.[66] Whereas preachers like Cotton Mather had urged his young listeners to listen to his sermons as the very voice of God, Sunday School and tract literatures emerged as more than capable replacements.

The impact of the diverse literary genres contained in Sunday School literature cannot be overstated. The atmosphere of American Christianity and its communicative practices were shifting. Charles Finney and those who followed in his footsteps spoke in plain language, eschewed doctrine for practical matters, aimed for the emotions, and utilized theatrics, which all achieved a great deal success (and not a little controversy).[67] The revivals introduced by Finney and others were wildly successful among young people.[68] Out of this perfect storm, the perceived need to create "interest" among listeners grew, and young listeners in particular. Jacob Abbot's tract *The Young Christian* is worthy of quoting at length:

> I have made no effort to simplify the language. It is not necessary to do this even for children. They will understand the language of maturity easily enough, if the logic and rhetoric are theirs. I have attempted, therefore, to present each subject in such an aspect, and to illustrate it in such a way as is adapted to the young mind, using, however, such language as has suggested itself spontaneously. It is a great but a very common error, to suppose that merely to simplify diction is the way to gain access to the young. Hence a sermon for children is seldom any thing more than a sermon for men, with easy words substituted for the hard ones. This goes on the supposition that the great difficulty is to make children understand religious truth. Whereas there is no difficulty at all in this. The difficulty is in *interesting them in it.*

"American Children's Periodicals: 1789–1820."

64. "The New Year."
65. Ibid., 6.
66. Society, *Second Annual Report*, 7.
67. Edwards, *History of Preaching*, 509–20.
68. Kett, *Rites of Passage*, 64.

> They will understand readily enough, if they are interested in the form and manner in which the subject comes before them. These principles will explain the great number of narratives, and dialogues, and statements of facts which are introduced to give vividness to the conceptions of my readers.[69]

Though Abbott is writing about writing, he points to the practice of preaching as an analogous task. Printed again in 1882, Abbott's advice about writing and preaching to young people codified.

The concern for interest found its way into what would become one of the most successful homiletics textbooks in America. In his lecture on "Preparation of Special Types of Sermons," John A. Broadus observes,

> Everyone notices how few persons succeed decidedly well in speaking to children. . . . In general, in preaching to children the three primary things to do are to interest, to instruct, to impress. Grown people may pay attention to what does not deeply interest them, but children do not, perhaps they cannot. In order to interest them, there must be clarity both in plan and style; they must understand. Two favorite words with children are pretty and funny. It is well, therefore, in seeking to interest children, to use the beautiful and the humorous; yet, neither must be overdone. In all sermons to children there should be instruction by illustrations that will appeal to the childish mind.[70]

Broadus's emphasis on interest, instruction, and impression parallels Augustine's advice from *On Christian Doctrine*.[71] Still, Broadus champions interest in the case of young people. In the transitional path, Abbott and Broadus retain the important themes associated with preaching from the previous era while bringing interest to the forefront.

The movement to generate interest, however, did not completely render young people as the subject of preaching. Sunday Schools possessed "a relatively youthful teacher corps," with most teachers in their teens and twenties.[72] As such, young people (both men and women) could occupy authorized spaces that did not require ordination or seminary training. Teachers led in Bible instruction and hymn singing, visited the sick, and endeavored to raise up young people in pious, righteous lives.[73] Rever-

---

69. Abbott, *Young Christian*, 4. Italics in text. Again, cf. Reynolds, "From Doctrine to Narrative."

70. Broadus and Stanfield, *On the Preparation*, 253–54.

71. See Augustine, *On Christian Doctrine*, Book 4, Chapter 12.

72. Boylan, *Sunday School*, 114.

73. Ibid., 41.

end Timothy Clowes, in preaching to the instructors of youth in Albany, New York said that teachers (public and religious) were invested with the characteristics of minister, parent, and preceptor for those under their charge.[74]

As the frontier pushed westward, the American population soared. But as the numbers multiplied, the number of young men educated for the ministry did not. As was the case with Charles Chauncy, Menzies Rayner declared that the teaching, exhorting, and public praying of young people occurred "in extempore effusions, with such an air of assurance, such extravagant and incoherent expressions, and such enthusiastic fervor, as puts common sense and modesty to the blush."[75] As a natural result, in the first quarter of the nineteenth century sermons begin to appear for the newly formed American Society for Educating Pious Youth for the Gospel Ministry. The convergence of religious institution-building, low numbers of educated clergy, and disdain for young exhorters precipitated the society's formation. This transitional path for young people was designed to harness their religious zeal and channel it into a properly educated and orderly ministry. The sermons before these meetings analyzed the numbers of a growing population as compared to the number of available ministers in a particular state. They then urged upon listeners (potential donors) that "above all, thousands of pious young men must be educated for the ministry; and this speedily. A little more sleep, a little more slumber, and all is lost."[76] The crisis of population growth would not lead to passivity in regard to those allowed to preach.

Emergent Paths in the Nineteenth Century

The American Society for Educating Pious Youth for the Gospel Ministry was reacting to the resurgence of exhortation by young people that occurred in the Second Great Awakening. Although this kind of exhortation may have exhibited patterned, over-determined characteristics, it is exemplary of what Graff calls an "emergent" path, in which "we begin to see the lines leading toward the modern understanding of growing up, a picture blurring at its edges with the transitional path. Hallmarks of the emergent path include conscious choice and self-direction, a search for opportunities including social mobility, the instrumental use of further (especially higher) education,

74. Clowes, *Sermon Delivered in St. Peter's Church*, 17. See also Boylan, *Sunday School*, 22.

75. Rayner, *Dissertation*, 46–47.

76. Pearson, *Sermon Delivered in Boston*, 19.

and risk-taking in the commercial marketplace.[77] In the emergent path, not only did young people take on the activity of preaching in greater numbers, but new themes began to emerge in adult preaching to youth. These themes accommodated the shifting social and religious contexts and anticipated the trends in preaching to young people to come in the twentieth century.

On the frontier, revivalist James McGready was astounded not only with the power of conversions among young people, but also in their ability to participate in the revivals. McGready observed

> I have likewise stood present, when the light of the knowledge of the glory of God in the face of Jesus broke into their souls; and to the astonishment of all around them, these little creatures have started to their feet, and told all present their sweet views of the lovely, precious Lord Jesus . . . to hear them speak upon these subjects, the good language, the good sense, the clear ideas, and the rational, scriptural light in which they spoke, truly amazed me. . . . They spoke upon these subjects beyond what I could have done.[78]

McGready narrates how these young boys and girls who so affected older adults that "they fastened more convictions at these times, than all the preaching."[79]

Richard McNemar recounted a meeting in 1801 where a twelve-year-old boy attracted the main body of the people and, crying, was held aloft while preaching for an hour. Dropping his handkerchief, the boy "cried out: 'Thus, O sinner! shall you drop into hell, unless you forsake your sins and turn to the Lord.' At that moment some fell, like those who are shot in battle, and the work spread in a manner which human language cannot describe."[80] Even though traditional pulpits were not open to young people, as revivals opened physical spaces for authorized proclamation, "revival practices also opened up *rhetorical* space for child exhorters. The genre of exhortation provided a well-established form of authoritative speech that children could perform."[81] These kind of experiences exhibit the emergent path for young people.

Rather than participate in extensive training for ministry, many young people filled with the enthusiasm of the frontier revivals exercised their freedom en route to more formal ministries. In 1801, sixteen-year-old Peter

77. Graff, *Conflicting Paths*, 32.

78. Presbyterian Church, "Short Narrative," 50.

79. Presbyterian Church, "Narrative," 101.

80. McNemar and Shakers, *Kentucky Revival*, 26.

81. Smith, "Out of the Mouths of Babes."

Cartwright attended a wedding with his family which gave rise to great consternation over his faith. At one camp meeting he debated and deposed a Jewish man who challenged the Christian faith, winning several converts.[82] Cartwright unexpectedly received his license to exhort at seventeen.[83] Later that year, Cartwright was given the duty to form a preaching circuit.

Young African Americans preached as well. Although there was no active revival at the time of Charles T. Walker's youth, he began his preaching career before a formal education or any licensing. Walker was baptized at fifteen years old and sensed the call to preach not long afterward.[84] After a few years of schooling, he was licensed to preach at eighteen and ordained at nineteen. Walker became fairly well known as the "boy preacher," and at some point earned the nickname of "the black Spurgeon."[85]

Young women of this era, even within the more permissive frontier revival context, toed the line of authorized speech. Rebecca Chaney Miller "struggled with 'deep anxiety and sorrow' after feeling called to preach at the young age of only sixteen, but when she attended her first camp meeting, she finally overcame her 'diffidence in public speaking.'"[86] Being young and a woman presented a double boundary. African American women faced another layer of limitation in their speech practices. Some managed to speak with authority by virtue of their marriage to clergymen. Others labored under more contentious conditions. Catherine Brekus records five women preachers in the nineteenth century under the age of twenty when they are first mentioned in historical records.[87] Through their preaching, young women worked to forge the emerging path for women Graff characterizes as "an intricate, highly contradictory process that remade home, family, childhood and adolescence, and womanhood itself."[88]

Finally, the major themes of adult preachers in the latter half of the nineteenth century signaled transitions in preaching, culture, and the perceived religious needs of young people. These emergent themes anticipated themes that would continue into the twentieth century. According to O. C. Edwards, "the Romantic preaching of liberal orthodoxy helped American Protestants to adjust to the great social change of the years after the Civil War, that of moving from an agricultural to an industrial society. Horace

82. Ibid., 51.
83. Ibid.
84. Floyd et al., *Life of Charles T. Walker*.
85. Smith, "Out of the Mouths of Babes," 35.
86. Brekus, *Strangers and Pilgrims*, 142.
87. Ibid., 344–46.
88. Graff, *Conflicting Paths*, 71.

Bushnell, Henry Ward Beecher, and Phillips Brooks all were concerned with the social problems they saw."[89]

As early as Ebenezer Hebard's 1814 sermon on Prov 22:1, we begin to see some of these emergent themes.[90] Hebard left behind his text almost immediately to extol the virtues of making for oneself "a good name." One forms character through making moral choices. This becomes a consistent refrain through the emergent preaching of this era, a markedly different expectation than the demands of early piety for salvation's sake. Howard Crosby's 1866 series of three sermons entitled *Social Hints for Young Christians* left behind the piety exhortations of Puritan preaching as well.[91] Crosby talked about humanity as a social creature, addressed the need for appropriate understandings of conversation, and helped young people explore the proper place of amusements in their lives. Samuel Barrett encouraged young people to not be "neglectful of health;" to attend to "what becomes them in the presence of their superiors;" to "stay much at home," which "is the nursery of nearly all the virtues," to understand "the nature and prerequisites of true freedom;" and to not be "misled by wrong ideas of what is manly," among other admonitions.[92]

The preaching of Henry Ward Beecher and Washington Gladden represent the emergent themes fully developed. Beecher's *Lectures to Young Men* are suggestive of the new themes: "Industry and Idleness," "Twelve Causes of Dishonesty," "Gamblers and Gambling," "Practical Hints," "Vulgarity," and "Happiness" are among a few. The rapidly urbanizing, increasingly independent young men would be helped by "warning them against the moral dangers of life in the city."[93] Beecher's three hundred plus pages cautioned against laziness while advocating industriousness, outlined social graces, cautioned young men about brothels and enticing amusements, and advocated the social practices which should lead to happiness.

Gladden's *Myrrh and Cassia: Two Discourses to Young Men and Women* bemoaned "the great decrease in family life, especially in our cities. . . . Many of the social conditions resulting from the introduction of the large system of industry—the aggregation of capital and the congregation of laborers are injurious to morals." [94] Gladden encouraged his audience to at-

---

89. Edwards, *History of Preaching*, 648.

90. Hebard, *Sermon Delivered at Brandon*.

91. Crosby, *Social Hints*.

92. Barrett, *Youths Void of Understanding*.

93. Edwards, *History of Preaching*, 635. Also note that they are called lectures rather than sermons.

94. Gladden, *Myrrh and Cassia*, 5.

tain high moral improvement, mental improvement, and to be responsible professionals as no other generation before had.[95] For young women, Gladden attacked those who portrayed "the kind of life that a young woman ought to live [which] is summed up in one word—uselessness. . . . That is about the estimate of women held by many men; and it goes without saying that it is an estimate readily accepted by the indolence and selfishness of many women."[96] Gladden paved a new way forward by addressing young women with an entire sermon and by championing educated, employed, powerful, and godly women who were not simply objects of beauty to placate men's desires.

Nineteenth-century preaching provides a canvas upon which to see the changes that occurred among America's young people. While some of the preaching stayed on traditional paths with respect to young people, transitional and emergent paths indicated a new concern for their place within society. The explosion of Sunday Schools carved out a niche in the church's relationship to young people that would only increase. The preaching characteristic of these paths also indicates young people's attention to their self-perception and an awareness of their agency. As we move forward, the preaching of the twentieth century will find expression alongside the rise of the modern adolescent.

MOVES TO THE MARGINS IN THE EARLY TWENTIETH CENTURY

If young people in the eighteenth and nineteenth centuries displayed a variety of engagement with preaching, both as listener and preacher, the first fifty years of the twentieth century paint a picture of decreasing diversity. While preaching to young people and young people preaching continue in the twentieth century, there were significant changes. The way people thought about growing up in America revolutionized as "the era of the adolescent dawned."[97] The seeds of new themes in preaching from the nineteenth century converged with innovative trends in preaching for an unrivaled confidence in young people. Religious education began to drive homiletic thinking about young people. A positive image of young people reigned in pulpits while cultural images of young people trended toward ambivalence.

95. Ibid., 12.
96. Ibid., 22.
97. Kett, *Rites of Passage*, 215.

Cultural Changes

The "era of the adolescent," as Kett calls it, was inaugurated through shifts in the cultural imaginary of Americans. Three interrelated shifts contributed to twentieth century constructions of the adolescent: (1) the development of a psychological focus on adolescents, (2) new social and economic policies that determined adolescent roles, and (3) the pursuit of adolescents through the market.[98]

The first of these shifts was taken up by many, but perhaps no more influential than G. Stanley Hall and his *Adolescence* (1904). Hall portrayed "adolescent experience as torn by dualisms which disrupted the harmony of childhood; hyperactivity and inertia, social sensibility and self-absorption, lofty intuitions and childish folly. . . . Hall insisted that the misbehavior and eccentricities of young people be viewed as normal outgrowths of biological maturation rather than as inexcusable departures from a fixed standard of behavior."[99] Hall's thoughts were not necessarily original, but his work brought together science and religion, and placed young people at the center of research.[100]

The psychological view also found its way into the social and economic policies of the early twentieth century. Adolescent populations declined (due to decreasing family size) in the first two decades of the twentieth century and the Great Depression made employment scarce for young people in the 1930s. National labor laws discouraged the hiring of young people and public high schools became increasingly well attended due to compulsory education laws. Franklin Roosevelt's 1935 act to establish the National Youth Administration "trumpet[ed] the motto 'Youth Must Be Served.'"[101] Social and economic policies placed young people into managed spaces and, taking a cue from Roosevelt, transformed young people from producers into consumers.

As the Depression ended and World War II commenced, many young people had more free time and disposable income. Eugene Gilbert's efforts to market products to young people eventually found great success.[102] Magazines, automobiles, movies, fashion, and music established empires while young people were less likely to produce goods and service. The relationship between market and adolescents emerged as a driving force in

98. Ibid., 215–72.
99. Ibid., 217.
100. Ibid., 221.
101. Palladino, *Teenagers*, 39.
102. See Ibid., 97–115.

the American economy in the first half of the twentieth century. The three major segments of the cultural imaginary (psychology, social and economic policy, marketing) also affected young people's relationship with preaching.

Adult Preaching to Young People in the Early Twentieth Century

Relatively few sermons or collections of sermons are available in the opening years of the twentieth century. In the years surrounding the Great Depression, however, there seems to have been a resurgence. The preaching in this time exuded confidence in young people. Preachers addressed young people concerning the progress of the era, social issues, character formation, and linked together country, work, and education. For some, modernism and fundamentalism surfaced as important issues that could affect young people. Sermons combined aspects of the Romantic and Social Gospel preaching of the earlier era with the influence of Harry Emerson Fosdick's "project" preaching method. Frank Fagerburg, for instance, said that young people "are certainly thinking and asking significant questions, sometimes very disturbing questions. . . . Young people's questions must be faced as candidly as they are asked."[103] All of Fagerburg's sermons were titled as questions and respond to questions prompted by young people.

Similarly, others characterize optimistic views of young people. George Crapullo noted in 1936 that

> Youth is on the march. Victims of an unprecedented period of hardship and insecurity, they have been plunged into the grim realization that all is not well with the world. The carefree, light-hearted, pleasure-seeking youth of the jazz age of yesterday have been supplanted by the serious-minded youth of the depression era, who are bent on doing something about the conditions that have made them the "lost generation." They are on the march to discover new ideals and new ways of living.[104]

This kind of optimism in the character of young people was closely tied to the future of the nation.[105]

The confidence in young people continued with preachers like Gaston Foote, who compared Jesus to a football player and encouraged young

---

103. Fagerburg, *This Questioning Age*, i.

104. Crapullo, *Messages to Modern Youth*, 7. Some of Crapullo's sermons were also framed as responses to young people's questions.

105. Ibid., 23.

people's similar self-determination and ambition.[106] W. B. Riley also exhibited such confidence with his collection of sermons entitled *Youth's Victory Lies This Way*.[107] While Riley's emphasis on young people as the future of church and nation was evident, he brings another dynamic to preaching to young people. His sermons are rife with polemic against the evils of modernism. He speaks of "'The Revolt of Youth' [which is] for the most part . . . wholly unorganized. It is the product of and accentuated by, liberal theology, loose morals, ill-advised luxury, and parental slackness."[108] He encourages faith in the integrity of the Bible while discouraging evolutionary thought and communism. In many circles, young people became a foil for arguments against liberalism.

Religious Education Eclipses Homiletics

In the early twentieth century, advice on religious education encompasses instruction to pastors on preaching to young people. Bushnell's *Christian Nurture*, the advent of psychology, the institutionalization of Sunday School, and movements in education coalesced in such a way that religious education as a discipline could speak authoritatively to preachers.[109] It is here that religious education, rather than preachers like Broadus or Mather, begins to instruct homiletics on the best practices for preaching to young people.

Writing on the role of religious education, Paul Morris, directed, "Speak the language of youth and of the particular age of youth with which you are dealing. This necessitates some knowledge of psychology. It is sometimes a mistake of age to attempt to talk to youth in the terminology of a past generation."[110] Furthermore, the pastor functioned as a "youth evangelist," who "with his superior understanding of the workings of the Spirit of God in the hearts of youth . . . has an unequaled opportunity and responsibility for leading youth to Christ."[111]

106. Foote, *Keys to Conquest*. This is quite a departure from the Puritan warnings to young people about games of the field. His sermons also intersect, at times, with the theology of "Muscular Christianity."

107. Riley, *Youth's Victory*.

108. Ibid., 30.

109. The Religious Education Association, for instance, was formed in 1903. See also Stock, *Church Work with Young People*, 1–15.

110. Morris, *Winning Youth for Christ*, 18.

111. Ibid., 13.

Harry Stock advocated a move toward more substantive periods of worship within the church's educational program.[112] In worship Stock wanted two elements: talks and stories. According to Stock, "talks are frequently a part of the worship service but they should seldom be regarded as the major element. . . . A five- or ten-minute talk in the usual Sunday morning period is all that should be expected."[113] Stock characterized stories in this way: "well read or told, [stories] are often more effective than addresses or sermonettes. Great care should be taken in the selection of materials. 'Sob stuff' must be avoided."[114] In a section entitled "The Pastor and His Young People," Stock advised the pastor to account for young people in sermon preparation for the Sunday morning service, and visualized the particular needs of a young person named "John Jones." Stock asked,

> What change needs to be made in the sermon for him? It will not be necessary to dilute the message; it may be necessary to simplify it or to couch it in terms which correspond with his present experience. There will need to be a certain concreteness which finds illustration in the realm of young life as well as adulthood. . . . This will not be talking down to youth; it will merely be a recognition that they are there—or ought to be. Such an ability to include young people within the range of the sermon thought and yet not to single them out for extended special treatment, and also to lift their minds to truths which they cannot yet fully comprehend but about which they should be thinking, will be in no small measure a result of the pastor's constant contacts with young life.[115]

In Stock's statement the religious educator becomes the preaching professor in trying to reach the young "rebels," "idealists," "drifters," and "perplexed."[116] Stock also indicated that young people's voices should be carefully managed, giving them some pulpit responsibility while hoping to turn them toward "full-time Christian service" (read: more adult-like and more effective).[117]

---

112. Stock, *Church Work*, 93–94.

113. Ibid., 101.

114. Ibid.

115. Ibid., 194–95.

116. Ibid., 210–16. Here again, the dichotomy of dangerous/beautiful exists in a classificatory system.

117. Ibid., 195–96.

The preacher also received direction from the religious educator in Nevin Harner's *Youth Work in the Church*.[118] Throughout the book, Harner described youth as a prize to be won. Harner warned ministers, saying "if they find [the sermon] dull and uninspiring, or monotonously the same every Sunday, or shot through with concepts and language which they do not understand, of course they will not come and continue to come."[119] Harner devoted an entire section to "Preaching to Young People." In it "the attractiveness of a church service to youth—still using the word in the best sense—will hinge to a considerable degree upon the sermon."[120] In this section, Harner the religious educator describes good preaching as dependent upon content and form. The preacher who successfully manages content will "build a bridge of words across the gap which separates them [meaning, doctrines and the issues of youth] so that spiritual help and strength can march out of our ancient Christian faith straight into the needy lives of youth today."[121] The more difficult matter was form. In order to understand the form of successful preaching to young people, Harner analyzed a book of sermons.[122] Harner counted the number of illustrations in each sermon, the clarity of its structure through number of divisions, use of humor, and any distinguishing uses of language. Upon his observations, Harner concluded that the most successful characteristics of preaching to youth were:

1. A rather free use of illustrations.

2. A clear-cut structure, easy to follow and easy to remember.

3. A speedy beginning, which enlists interest and gets at the heart of the matter quickly without the tedium of a long-drawn-out introduction.

4. Pungent phrases, which rivet attention and stand to be remembered.

5. A considerable understanding of what youth are thinking, what they are saying, and what they are worrying about.[123]

Harner summed up his understanding in this way: "Here, then, is a beginning at least of the science of preaching and speaking to youth."[124]

118. Harner, *Youth Work*.

119. Ibid., 91. Interestingly, this work comes out at the leading edge of the years Palladino calls "the advertising age."

120. Ibid., 96.

121. Ibid., 97.

122. Weston, *Sermons I Have Preached*.

123. Harner, *Youth Work*, 99–100. This train of thought continues later in Conrad, "Preaching to Young People," 144–50.

124. Harner, *Youth Work*, 100.

In Harner, we find the religious educator determining the science of good preaching. Harner also suggested the measured use of young people to determine the direction of regular preaching. Harner set young people up as a focus group (a marketing technique!) designed to help the preacher find material that appealed to young people.[125] This was careful management of the space and authority of young people.

As religious education as a discipline emerged, it asserted its own authority about preaching as far as young people were concerned. Young people in this literature were characterized as largely passive subjects. In this, the contemporary formulations of the passive adolescent listener come to fruition. This does not mean, however, that they ceased their roles as speakers.

Young Preachers in the Early Twentieth Century

Young preachers in the early twentieth century were increasingly encouraged to pursue formal Christian ministries. As we have seen, Stock believed young people's preaching was the best way to turn young people toward full-time Christian ministry though the effect of this preaching on the religious communities is not mentioned. Young people's exhortation was not celebrated in the same manner as it had been in the frontier revivals. Rather than a celebrated but limited ecstatic occurrence, young people who showed promise for preaching were directed toward formal education and ministerial training.

R. N. Hogan, an African-American in the Church of Christ tradition, experienced the combination of an apprentice and educational model, as Hogan went on preaching tours with his mentor G. P. Bowser. Hogan "became known as the 'boy evangelist' and converted over seventy people in his first three years of preaching. Bowser schooled Hogan thoroughly in the art of preaching, and Hogan mastered the creative synthesis of the rational and black preaching traditions that Bowser taught."[126] Though Hogan had a large number of converts through his preaching, the situations and style of his preaching were managed. In addition, the moniker "boy evangelist"

125. Ibid., 101. Compare with the contemporary "roundtable" approaches of John McClure and Lucy Rose that concede much more authority to all on both the issues of theology and preaching.

126. Casey, *Saddlebags*, 140. The apprenticeship model, most prominent in African American and Latino/a preaching traditions, will continue to be an important way that young people engage preaching into the twentieth and twenty-first centuries, and one that holds potential for the kind of liberative and formative processes I describe later.

signified that Hogan was doing something unusual and the number of conversions was worthy of recording.

Mary G. Evans experienced a similar set of circumstances. Bettye Collier-Thomas records that Evans was a young African American woman who felt called to preach at age twelve.[127] Like the nickname given to Hogan, Evans was "dubbed the 'girl preacher,' [and] she was highly praised for her sermonic discourses. At fourteen, she received her local preacher's license at the AME District Quarterly Conference."[128] Only a short time later, she felt the need to be educated for ministry and entered Payne Theological Seminary, graduating at age twenty.

Among African Americans and whites, women and men, this emerges as a common pattern in the twentieth century. Young people are encouraged to preach through carefully managed preaching opportunities, then take up more education through apprenticeship and/or formal education.

SUMMARY

Young people's relationship with preaching through American history is one of varied experiences and ways of engaging preaching. Prior to the emergence of the passive teenage listener who needs to be reached through special means, young people championed preaching, spoke through adult preaching, and spoke themselves. Preaching helped shape perceptions of young people. They have been characterized as sinners who endanger themselves and society. Conversely they have been depicted as the brightest hope of the church and world. Young people have spoken back to preaching in important ways as much as preaching has spoken to them. Young people's historical relationship with preaching calls into question the lack of inclusion and involvement of youth in contemporary preaching studies, and calls forth a theological and ethical foundation that can more appropriately fund their relationship with preaching. The next chapter explores the ways that the relationships between young people and preaching continue to ossify in distinctly different, yet related literatures of the late twentieth century.

127. Collier-Thomas, *Daughters of Thunder*, 148.
128. Ibid.

2

Silence and Deficiency

Contemporary Pictures of Youth and Preaching

In contemporary preaching literature and in churches today, the relation-ship between preaching and adolescent youth seems tenuous. Even as young people populate weekly worship services and stand in pulpits across North America, their preaching activity receives meager reflection in literature concerned with either preaching or adolescents. This disposition reflects the historical process charted in chapter 1, where religious education eclipsed preaching. Although the exclusion of young people has not been deliberate, this chapter will explore how preaching and homiletics has maintained this alienated relationship with adolescents.[1] Public images of adolescents have been uncritically incorporated into the work of mainline denominational, university-based homiletics and youth ministry literature on preaching, even though these two literatures rarely interact. Additionally, this chapter will also take account of how the literature of childhood studies, childhood studies in religion, critical youth studies, and recent scholarship in the reli-gious education of youth helpfully reframe the public images of adolescents

1. Though the distinction between "preaching" and "homiletics" can be false, I mean that preaching is the practice of gathered listeners and preacher, while homiletics is the disciplinary reflection on that practice. Thus I am interested in how adolescents are depicted in their relationship to preaching as a practice as well as how they relate to homiletics as a discipline.

and their religiosity, but are unconcerned with preaching. In order to offer a type of preaching discourse that helpfully weaves and corrects these threads, the chapter surveys the ways that different disciplines either ignore adolescents, narrowly construct them in ways that deny difference and/or agency, or disregard preaching activity as an important locus of youthful religious practice.

MAINLINE DENOMINATIONAL, UNIVERSITY-BASED HOMILETICS AND ADOLESCENTS[2]

Listener-Centered Homiletics

Homiletic discourse originating in mainline denominational and university-based research programs over the past fifty years has focused its attention on the listener. In order to understand the contemporary picture of homiletics and adolescents' place within it, two schemes for categorizing North American homiletics and the development of a listener-centered approach are important.

Lucy Atkinson Rose narrates the role of the listener in North American homiletics through the metaphor of an ever-expanding group of gatherers around a table whose focus is the Christian scriptures. In late nineteenth and early twentieth century North American homiletics, the preacher's task is transmission of a truth to listeners, or what she calls "traditional theory."[3] The passive role of the listener shifts very little and the preacher's role decreases significantly in what Rose calls "kerygmatic theory." According to Rose, in kerygmatic theory, "the gap between the preacher and the congregation [widens] because of the conviction that in the sermon God speaks."[4] In more recent years, through what has become known as the New Homiletic, preaching has focused on creating an experience for listeners.[5] Rose calls this development "transformational theory."[6] Rose's proposal for a new focus envisions preaching as "marginal voices" gathering around the table where preacher and congregation are inter-connected explorers of

---

2. I choose university-based and mainline denominational homiletic discourse as a mode of discourse because it has been a location of diverse thought and because it is the primary site of my own training in preaching.

3. Rose, *Sharing the Word*, 15.

4. Ibid., 38.

5. Ibid., 59.

6. Ibid., 61.

texts, meaning, and mystery.[7] Rose narrates a theological-ethical account of communication theory in North American homiletics where power for interpretation and communication via the pulpit has shifted.

John McClure also proposes a scheme for understanding the preacher/listener relationship in the North American homiletic tradition.[8] Rooted in a positive attempt to negotiate the religious terrain in the post-World War II era, "the idea that speakers and hearers can link arms and share a common experiential journey toward the meaning of the gospel was essential" for New Homiletic writers.[9] These accounts of preaching have, by and large, carried the day. But McClure indicates that post-World War II homiletic thought has also been on a trajectory towards ever-widening accounts of experience. [10] The preacher is no longer able to speak authoritatively and universally about human experience with the same confidence found in the New Homiletic.

These accounts suggest that preachers are realizing that simplistic or universalized accounts of human experience, or traditional notions of authority, are no longer adequate.[11] Still, in an era attuned to the varieties of human experience, adolescents have not garnered the attention that others have found in recent thought. Instead, either silence toward youth or broad stereotypical ontological adolescence stand in for young people in this literature.

Deficient and/or Missing Youth

Adolescent responses to preaching are often assumed. For instance, Fred Craddock opines, "some of the congregation *especially the young people*, find the 'points' useful for estimating the hour and minute when the terminus can be expected. The process is simple arithmetic: time the first point, multiply that by the number of 'points' announced ('I have three things to say about this matter this morning'), and one has not only something to anticipate but a fair estimate as to when to expect it."[12] Adolescents are caught in the

7. Ibid., 90.

8. McClure, *Other-Wise Preaching*, 47–66.

9. Ibid., 48.

10. Ibid.

11. See, for instance, the ways the rich texture of human experiences are honored in McClure and Ramsay, *Telling the Truth*; Black, *Healing Homiletic*; Nieman and Rogers, *Preaching to Every Pew*; Smith, *Preaching as Weeping, Confession, and Resistance*; Smith, *Preaching Justice.*

12. Craddock, *As One Without Authority*, 115. Italics mine.

middle of Craddock's argument against deductive preaching. They function as the superlative "straw man," an undifferentiated group of preaching time keepers who impel preachers toward inductive movement.

Likewise, in his book *Celebration and Experience in Preaching*, Henry Mitchell instructs preachers on concrete images, familiar language, familiar details, and timing for preaching.[13] In a section on the necessity of familiar language for language to form in consciousness, he states

> This insight is evident in the way some people relate to youth. No matter how old the speaker is, the use of the latest youth lingo will procure her or him a bond with the teenagers. No matter how young the speaker is, the use of what seems to be stilted and strange lingo will result in inattention or being tuned out, for being perceived as "out of touch." Familiar language is a way of saying that the speaker identifies with the hearers, whatever the genre being used.[14]

Certainly to an extent, Mitchell is correct. According to Mitchell, however, if preachers cannot speak the peculiar linguistic practices of adolescents, then no hearing can be gained. Mitchell assumes a unified youth culture where adolescents by and large share a common "lingo" and that youth are unable to participate in "adult" lingo.[15]

Other references to adolescents are more ambiguous in nature. Paul Scott Wilson describes the task of the "four page" sermon with the metaphor of movie making. Sermon writing as movie making requires preachers to "shift the mental image of sermon composition from essay writing to movie making . . . a tremendous change in how we arrange our thoughts" and "more than simply telling plots, or becoming one character in a narrative, we will create entire worlds that address the senses, the mind, and the heart."[16] An almost negligible line is inserted within this paragraph on preaching-as-movie-making: "If preaching is to reach youth and teenagers

---

13. Mitchell, *Celebration and Experience*.

14. Ibid., 81. This section of the 1990 text did not make it into the revised version in 2009.

15. Two commitments undergird Mitchell's statement: (1) Use of Kenneth Burke's understanding of "identification" and "consubstantiality." Burke says, "You persuade a man only insofar as you can talk his language by speech, gesture, tonality, order, image, attitude, idea, identifying your ways with his." See Burke, *Rhetoric of Motives*, 2. (2) David Buttrick's understanding of how "language forms in consciousness." The preacher's theological task is to search for the images and language most appropriate to the context in which the preacher is speaking.

16. Wilson, *Four Pages of the Sermon*, 11.

especially, it needs an approach like this movie making idea."[17] There is no explanation or cited research to indicate why this is true. Wilson's intention seems to be rather benign. But much like Craddock's statement, adolescents are caught in the crossfire between one preaching theory and a new and improved theory which, as if to tout the extent of its effectiveness or to establish the viability of preaching in the future, can garner even the attention of young people.

These statements provide examples of what communication theorists call "marked" and "unmarked" language.[18] "Youth" and "teenagers" are marked elements of preaching discourse that signify listeners who need special attention. When "youth" or "teenager(s)" appear in this literature, they function as a kind of tacit assent to a universal idea of who youth are in relation to preaching. They are, in some sense, deficient as listeners and function this way without the need for elaboration on the part of the author. On the other hand, "adult" (which does not need to be stated) functions as the unmarked, oppositional term and indicates a more mature sermon listening ability.

Some homiletic studies unintentionally exclude adolescents, resulting in a kind of silence. Christine M. Smith's otherwise helpful text *Preaching as Weeping, Confession, and Resistance: Radical Responses to Radical Evil* maps out a response to ageism and her focus on age suggests that homiletics might also attend to youth. [19] As she narrates the increase of the aged population in America, she notes that "our sermons and our ministries need to portray older adults as pictures of strength, resourcefulness, and endurance. Through ministries of word and action we need to call our congregations into conscious advocacy of the special kind of assistance that is needed for older adults to remain independent in the community."[20] She offers a useful corrective for preaching and Christian ministry but does not include youth in this helpful discussion on age.

Detailing the challenge of preaching to a multi-generational audience, Joseph Jeter and Ronald Allen outline characteristics of different generations in *One Gospel, Many Ears*.[21] Jeter and Allen outline the multiple features of generations and how those defining features influence preaching. They also recognize a challenge for their own work:

17. Ibid.

18. See O'Brien, "Boundaries and Contradictions," 426–42. See also the discussion on Lesko's "confident characterizations" of youth, below.

19. Smith, *Preaching as Weeping*, 38–61.

20. Ibid., 45.

21. Jeter and Allen, *One Gospel, Many Ears*.

> Even as we write and read, of course, a new generation is enter-
> ing adulthood—those who have been born since 1981 (or so)
> that we have heard described as the Millenial Generation. The
> church needs *now* to begin to identify distinctive qualities in
> this rising group, and to learn both how to speak the gospel in
> the generation's language and how to help the newest generation
> speak gospel language.[22]

Later in the book they devote time to talking about children and preaching as well as faith development and preaching, but they do not go beyond
the recognition that *someone* should devote time to this group. Though
they recognize adolescents as important, silence about adolescent listeners
persists.

In a similar volume, Thomas Troeger and H. Edward Everding, Jr.
apply Howard Gardner's theory of "multiple intelligences" to preaching.[23]
While Gardner's theory ostensibly applies to all ages, Troeger and Everding
explore preaching to the whole congregation in two chapters: "Preaching
and Children's Ways of Knowing" and "Preaching and Adult Ways of Knowing." Adolescents receive no attention in either of the chapters and receive
no chapter of their own. Occupying a liminal space—no longer children
and not yet adults—adolescents are missing.

Finally, the Listening to Listeners research group provides invaluable
resources from their study of congregants' thoughts on preaching. They set
out to interview "slightly more than 260 laity" in order to understand how
listeners hear and process sermons.[24] Though the study worked across denominational, ethnic, geographical, and gender lines, when it came to age
the Listening to Listeners project "tried to interview people from different
age groups—older *adults*, middle-aged *adults*, and younger *adults*."[25] Two
fifteen year olds and two nineteen year olds were also interviewed, amount-
ing to four interviewees in the project.[26] This counts for about 1.5 percent
of the attention of the study, hardly representative of the adolescents in
churches, denominations, or the general population.[27] A limited data pool

---

22. Ibid., 47.

23. Troeger and H. Everding, *So That All Might Know*. See their references to Gardner's works in the notes. See also their references to James W. Fowler's work.

24. McClure, *Listening to Listeners*, 184.

25. Ibid. Italics mine. It is not my intention to criticize the work of the Listening to
Listeners group; in fact, their work in many ways sets an agenda that will be discussed
below.

26. Many thanks to John McClure for acquiring this information from Ron Allen.

27. According to the 2000 U.S. Census, people age ten to fourteen make up 7.3
percent of the population and fifteen to nineteen, 7.2 percent of the population.

is understandable, but the choice to limit their pool to an overwhelming percentage of adults as sermon listeners reveals assumptions about who is able to give meaningful feedback on preaching.

Some Openings in the Conversation

The news about mainline denominational and university-based homiletics is not entirely bleak. Most recently, the *New Interpreters Handbook of Preaching* contains two article entries on preaching and young people.[28] Kenda Creasy Dean and Mark DeVries, both scholar-practitioners in youth ministry, encourage preachers to overcome unfair stereotypes of young people as listeners and champion the use of story/storytelling, testimony, and object lessons as preaching solutions for adolescents, albeit with little technical insight or nuance.[29]

More significantly, Anna Carter Florence devotes two essays to preaching's relationship with adolescents. Florence's essay, "Preaching to the Exiles Who Live at Home: Youth, Testimony, and a Homiletic of 'True Speech'" indicts the academy concerning its silence concerning adolescents: "In the academy, too, silence reigns: only a very few scholars are writing about youth and preaching [she does not identify who!], and virtually none of them are homileticians. The message to our seminarians and churches is clear: *this is not an issue worth serious time and study.*"[30]

In this first essay, Florence's argument hinges on the notion that youth are, in the popular theological idiom, "exiles." In her opinion, "'exile' is a potent metaphor for youth. We preach to youth in exile from the church, and a church in exile from the culture. Everyone is disoriented; no one feels at home."[31] Building on Walter Brueggemann's work on testimony and counter-testimony, she believes that counter-testimonial speech helps youth form alternative identities amid exile, even as they learn the "mother tongue" of the church's speech practices.[32] She urges preachers to engage youth and youth culture, invite youth to openly discuss sermons and Scrip-

28. See Dean, "Preaching to Youth," 281–83. And also DeVries, "Youth Ministry," 337–42.

29. I believe this is suggestive of a divide in practical theology, carried forward from the history explored in chapter 1.

30. Florence, "Preaching to the Exiles," 24.

31. Ibid., 27.

32. For Brueggeman's work, see Brueggemann, *Cadences of Home.* For an argument similar to how Florence expresses that youth learn the church's "mother tongue," see "Youth and the Language of Faith," 113–28. Although Dykstra does not talk about preaching, he does express a similar frame of reference to Florence.

ture passages ("true speech"), and ultimately, to open the pulpit to youth beyond special occasions. For Florence, youth will experience preaching most effectively when "they see the church as offering an alternative identity in exile through distinctive, peculiar patterns of true speech; their pastors help them to 'get it' and proclaim it."[33]

Florence's thought is influenced not only by Brueggemann's use of "exile" but also by Yale school postliberal theology, and in particular the stream made popular by Stanley Hauerwas and William Willimon.[34] In this stream of thought, culture functions with clear boundaries: church versus wider culture, and in Florence's version youth religious culture versus adult religious culture. As a result, youth function as exiles among exiles. In order for youth to get past the first level of exile from church, "the church's mother tongue must be spoken, modeled, and taught in all of its true speech practices . . . the biblical pattern itself must be lived and learned through the community's engagement of life and text."[35]

Her second essay, "A Prodigal Preaching Story: Paul, Eutychus, and Bored-to-Death Youth," elides the story of Eutychus from Acts 20 and contemporary preaching.[36] Florence imagines that Eutychus was "killed because he was literally marginalized . . . it was the church's preaching (not to mention its spectacular lack of awareness) that actually put him at risk. . . . When performed in the local congregation, it is more like a text of terror—for youth, for preachers, and for the church."[37] The danger of preaching like Paul in this instance becomes the realization that a youthful audience "is of no consequence to the rest of us. They know the *rules* for sermons (no talking, fidgeting, pinching, fussing), but not the *art of listening*, of entering the world of a sermon; that is a much more difficult and subtle process that requires spiritual mentorship and companionship."[38] Florence advocates more attention to youth as they learn to listen to preaching and more compassion from churches as they engage youth through preaching. Ultimately, she encourages preachers to embrace youth and speak about the life that is in them.[39]

33. Florence, "Preaching to the Exiles," 29.

34. See, for example, Hauerwas and Willimon, *Resident Aliens*; Willimon, *The Intrusive Word*; Willimon, *Peculiar Speech*.

35. Florence, "Preaching to the Exiles," 27.

36. Florence, "A Prodigal Preaching Story," 233–43.

37. Ibid., 236.

38. Ibid., 238.

39. Ibid., 242–43.

Florence presents a model of adolescents' marginality based on the church's relation to culture and the church's inadequate relation to adolescents. In the end, however, her ideas fail to challenge essentialized versions of adolescent religiosity and trade on ideas within the dominant culture that adolescents are artless religious listeners and religious exiles, when, in fact, the opposite might often be the case. A more constructive response might recognize the interaction between culture, experience, and adolescent religious agency. Kathryn Tanner believes there is "no reason to insist on a culture's sharp boundaries," which renders culture as a much more multifarious scene than Florence.[40] Approaching culture this way, the exile metaphor fails to hold together as church and culture's boundaries become less definite and notions of adult and adolescent cultures (and their religious speech/listening practices) are seen in more robust interaction. Still, we can concede the main points: adolescents can and do experience distance from preaching. Likewise, the art of sermon listening is not high on the agenda of many youth. If, however, we adopt a revised understanding of the relationship between subcultures, we prevent distance in preaching from becoming a rigid marker of adolescent religiosity, and we allow that adolescence may be an important time in which a range of practices for listening and speaking are deployed.

YOUTH MINISTRY LITERATURE

The literature of youth ministry exists alongside, but with little to no interaction with mainline denominational and university-based homiletics. Of course, preaching and youth ministry often go hand-in-hand, particularly at retreats, camps, conferences, and separate youth worship services. A specialized industry supports youth ministry and thus there is literature concerning preaching specifically to youth.[41] Here we see how communication theory, theologies of preaching, and the person of the preacher operate among those who specialize in youth ministry, exhibiting a relationship with contemporary homiletic theory that is distant at best. Even as this literature places adolescents at the center, it reveals a narrow construction of adolescents as an undifferentiated audience which demands specific communication skills.

40. Tanner, *Theories of Culture*, 53. See also Chapter 5, "Christian Culture and Society" for Tanner's critique of Yale school postliberal theology.

41. This may be Anna Carter Florence's reference to "evangelical circles, where a distinct homiletic about preaching and youth already exists and flourishes." Florence, "Preaching to the Exiles," 23.

Creating Interest

Ken Davis's *How to Speak to Youth . . . And Keep them Awake at the Same Time* seeks to convey the "technical aspects of communication, as well as the heart of good communication."[42] One of few books to receive a second, revised edition in the field of youth ministry, Davis's book could be classified as a "standard" in the literature. While Davis spends most of his time developing hints and helps for communicating to adolescents, he does spend a moment characterizing them as a group. Davis's characterization of their religious capacity is not unfamiliar when viewed in historical perspective. In terms of other character traits of youth, preachers

> have the opportunity to address the most challenging, unique, and wonderful audience in the world. On the one hand, young people are hostile and skeptical, spoiled by a barrage of top-quality entertainment and turned off to much of traditional religion. On the other hand, they are moldable and tender, capable of great loyalty and commitment. Our audience is a self-conscious group of teenagers, who spend much of their lives wondering what their friends will think and giving very little thought to their own goals. They grow up in a culture that teaches them to avoid sacrifice and pain. Many kids live only for themselves and for immediate gratification. They want to believe they will live forever, yet they fear death and try to cram all of life into today. Many teenagers are lonely even in the midst of a crowd of their peers. They want to be noticed but are afraid to be different unless there is a group willing to be different with them. Many of their roles models present a message that is the antithesis of the Gospel.[43]

For Davis, the cultural manifestations of adolescence may change, but the essence of adolescence remains fixed. Of the adolescents of the 1990s, the time at which the revised edition was written, Davis believes that "if ever there was a lost generation, this is it."[44] Davis's ideas draw deeply upon the religious and cultural construction of the adolescent rooted in early American preaching, especially ideas that youth represent beauty and danger. By identifying an audience with unique needs and exercising the ability to describe its universal characteristics, Davis is able to develop and

---

42. Davis, *How to Speak to Youth*, 10.
43. Davis, *How to Speak to Youth*, rev. ed., 22.
44. Ibid., 23.

market communicational competencies (methods for creating and delivering "talks"[45]) for those who speak to this specific audience.

Part of this approach involves beginning with topics that assume and address the universalized adolescent. Propositions take the following form: "Every _____ should/can _____ because/by _____."[46] For example, Davis gives this statement as a demonstration: "Every Christian can learn to love his or her neighbor by applying three principles of neighborly love."[47] In Davis's estimation, speakers should be clear about whether their speech communicates an "'obligation,' telling kids they *should* do something; or an 'enabling' speech, telling them they *can* do something."[48]

Davis's argues for a specific type of logic for the purposes of capturing attention. He employs what he calls the "SCORRE method" for planning talks. This anagram stands for "Subject, Central Theme, Objective, Rationale, Resources, Evaluation."[49] He believes that "if you follow this process, your audience will listen *because you know how to make them listen*."[50] The speaker communicates a rationally conceived proposition supported by appropriate resources and possesses the ability to make listeners listen. He conceives of speaking with the metaphor of aiming at a target, as in hunting, or the idea of a niche- or target-market. This concept of speaking is not limited, however, to arrangement of ideas.

Davis discusses the physical aspects of preaching to youth: use of notes, aspects of the physical space of preaching, and use of sound systems and microphones. He suggests that audiences build rapport with a speaker through his/her confidence displayed through "command of the language . . . choice of words . . . use of effective illustrations . . . clear presentation of the speech's objective . . . good eye contact, powerful gestures, an aggressive stance."[51] Again, all of this is suggestive of the hunt, with the exception of the advice to be vulnerable, which "makes members of the audience believe you are communicating with them, not delivering a canned speech at them."[52] This simultaneous presentation of power and vulnerability expresses Davis's views on the submissive role of undifferentiated adolescent listeners.

---

45. As below with Fields/Robbins, Davis does refer to the communicational event as speaking or giving a speech or talk.

46. Davis, *How to Speak to Youth*, 52–60.

47. Ibid., 61.

48. Ibid., 44.

49. Davis, *How to Speak to Youth*, rev. ed., 44.

50. Ibid. Italics mine.

51. Ibid., 101.

52. Ibid.

Speakers are in control of the situation, able to manipulate listeners (benevolently, of course) in such a way that their messages are received.

Davis presents adolescents' lack of ability to maintain "interest" and "attention" as defining characteristics of the universal adolescent audience. In order to keep teenagers' attention, Davis explores the use of humor and use of the Bible. Humor, according to Davis, "gets the blood flowing and creates great interest."[53] He suggests always reading the Bible in understandable language, presenting biblical characters as real characters, avoiding over-spiritualizing details of the biblical text, and providing applications of the Bible to real life.[54] Rather than a rigorous attempt at biblical contextualization, Davis presents a more focused attempt to attract and sustain interest.

Dan Webster and Jana Sundene's essay, "Speaking to High School Students" describes how the youth minister can be an effective communicator when the youth minister can *understand his* (sic) *target audience* (the students), know how to *apply biblical truths to a student's life,* and *develop practical communication skills.*[55] The youth minister is called to four different areas (presented in overlapping circles): (1) understanding students, (2) knowing content, (3) developing communication skills, and (4) knowing the power of the Holy Spirit.[56]

Speakers understand students by recognizing four major developmental issues for youth: "experiencing physical and emotional changes, struggling with self-worth, and tending toward conformity and mental confusion."[57] They also observe four cultural forces on adolescents: fragmentation, a "me-istic culture," relativism, and escapism.[58] Like Davis, Webster and Sundene attempt to build a preaching method built upon universal assumptions about adolescents which are predominantly negative—deficiencies which can be corrected through the kind of practices they describe. Adolescents are enveloped in a time of *sturm und drang.* They are struggling spiritually, physically, emotionally, psychically, socially, and mentally, inescapably caught up in the nefarious pressures of "culture." The 1980s generation about which Webster and Sundene write is ostensibly as much a "lost generation" as Davis writes about in the late 1990s. These tropes bolster the

---

53. Ibid., 135. Notice also the subtle arrangement of Davis's instruction by some of the categories of classical rhetoric: invention, arrangement, and style/delivery.

54. Ibid., 143–50.

55. Webster and Sundene, "Speaking to High School Students," 326.

56. Ibid., 327.

57. Ibid., 330.

58. Ibid., 330–32.

heavy-handed authority of preaching to adolescents while simultaneously perpetuating the idea of ontological adolescence.

Knowledge of content is demonstrated by messages that are "grounded in biblical truths" and that interface with the developmental/cultural needs of students.[59] Regarding the development of communication skills, speakers are told that logic, interest, and application of a message to youth will increase the possibilities of listening.[60] Webster and Sundene identify competencies that the speaker to young people must develop in order to gain a hearing. "Interest" is fundamental and the language of transaction—giving a message to students—is used for the nature of communication. They propose that "illustrations and humor are two *essential* ingredients in speaking to high school students."[61] Again, this advice is based on universal assumptions about youth—that they lack "interest" or the ability to discern difficult ideas and must therefore have ideas "illustrated" (read: simplified) and made humorous.

A more recent text takes a similar approach, but it is more important to see in this text the relationship between youth ministry and mainline denominational, university-based homiletics. Doug Fields and Duffy Robbins's *Speaking to Teenagers: How to Think About, Create and Deliver Effective Messages* is poised to become a standard text since Fields and Robbins are popular pastors/youth ministry experts.[62] This self-proclaimed "advanced" youth ministry text tends to take an adversarial approach to homiletic theory or at least homiletic pedagogy. While both authors claim a valued seminary education, one of the authors writes

59. Ibid., 333.

60. Ibid., 334.

61. Ibid., 337. Italics mine.

62. Robbins and Fields, *Speaking to Teenagers*. Fields and Robbins share some of the same assumptions about adolescents as Davis and Sundene/Webster. For instance, similar to Davis's "lost generation," they point out "Obviously, our audience is a lot younger than most of the folks who sit in those pews on Sunday morning, but the reality of their pain and needs is just as real. There are hurting kids everywhere dying to know the good news of God's love" (16). The trope of hurting/angst-ridden/troubled adolescence remains, but they are simultaneously ripe for gospel preaching. And likewise, they pose six questions concerning potential blocks to communicating with young people: "1. First, we have to get them to pay attention to the message . . . 2. And if they hear it, we need to make sure they understand it . . . 3. Then even if they hear it and understand it, that doesn't mean they'll actually believe it . . . 4. Even if they believe the message in that moment, there's still the challenge of helping each of them to retain it in their active memory . . . 5. And then, of course, there is the question of obedience . . . 6. And of the number who retain the message and have some measure of resolve to obey the message, there's finally this question: Will they actually flesh out the decision by taking action?" (18–19). Again, interest is a main feature followed by the need for clarity.

When I was a seminary student, my homiletics professor was very difficult to impress. . . . He was a good man, a great preacher, a very tough grader, and someone I really wanted to impress when I was a young communicator. But even today, I've got to force myself to remember he's no longer my audience and I'm not competing for a grade. When we study, we want to study for our real audience—that group of teenagers to whom we plan to speak, not the imaginary audience we want to impress. . . . We've all heard youth ministry speakers who might have been very effective had their audience been a panel of seminary and college professors. Unfortunately, the profs couldn't make it to youth group, and the teenagers who did show up were left confused and disconnected—and therefore bored with the content. It's nice that you still remember how to parse verbs and can articulate the historical context for the use of mud as Jesus' healing agent of choice. But it's far more important that you study with the intention of gaining knowledge so teenagers can recognize that God's Word is understandable, relevant, and has the power to transform their lives even in the twenty-first century.[63]

This, of course, is not a new thought for preachers and critics of preachers. In fact, their statement perhaps unknowingly echoes Harry Emerson Fosdick's classic criticism:

They [preachers] take a passage from Scripture and, proceeding on the assumption that the people attending church that morning are deeply concerned about what the passage means, they spend their half hour or more on historical exposition of the verse or chapter, ending with some appended practical application to the auditors. Could any procedure be more surely predestined to dullness and futility? Who seriously supposes that, as a matter of fact, one in a hundred of the congregation cares, to start with, what Moses, Isaiah, Paul, or John meant in those special verses, or came to church deeply concerned about it? Nobody else who talks to the public so assumes that the vital interests of the people are located in the meaning of words spoken two thousand years ago. . . . Somehow or other, every other agency dealing with the public recognizes that contact with the actual life of the auditor is the one place to begin. Only the preacher proceeds still upon the idea that folk come to church desperately anxious to discover what happened to the Jebusites. The result is that folk less and less come to church at all.[64]

63. Ibid., 108.
64. Fosdick, "What is the Matter," 10.

At first glance, Fields's and Robbins's outlook is a wholesale adaptation of Fosdick's own "project method" of preaching whereby "preaching's primary concern is people's real problems."[65] This kind of personal pastoral preaching, however, is not the goal nor is it the starting point for Fields and Robbins. Instead, they cite persuasion and teenagers' obedience as the ultimate goals of "messages."[66] In fact, the entire framework of their book is built on a classic rhetorical model of *ethos*, *pathos*, and *logos* (in that order).[67] Fields and Robbins desire to construct a way of communicating that primarily relies on the relationship of speaker to audience and on being able to effectively persuade the audience through their needs/interests/emotions, which differs from providing therapy through preaching.[68]

Only after heavily treating *ethos* and *pathos* as avenues toward creating primary bridges of communication do they engage the *logos* aspect of communication. Fields and Robbins envision messages crafted by speakers that "S.T.I.C.K.," which stands for the different processes of writing messages: (1) Study, (2) Think, (3) Illustrate, (4) Construct, and (5) Keep focused.[69] Within this framework there are some expected assumptions about preaching from the Evangelical perspective. For instance, Fields and Robbins present the rationale for study: "The goal of study is to gain a greater understanding of Scripture so you can—(a) Allow the text to speak for itself, untarnished by your own assumptions and preconceptions. (b) Identify the timeless message that God has for his (sic) people. (c) Consider what these timeless truths mean for your life and for the lives of your students."[70] This focus on the timelessness of a text's message, the text's pristine voice, and absence of any human hermeneutical element uncovers a great distance between so-called Evangelical homiletics and mainline denominational,

65. Ramsey, *Care-Full Preaching*, 14.

66. Again, this is a rhetorical model not foreign to traditional homiletic theory, but also not explicitly acknowledged. For instance, see J Broadus and Stanfield, *On the Preparation*, 170. See also Robbins and Fields, *Speaking to Teenagers*, 37–43. Not once do they claim their own activity as "preaching."

67. There are only two references in the book to homiletics texts. The rest come largely from communication theory.

68. It also extends to their treatment of how room arrangement and delivery affect these elements in the final chapter.

69. Robbins and Fields, *Speaking to Teenagers*, 89.

70. Ibid., 110. This kind of thinking about the nature of the biblical text in concert with their advice to consult traditional exegetical tools (based in human reason) lies somewhere between Donald McKim's descriptions of how "fundamentalist theology" and "neo-evangelical theology" use the Bible. It also lies between John McClure's "scriptural code" categories of "translation" and "transition/traduction."

university-based homiletics. The latter would not advocate applying time-less messages to timeless forms of experience.

Unexpected, however, is their emphasis on the construction of a "talk" through principles of inductive communication.[71] From this we can sur-mise that Fields and Robbins desire to create common experiences within communication that are transformative for all listeners. By this logic, "con-cretes" are grounded in assumptions that human experiences are, in fact, universal experiences. Inductive communication disregards the varieties of human experience that actually take place among adolescents in favor of (1) an assumed common lived experience on the part of listeners or (2) creating a common listening experience for all listeners.[72] So as Fields and Robbins advocate using "concrete life" without nuance, they end up holding up universal experiences as the "doorway" to truth.[73]

Forays into Narrative, Experience, and Imagination

Mark Miller's *Experiential Story-Telling: (Re)Discovering Narrative to Com-municate God's Message* has more recently entered the youth ministry mar-ket with the intent to bring about a narrative orientation for preaching to youth.[74] It is important to also see his work alongside mainline denomina-tional, university based homiletic theory. He explains an encounter with a friend in youth ministry who opines, "Nothing works anymore. Everything I was taught about effectively communicating God's Word doesn't work like it used to. Today's teens just don't learn in the same ways."[75] This vignette opens Miller's first chapter and in much the same way that adolescents func-tion in other literature above, here they also provide the impetus toward

71. Robbins and Fields, *Speaking to* Teenagers, 163–64.

72. McClure, *Other-Wise Preaching*, 51.

73. As they go on to detail what they mean by inductive communication however, it is obvious that the distance between the youth ministry material and university-based and mainline homiletic material can be found in no larger relief than here. There is no mention of or allusion to Fred Craddock in this section, who pioneered and popular-ized principles of induction for preaching in the mainline, university-based camp or even of Haddon Robinson's understanding of induction through a more evangelical lens. See Robinson, *Biblical Sermons*.

74. Miller, *Experiential Storytelling*. This book is also part of Zondervan's publishing partnership between Youth Specialties and "emerging church" leaders as a part of its "emergent ys" titles. The Youth Specialties partnership has since been dissolved, though Zondervan continues to publish Youth Specialties and titles from emerging church leaders separately. The relationship between youth ministry and emerging church lead-ership has often been quite strong.

75. Ibid., 11.

new preaching methods because they are chief among those who cannot or do not listen. Miller assesses the preaching situation with his own epiphany that "experience is the new king of the mountain. There are no passive participants"[76] which prescribe "nothing less than a complete reconstruction of how we communicate."[77]

In order to initiate that reconstruction, Miller reproduces the logic of Jesus as exemplary storyteller as a model for contemporary preaching.[78] The motivation behind mimicking Jesus the storyteller is the perception that sermons are authoritative, closed, and directive while story invites open-ended, free-thinking interpretation from listeners.[79] He unwittingly verbalizes some principles of the New Homiletic: "the story is no longer simply heard, but also experienced. With this experiential immersion, the 'hearer' can listen on several levels and receive what's communicated in a form that disarms any fears of conquest. Experience by nature has a collaborative feel. It engages more of our senses and gets individuals involved in the story."[80] Miller paradoxically argues for both an authoritarian and communitarian model of preaching simultaneously. The appearance of collaboration is merely a veneer since the listener remains a "receiver" and story works as an instrument to "disarm" fears. As a result, instead of preaching deductively *to* or *at* an assumed form of experience (Davis), Miller advocates a shift to preach narrative experiences *from* or *toward* the same universalized form of experience.[81] The goal of this kind of communication for Miller is life transformation, rather than acceptance of facts.[82]

Sarah Arthur exhibits a similar storytelling orientation to youth ministry (rather than preaching only), but through a more sophisticated, intentionally theological lens, in her book *The God-Hungry Imagination: The Art of Storytelling for Postmodern Youth Ministry*.[83] Her use of narrative is

76. Ibid., 15.

77. Ibid., 25.

78. Ibid., 39–41. For a critical perspective on this logic, see Charles L. Campbell, *Preaching Jesus*, 178–80.

79. Miller, *Experiential Storytelling*, 41.

80. Ibid., 86.

81. This is also a general critique of Fred Craddock's confidence in the openness of inductive preaching as well as others constitutive of the New Homiletic (Lowry, Rice, etc.). Craddock's work remains unanalyzed by Miller.

82. See Rose, *Sharing the Word*, 37–56. Miller seems to be unaware of the larger conversation of narrative and imagination in preaching, with its emphasis on transformation which precedes him by over thirty years.

83. Arthur, *God-Hungry Imagination*. Though her book does not center on preaching, I include it here because her orientation toward narrative for the trajectory of ministry as a whole echoes that of recent narrative homiletics, and more specifically,

helpful not for its relation to homiletic theory (or lack thereof), but rather her use of theological method to describe adolescents and their religious needs/tendencies. The impetus for her work, she says, comes from the desire for meaningful content in youth ministry along with findings from the research of Christian Smith and Melinda Lundquist Denton that diagnoses teenagers with "pervasive teen inarticulacy" in regard to faith.[84] Her solution is a reorientation to youth ministry that nurtures the relationship between imagination, story, and spiritual formation.

Arthur's response consists of "reclaiming the imagination's vital role in spiritual formation" and "reclaiming the church as the living story" while the youth pastor and leaders function as "bards: poets charged with the task of keeping and imparting the stories, language, values, and beliefs of a culture."[85] Each of these phrases are incredibly rich with theological import, as is the diagnosis that all people "wear natural blinders that bias us toward a particular worldview, and this bias can (often unintentionally) eclipse the authority of both scripture and the church for our lives and ministries."[86] Arthur's diagnosis and response relies on theories of narrative whereby humans live a storied existence with different competing narratives.[87] In order to function as the church in the world, ministry must rightly story the world for Christians. As the resident "bard," the youth minister's task is to help form a storied ministry.[88] This model creates a strong affinity with the catechizing function of ministry. The "bard" functions as a teacher of the church's culture, helping form young people's imaginations with the church's own distinctive stories, language, and images.[89]

---

as I will show, postliberal streams of narrative homiletics. Arthur's work is perhaps the chief example of the breakdown of the neat dichotomy of "mainline" and "evangelical" in youth ministry literature.

84. Ibid., 17–18. See Smith and Denton, *Soul Searching*.

85. Arthur, *God-Hungry Imagination*, 29–31. Arthur's theological model is not far from Florence's working assumptions about youth and theology, above.

86. Ibid., 32.

87. See McClure, "Narrative and Preaching," 27. Arthur's use of narrative would be classified as "narrative world view," whereby those who speak of narrative speak about its power to establish worldview. Although she does not refer to it, postliberal homiletics and testimonial homiletics advocate these views.

88. Arthur, *God-Hungry Imagination*, 126. Arthur directly quotes Lindbeck, *Nature of Doctrine*.

89. See also Green, *Imagining God*; Hauerwas and Willimon, *Resident Aliens*; Brueggemann, *Finally Comes the Poet*; Brueggemann, *Texts under Negotiation*; Kenneson, "Gathering." Arthur does not emphasize the communitarian aspect as greatly as do Hauerwas/Willimon and Kenneson.

Unsurprisingly, Arthur depicts adolescents as bored with church, particularly its rationalistic and linear orientation, and its dead theological language. Most problematic is "the astounding illiteracy and inarticulacy of the mainstream populace regarding theological and biblical concepts. Ask any middle schooler in your youth group what the word *idol* means, and she or he will probably say, 'It's, like, someone you look up to who sings really good.' Meanwhile, relativism and pluralism now infuse so much of popular culture that our young take it all for granted."[90] For Arthur, young people lack a sophisticated theological vocabulary and thus a robust faith. In addition, youth are completely unable to sort through the range of religious ideas presented to them in wider cultural arenas. They are passive in the face of cultural and religious options, wholly consuming the religious values offered in popular culture. This narrow construction necessitates the singular theological and homiletic solution Arthur articulates.

Her short statement from the imaginary middle school youth group member is significant. She posits "any" middle school student is likely to give similar responses. Adolescents are categorized as ignorant concerning words with theological origins, such as *idol*. Popular culture has co-opted the church's language and displaced its primary meanings (as seen in the reference to the popular television show *American Idol*). Adolescents also communicate in a broken down version of the English language, showing a kind of inarticulacy from the reference of more proper adult, white, and educated versions of English. The filler word "like" operates under the "valley girl" stereotype while the phrase "sings really good" violates grammar rules. And finally, while the entire American culture suffers from relativism and pluralism, it is "our young" who suffer the brunt force of the attack. Again, young people become the most victimized or the chief of sinners (or both). All of this fuels Arthur's confidence that the specialized "bard"/catechist can help young people live faithfully into the Christian story. Arthur conceives of young people within a theological framework that depends on them being unformed, deficient religious subjects in need of formation by the church's tradition in opposition to the formation offered by culture. Although the arch towards formation is an impulse not unworthy of our attention (and indeed it will characterize our discussion going forward), it needs to be tempered by a more broad theological understanding.

In youth ministry literature, adolescents function as a double sign. Joe Austin and Michael Nevin Willard observe through recent American history "the bifurcated social identity of youth as a vicious, threatening sign

90. Arthur, *God-Hungry Imagination*, 23. Arthur works with a post-Christendom model which the postliberal theological camp simultaneously celebrates and mourns. At the very least it opens up opportunities for new traditioning in the church's language.

of social decay and 'our best hope for the future.'"[91] Whereas the mainline denominational- and university-based homiletic literature either ignores adolescents or stereotypes them as deficient listeners, youth ministry literature centers its focus on adolescents, doing so with the assumption that there is simultaneous danger and beauty in adolescents that preaching can address. Unfortunately, none of these authors interact with homiletic theory for a more nuanced understanding of preaching. And while homiletics could be a potential site of knowledge for understanding and ministering to/with adolescents, it does not yet frame adolescence sufficiently. There are, however, helpful frames for understanding adolescence outside the bodies of literature we have examined thus far.

STUDIES IN THE SOCIAL SCIENCES AND RELIGION APART FROM HOMILETICS

A tremendous volume of literature concerning children and adolescents has emerged over the past twenty-five years in the social sciences and education, with some of the literature focusing on religion as well. We turn toward this literature for two main reasons. First, research emerging out of the fields of childhood studies, childhood studies in religion, critical youth studies, and religious education concerning adolescents helps frame adolescence in new ways. Second, even though this literature remains unconcerned with theories and practices of preaching, the possibility for a new way forward for preaching's relationship with youth emerges from the frames we find here.[92]

Framing Adolescence: Childhood Studies and Childhood Studies in Religion

In order to begin the work of reframing adolescence from the views we find in homiletics and youth ministry, we will look at the fields of childhood studies and childhood studies in religion.[93] Philippe Ariès's *Centuries*

---

91. Austin and Willard, *Generations of Youth*, 2.

92. As such, the second of these foci functions as a representative examination of homiletic method, specifically concerning the relationship of homiletics with practical theology and the academy at large.

93. Since there is no clear line of demarcation between childhood and adolescence, much of the emerging literature purports to cover the range of childhood and adolescence. Whether they actually do attend to adolescence effectively is up for debate, but the place for that argument is not here. Regardless, the methods by which they address childhood and adolescence are at stake here and prove to be quite helpful.

of Childhood: A Social History of Family Life is generally regarded as the first and most significant work to question modern presumptions of a fixed nature of childhood.[94] His thesis, supported by material history, proposes that children in the middle ages through the fifteenth century were regarded as "little adults" and only more recently transitioned into sentimentalized individuals segmented from adults. Although his thesis has since been brought under more critical scrutiny, Ariès charted a new course for the study of children in the social sciences.

Since Ariès, scholars like Alan Prout and Allison James have articulated theoretical shifts within the field. They start with what they call "the dominant framework surrounding the study of children and childhood," which, relatively unquestioned until the 1970s, depicted children as being less rational than adults, having a natural simplicity, and that their nature was a universal feature regardless of any other social factors.[95] This materialized in various developmental models: physical, psycho-social, and cognitive. Children within this framework are essentially less than adults but function on a patterned, predictable journey toward adulthood.

In contrast, James and Prout summarize the features of contemporary research in childhood. This emergent paradigm in childhood studies displays the following key features/commitments:

1. Childhood is understood as a social construction. As such it provides an interpretive frame for contextualizing the early years of human life. Childhood, as distinct from biological immaturity, is neither a natural nor universal feature of human groups but appears as a specific structural and cultural component of many societies.

2. Childhood is a variable of social analysis. It can never be entirely divorced from other variables such as class, gender, or ethnicity. Comparative and cross-cultural analysis reveals a variety of childhoods rather than a single and universal phenomenon.

3. Children's social relationships and cultures are worthy of study in their own right, independent of the perspective and concerns of adults.

4. Children are and must be seen as active in the construction and determination of their own social lives, the lives of those around them and of the societies in which they live. Children are not just the passive subjects of social structures and processes.

94. Ariès, *Centuries of Childhood.*
95. Prout and James, "New Paradigm," 10.

5. Ethnography is a particularly useful methodology for the study of childhood. It allows a more direct voice and participation in the production of sociological data than is usually possible through experimental or survey styles of research.

6. Childhood is a phenomenon in relation to which the double hermeneutic of the social sciences is acutely present (see Giddens, 1976). That is to say, to proclaim a new paradigm of childhood sociology is also to engage in and respond to the process of reconstructing childhood in society.[96]

This new paradigm is embodied in a number of perspectives in the social sciences including more recent historical studies, sociological studies, education and social policy research, cultural studies, as well as studies centered on family life.[97]

These studies invite new inquiries and methodological frameworks for studying children's agency, voice, and identity. With different ends, childhood studies engage children's worlds with the intent to discover voice, which is composed of the "cluster of intentions, hopes, grievances, and expectations that children guard as their own. This voice surfaces only when the adult has learned to ask and get out of the way."[98] And "by agency," Pufall and Unsworth "refer to the fact that children are much more self-determining actors than we generally think."[99] In terms of identity, Pufall and Unsworth also highlight two important questions of childhood studies, "What is a child?" and "When is a child?"[100] For childhood studies, identity encompasses more than biology or narrow constructions of what a child should be doing physically/emotionally/socially at certain ages. Instead, childhood studies attend to the ways that children perform identities.

Only very recently have scholars of religious studies and theology sought to overcome Marcia J. Bunge's criticism that "despite the rising concern for and curiosity about children, scholars of religion, theologians, and

96. Ibid., 8. See also Pufall and Unsworth, "Imperative and the Process for Rethinking Childhood" and Allison James, "Understanding Childhood from an Interdisciplinary Perspective: Problems and Potentials."

97. In addition to the above, see Graff, *Conflicting Paths*; Hiner and Hawes, *Growing up in America*; Steven Mintz, *Huck's Raft*; Scheper-Hughes and Fishel Sargent, *Small Wars*; Jenkins, *Children's Culture Reader*.

98. Pufall and Unsworth, "Imperative," 8.

99. Ibid., 9. Discussions of "agency" in regard to children/childhood are also explored in Miller-McLemore, *Let the Children Come*, 137–60; Miller-McLemore and Browning, "Introduction," 7–8.

100. Pufall and Unsworth, *Rethinking Childhood*, 12–19. These of course, are questions asked of the historical narrative in the preceding chapter.

ethicists across religious lines have had little to say about children, and they have had little to contribute to the growing political and academic debates about children or our obligations to them."[101] A flurry of publishing activity now extends beyond religious education alone, which is also rethinking its understandings of children.[102]

In terms of approach, Bonnie Miller-McLemore and Don Browning outline two "prominent frames of interpretation on contemporary childhood" at work in religious studies.[103] The first frame, "the family modernization hypothesis," proposes children's lives are affected by technical rationality that increases separations in social systems along the lines of age and life becomes "increasingly oriented around market values, individual rights, self-actualization, and secularism."[104] The second, more widely used in childhood studies, is the "social constructionist hypothesis," which "argues that even though childhood has distinct biological parameters, societies and social groups construct the meaning and nature of childhood to a considerable extent around powerful economic, political, and religious ideas."[105] It is in this second hypothesis that childhood studies in religion forge a strong relationship with the foundational assumptions at work in the social sciences.

Christian ethicist John Wall presents a taxonomy of Christian ethics' approaches to childhood, articulating how concern for children has diversified in theological approach.[106] Wall traces one of the first approaches as "communitarian" ethics, popularized most prominently by Stanley Hauerwas, and "argues that children fare poorly in the contemporary world primarily because they lack strong families, traditions, and social narratives under which to develop civilized and meaningful social values. Children are not just individual or autonomous agents but need to be socialized into the larger values and virtues of coherent moral communities."[107] We have already seen the reach of this approach in the work of both Anna Carter Florence and Sarah Arthur. "Liberationist" thinkers in the early 1990s share "what could be called a 'bottom-up' approach that starts in children's own

101. Bunge, "Child, Religion, and the Academy," 551.

102. Ibid., 555–56.

103. Miller-McLemore and Browning, "Introduction," 3.

104. Ibid.

105. Ibid., 4.

106. Wall, "Childhood Studies." Wall presents the strengths and weaknesses of each of the different approaches, which are important, but tangential at this point. Here I simply want to name the different ways of approaching children/childhood in contemporary Christian theological ethics.

107. Ibid., 530.

actual lives, voices, agency, and experiences. Their reason to engage theologically with childhood is that . . . children 'are often the ones with no voice, the unconsulted and sometimes undeserving victims of oppression."[108] Because children are unable to advocate for themselves in the academy, this kind of liberationist concern provokes what David Jensen calls a type of "advocacy theology" on behalf of children.[109] Finally, Wall describes the most recent (mid-1990s) theological ethical approach to childhood, which he labels "progressive familism."[110] While many of those Wall ascribes to this group articulate strong foundations in liberationism and feminism,

> they also believe that the well-being of children is uniquely dependent on others and particularly on parents (hence "familism"). Significantly, progressive familists are deeply engaged with the fields of developmental and evolutionary psychology, partly because these fields offer empirical insight into families, but also, and perhaps even more importantly, because they help describe how children become—rather than just already are—competent social agents. In other words, children's social agency is not just a given but also a developmental task falling first and foremost on families.[111]

Beyond theological ethics, childhood studies has branched out to areas within the theological academy such as historical theology, systematic/constructive theology, biblical studies, and practical theology who all reflect one or more of Wall's categories.[112]

There remains some ambivalence, however, as to whether these studies are concerned with adolescents. This ambivalence is evident in the use of "children" to refer to those under the age of eighteen in childhood studies, while the general public rarely includes in "children" those in the age range of thirteen to eighteen. This unreflective use of the terms "child" and

108. Ibid.

109. Jensen, *Graced Vulnerability*, xiii. Jensen says "an advocacy theology seeks to speak with those whose voices are often not heard. Children's voices often drown in the cacophony of commercialization and violence that characterized the (post)modern world. Attempting to hear them is fraught with peril: often we think we hear their voices when we really are hearing only ourselves and our intentions for children."

110. Wall, "Childhood Studies," 531.

111. Ibid.

112. See, for instance Bunge, *Child in Christian Thought*; Herzog, *Children and Our Global Future*; DeVries, "Toward a Theology of Childhood"; Jensen, *Graced Vulnerability*; Carroll, "Children in the Bible"; Capps, "Curing Anxious Adolescents"; Parker, "Hungry for Honor"; Miller-McLemore, *Let the Children Come*; Mercer, *Welcoming Children*.

"children" by childhood studies has led to an unintentional, but nonetheless problematic, oversight about variations across age groups and a neglect of those thirteen and over who are no longer children in many ways, but not yet fully adult in others.[113]

Framing Adolescence: Critical Youth Studies and Religious Education Concerning Adolescents

The ambivalence toward adolescents in childhood studies and childhood studies in religion leaves a gap filled by two important fields of discourse. Critical youth studies works with many of the same foundational methodological principles as childhood studies, but for many this research concentrates on the "teenage" years. This focus on biological age provides a functional delimitation for study, effectively eliminating the ambivalence found in childhood studies. The leading foundational commitment is understanding adolescence as a social and cultural construction, with historical studies demonstrating adolescence as a historically contingent phenomenon.[114]

One of the chief aims of critical youth studies is to overcome the universalized versions of adolescence which have hardened in the public imagination, or what has been termed here as "ontological adolescence." Nancy Lesko uses much softer language, identifying four "confident characterizations" concerning adolescents.[115] These characterizations identify ways in which adolescents are largely understood in the public imagination while also exposing how the characterizations circumscribe the power of description to adults. Lesko begins with the characterization that "teenagers are 'at the threshold' and in 'transition to adulthood.'"[116] Popular developmental models commonly frame adolescence this way and have influenced cultural structures. Second, Lesko points to the characterization of youth as uncontrollably captive, physically and emotionally, to the power of "raging hormones" which "links the power to sexuality, and offers these facts as biological and beyond social intervention."[117] Third, adolescents are commonly characterized as "peer-oriented" which "claim[s] that teenagers are

---

113. Miller-McLemore, Personal Conversation, 15 February, 2011.

114. There are a number of histories of adolescence in addition to the histories of childhood, which are commendable. See Kett, *Rites of Passage*; Palladino, *Teenagers*; Wallach, *Obedient Sons*; Austin and Willard, *Generations of Youth*; Hine, *Rise and Fall*.

115. Lesko, *Act Your Age!*, 2.

116. Ibid., 3.

117. Ibid.

less individuated than adults. . . . To demean peer pressure also has the effect of privileging an individualism that is historically associated with middle-class, white males and is largely alien to the experiences of many people of color and women."[118] Finally, Lesko demonstrates that age becomes a signifier for adolescence, such that when the age of a teenager is spoken/written, the age provokes "volumes of information and references: developing bodies, strange music, moody distancing, laughter alternating with sullenness, expectations of diffidence, passionate arguments, and talking endlessly on the phone. . . . Age is a shorthand, a code that evokes what amounts to an 'epidemic of signification.'"[119] Her work is representative among the field of critical youth studies which has been interdisciplinary and overlaps with various subfields including not only critical histories but also media studies, cultural studies, sociology, psychology, communication, and education.[120]

Despite that proliferation across disciplines, religious studies and religion is hardly a concern for many of the monographs that have appeared over the last fifteen years.[121] A small number of Christian educators, however, have appropriated this new framework for analyzing adolescence. These scholar-practitioners ask how critical approaches to adolescence can help theologians and ministry practitioners engage adolescents in renewed

118. Ibid., 4.

119. Ibid. This last observation is perhaps the most significant for the homiletic purposes of this study. The characterization translates into a helpful diagnostic for the homiletic literature analyzed above. Inasmuch as a numerical age functions as a signifier, so do the labels "teenage(r)," "adolescent," and "youth." Thus, one of the primary purposes of analyzing the homiletic literature above is to uncover how "teenage(r)," "adolescent," or "youth" function as a signifier and what their respective significations say about adolescents as listeners of preaching/religious subjects. They operate, more often than not, as indicators of difference, note the inability to listen/process sermons as adults do, and alert to the need for special (read: less sophisticated than adult) sermonic rhetoric and logic. They seem to at least have the potential to include Lesko's other "confident characterizations" within their realm of signification.

120. Work has been quite expansive over a short period of time, producing a number of quality monographs. See, for instance Fornäs and Bolin, *Youth Culture in Late Modernity*; Jagodzinski, *Youth Fantasies*; Weiner, *Enfants Terribles*; Mazzarella, "Constructing Youth: Media, Youth, and the Politics of Representation"; Hall and Jefferson, *Resistance through Rituals*; Acland, *Youth, Murder, Spectacle*; Kitwana, *Hip Hop Generation*; Campbell, *American Youth Cultures*; France, *Understanding Youth in Late Modernity*; Skott-Myhre, *Youth and Subculture as Creative Force*; Best, *Fast Cars, Cool Rides*; Haenfler, *Straight Edge*; Côté and Allahar, *Generation on Hold : Coming of Age in the Late Twentieth Century*; Côté, *Arrested Adulthood*; Williams and Thurlow, *Talking Adolescence*; Vadeboncoeur and Patel Stevens, *Re/Constructing "the Adolescent."* See also the interdisciplinary work of Henry Giroux, who writes at the intersection of youth, politics, education, and media.

121. A notable exception is Luhr, *Witnessing Suburbia*.

ways. Their work is rooted in a social constructionist understanding of adolescence which also accounts for adolescent agency rather than leaning solely on developmental models.[122] For instance, in the foreword to "Youth Ministry Alternatives" books series, series editors David White and Faith Kirkham Hawkins acknowledge that "youth ministry as it has evolved over these decades lacks significant critique of the shift in the social roles of young people in the second half of the twentieth century and into the twenty-first century, in which youth are increasingly ghettoized as passive consumers rather than treated as agents of faith influencing the common good."[123] This statement suggests significant influences from critical youth studies. Elsewhere White articulates an ideological approach whereby he weaves together a materialist account of postmodernity that narrates the conditions of contemporary adolescence(s) in order to help adolescents and those who work with them faithfully discern their vocation.[124]

Evelyn L. Parker roots an ethnographic approach in womanist thought, "fostering a Christian spirituality in African American adolescents whereby they live holy and hope-filled lives, guided by the Spirit of God, while engaging in the challenges of social justice."[125] Parker's ethnography of African American youth takes the view that youth are religious agents lacking social capital (namely, the ability to write and publish), helping her produce a constructive theological scheme "from below." Parker also invites theological reflection from adult female theologians and adolescent girls, seeking to articulate more fully the nature of spirituality among North American adolescent girls.[126] Similarly, Dori Grinenko Baker offers what she calls "girlfriend theology," which "is about girls and women creating spaces . . . so that we might discern the trace of a living, breathing divine presence who seeks our companionship as much today as on the fresh new dawn of creation."[127] Baker encourages a model of religious education that utilizes the stories of girls and women for Christian practical theological reflection.

122. David White and those among the authors of the *Youth Ministry Alternatives* series are guided by the impulses found in childhood studies. Many contemporary Christian educators, however, have not given up perspectives from developmental psychology, even as they tacitly assume some social constructivist views. Kenda Creasy Dean, for instance, uses a theological understanding of Erik Erikson (in the vein of her mentor, James Loder) to advocate for renewed practices of youth ministry. See

123. White and Kirkham Hawkins, "Foreword," vii.

124. White, "Illusions of Postmodern Youth Ministry," 19. The language of development is not abandoned among these authors. Rather it is reframed contextually and theologically. See also White, *Practicing Discernment with Youth.*

125. Parker, *Trouble Don't Last Always*, vii.

126. Parker, *Sacred Selves.*

127. Grinenko Baker, *Doing Girlfriend Theology*, 2–3.

The recent reflection in Christian education takes great strides beyond older models that fix adolescents to passive roles and universal, static, developmental tasks. They promote thinking about adolescence in critical frames; critique previous youth ministry approaches while prescribing contextual education and pastoral care of adolescents; and collaborate with youth for theological reflection. Unfortunately, for all its benefit, homiletic reflection is absent. For example, although Fred Edie incorporates Gordon Lathrop's conception of Christian worship as a "source and resource" for youth ministry, Edie does not mention preaching.[128] This kind of absence compounds a practical theological divide between religious education and homiletics. This problem is compounded when homiletics neglects youth, and when youth ministry literature neglects homiletic reflection. How should preaching proceed in light of this problem?

HOMILETICS AND ADOLESCENCE: AN ISSUE FOR PRACTICAL THEOLOGY

Tracing the literatures above portrays a significant gap in practical theological reflection, and particularly on the part of homiletics. The disconnects among the literatures we have examined above prove Bonnie Miller-McLemore's diagnosis that reflection on children "challenges the usual division between biblical, historical, systematic, and practical theology. Its reintroduction into academic study requires fresh rubrics that cross over and work between these categories."[129] For homiletics the subject of children and youth "has been a bit like the housework of the theological school: no one wants to do it."[130]

Preaching has a significant internal problem to overcome concerning young people. Even though religious education has appropriated frameworks for understanding contemporary adolescence(s) toward renewed practices, homiletics cannot simplistically import their work because preaching theories and practices are not necessarily within their scope.[131]

128. Edie, *Book, Bath, Table & Time.* See also Gordon Lathrop, *Holy Things.* When Edie summons the portion of Lathrop's *ordo* having to do with the Bible, Edie relegates adolescent engagement with the Bible to performance of biblical texts along the lines of how Nicholas Lash conceives performing scriptures as script in Lash, *Theology on the Way to Emmaus.*

129. Miller-McLemore, "Children and Religion," 385.

130. Ibid., 396.

131. See, for example, the ways that Dean and DeVries' articles on preaching and youth, above. The same also would apply for using childhood studies and critical youth studies, since their concern is predominantly not religion and certainly not homiletic theory and practice.

Furthermore, importing the frameworks of adolescence found in Christian education or pastoral care releases homiletics from its responsibility to adolescents. In such a practical theological relationship, no engagement with young people is necessary, if there is any concern for them at all.

Instead, preaching must proceed with a sense of being interconnected with other disciplines, theological and otherwise, with a committed relationship to youth. As such, homiletics can move forward to contribute a specific reflection on adolescence that also articulates renewed theories and practices of preaching for, to, with, and by adolescents. In order to do that, the study of preaching must begin to overcome its detachment from the lives of adolescents. Probing the historical materials and contemporary literature only provides ways to understand how the situation has come to exist. Homiletics can initiate a homiletic discourse that honors the rich texture of adolescents' lives, not dependent on images informed by ontological adolescence. In order to fund the kind of practical theology of preaching that interacts with young people, I will now outline a theological and ethical corrective that can renew the adolescent-adult preaching relationship and sets the stage for a project of listening to young people.

3

Renewing the Relationship

Liberation and Formation in the Way of Mutual Critique

Chapters 1 and 2 narrated the gradual decrease in attention given to adolescents by homiletics which resulted in contemporary representations of adolescents that are either characterized by silence, ontological adolescence, or deficiency. In response, I want to develop a theological and ethical corrective for preaching that can fund a renewed public homiletic space, test the limits of doing homiletics from the margins, and discern how youth can inform preaching theories/practices, even as the exigency of certain kinds of formation are apparent.

In the interest of renewing homiletic space, I propose moving between two poles, *liberation* and *formation*, as a normative theological and ethical disposition for how youth and adults engage each other through preaching.[1] This disposition will help preachers to develop approaches to youth

1. I intentionally choose the word "disposition." Use of the term "disposition" is more closely akin to a component of what Pierre Bourdieu calls "habitus," which are "systems of durable, transposable dispositions, structured structures predisposed to function as structuring structures, that is, as principles of the generation and structuring of practices and representations which can be objectively 'regulated' and 'regular' without in any way being the product of obedience to rules, objectively adapted to their goals without presupposing a conscious aiming at ends or an express mastery of the operations necessary to attain them and, being all this, collectively orchestrated without being the product of the orchestrating action of a conductor." Bourdieu, *Outline of*

grounded in listening to, learning from, and critically reflecting upon adolescents' communicative practices. Listening of this kind grounds a relationship that can foster the development of preaching practices for, to, by, and with adolescents.

The disposition of liberation and formation articulated here will protect against what we might call nostalgia. Young people will not be encouraged to uncritically appropriate, for instance, the image of the free and unfettered nineteenth-century frontier revival young preacher. A disposition of liberation and formation will avoid idealizing "the bourgeois liberal concept of the autonomous individual," which fails to account for the number of ways that young people's communicative practices were and are constrained.[2] Before we can explore the contours of the two poles, however, we first must define and reframe some key critical terms. Secondly, we will work toward an emerging homiletic ethos that can fund this relationship. This ethos integrates components already at work in contemporary homiletics and aspects of the communicative ethics of Jürgen Habermas. This will lay groundwork for the interactive relationship of listening tempered by liberation and formation.

REFRAMING OPPRESSION, MARGINALITY, AND SELF-REPRESENTATION

As a preliminary note, if we are to talk about "liberation" with regard to preaching and youth, we should recognize that the experiences of adolescents are different than those of other groups who experience oppression (i.e., African Americans, Latin Americans, feminists, womanists, disabled persons, etc.) and, as such, the concepts of "oppression" and "marginalization" need reframing. We have seen how there is either a dearth of discussion of young people in the literature of preaching and Christian ministry, or young people have been depicted with representations characteristic of

---

a Theory, 72. Bourdieu further defines "disposition" as "particularly suited to express what is covered by the concept of habitus (defined as a system of dispositions). It expresses first the result of an organizing action, with a meaning close to that of words such as structure; it also designates a way of being a habitual state (especially of the body) and, in particular, a predisposition, tendency, propensity, or inclination" (214). It is the "result of an organizing action," the structured action, and the character of a "way of being" that I attempt to describe in this chapter, particularly concerning how adults live in homiletical relationship with young people. As a disposition is a component of a habitus, I believe that the particular disposition I describe here fits into the overall larger habitus of homiletics as it relates to the marginalized.

2. Williams and Chrisman, *Colonial Discourse*, 6.

an ontological adolescence, including characterizations of deficiency. But this is not necessarily oppression and thus invites us to reframe how this concept applies to youth and preaching.

Postcolonial theory helps us to revise the concept of oppression and provides a preliminary foundation for the movement toward an emancipatory pole of homiletic discourse and practice for youth. While postcolonial theory might seem to be an odd fit for understanding adolescents' relationship with preaching,[3] at a basic level postcolonial theory focuses on "the process of production of knowledge about the Other."[4]

Nancy Lesko describes how "recapitulation theory," a core nineteenth-century anthropological theory, "established a threefold parallelism across animals, savages, and children: children were like savages, savages were like animals, and animals were like children."[5] Though recapitulation theory has now faded, the theory remains sedimented in the North American cultural imaginary. Lesko summarizes the contemporary effects of recapitulation theory:

> First, the modern concepts of child and adolescent development have a color and gender. Second, recapitulation theory links ideas about developing children and adolescents to a paternalistic and exploitative colonial system, which endlessly reiterated the inadequacies of the natives and the need for Western rule. Finally, recapitulation theory's intimacy with colonialism suggests that knowledge will provide a continuing gloss of and cover for the exercise of subordinating power that speaks of immaturity, emotionality, conformity, and irrationality.[6]

Lesko narrates a historical discourse of young people that intermingles nationalism, race theory (and racism), science, anthropology, gender, and much more. Through that narration, she describes how "the adolescent was an object that could be discussed, diagnosed, scientized, differentiated, and familiarized."[7]

As a byproduct, models of adolescence emerged within developmental psychology.[8] The developmental frameworks that proliferated in the twen-

---

3. As Nancy Lesko observes, "modern conceptions of children and youth are not usually located in historical frameworks that include colonial relations." Lesko, 33.

4. Williams and Chrisman, eds., *Colonial Discourse*, 4, 8.

5. Lesko, *Act Your Age!*, 33.

6. Ibid., 35.

7. Ibid., 46–47.

8. I have not approached developmental theories to this point, partly because of its entanglement in colonialist and structuralist foundations. This does not mean,

tieth century often hinged on scientized depictions of adolescence. Lesko's description of the objectified adolescent has been embodied in models that prescribe the norms of physical, cognitive, emotional, psychological, and even spiritual functions within each stage of development.[9] In other words, they act as models that "codify knowledge" about "non-developed," "undeveloped," or "under-developed" adolescents.

In addition to scientized accounts, adolescent experience has become, in many ways, normalized in the cultural imaginary, despite postmodern critiques of common human experience. Cultural and educational theorist Henry Giroux observes:

> Needless to say, simplistic Hollywood portrayals of working-class youth as either potential muggers or dead from the neck up legitimates real futures that offer the horrifying images of the prison, mental hospital, or local fast food outlet. As youth are conceived in images of demonization, sexual deviance, and criminality, the only public sites that appear available to them are unskilled work, highly policed public spaces, or the brute reality of incarceration.[10]

As a result, there appears to be some similarities between developmental models as colonialist discipline and mass media images, market, education, and differentiation of civic space according to age. Both have normalized the activity of youth in the cultural imaginary and in real public spaces.

More recently, Giroux has identified two tracks of representation for youth in the United States where "global corporations and the punishing state are now the dominant story tellers and influence in children's lives, shaping their futures according to the interests of the market."[11] Those who are unable to excel in the "pedagogy of commodification" are rendered "disposable" and often suffer under the effects of the "youth crime complex."[12] The complex network of corporations, media, government, the health care industry, and educational institutions come together to offer representations

---

however, that theories like those popularized in Erik Erikson's work (or any of the developmental literature) are unimportant or unworthy of study, or that they do not provide frameworks that can help in the church's ministry to youth. It does necessitate, however, a view embodied in the work of "critical psychology," which attempts to account for the ways that psychology's assumptions, methods, and findings are culturally and ideologically driven.

9. See, for instance, the textbook by Muuss et al., *Theories of Adolescence*.

10. Giroux, "Teenage Sexuality," 31.

11. Ibid., 28.

12. Ibid. Giroux also points to how these points of departure are largely racialized.

(commodification or disposability) of young people that narrate their lives in limited ways.

In order to further describe the limitations of self-conception among adolescents and particularly for preaching as a *discursive* practice, it is helpful to revisit briefly how postcolonial theory has considered Gayatri Spivak's influential question, "Can the subaltern speak?" The responses to this question bear fruit for exploring what it means for adolescents to have voice as preachers and/or participants in the shaping of homiletic discourse. Spivak believes that the subaltern is so entangled in the pull of colonial discourse that she is unable to recognize how her speech is conditioned and thus unable to have some sense of authentic voice.[13] Even in her own speech, the subaltern is always represented by others. On the other hand, Benita Parry contests Spivak's stance, suggesting that colonial forces are never able to fully control the subaltern's speech.[14] For Parry, some sense of authentic voice is always available. The extremes that Spivak and Parry present might best be avoided; the disagreement, however, provides a theoretical spectrum upon which to posit the boundaries of adolescents' abilities to speak with agency and voice.

In a sense, the issues of self-representation concerning young people and preaching have already been at work in chapters 1 and 2. Postcolonial theory helps bring those issues into view more clearly. For instance, we might ask, "Did young people in early America speak and endorse preaching with their own "authentic" voices or were they entangled in hegemonic ideas (religious, political, economic, social, familial) that anticipated their limited, controlled responses?"[15] The truth is likely somewhere in between. Adolescents' religious speech practices likely indicate their entanglement in larger cultural hegemonies. But this does not preclude attempts at resistance to those hegemonies.

As outlined in chapter 2, contemporary homiletic discourse often carries a distant, even combative rhetoric toward adolescents. Postcolonial theory helps paint a more textured picture of the sources and effects of this kind of language. Adolescents have been regarded more as "becoming" rather than "being."[16] As a result, they are always on the way toward sophistication in preaching, but never able to arrive. They do not possess inherent homiletic wisdom, but are timekeepers (Craddock) or in need of specific

13. Chakravorty Spivak, "Can the Subaltern Speak?," 78.

14. Loomba, *Colonialism/Postcolonialism*, 196.

15. Or, in the words of Pierre Bourdieu, were young people engaging in "regulated improvisation"? Bourdieu, *Outline of a Theory*, 78–79.

16. Lesko, "Denaturalizing Adolescence."

schemes of preaching (Wilson). They are generally regarded as passive recipients of preaching, rather than active listeners or religious communicators. According to Henry Mitchell and Sarah Arthur, adolescents speak in degenerate forms of the English language that preachers must engage through a type of cross-cultural analysis (perhaps even missiological in nature) and then subsequently manipulate in order to communicate effectively. Their "subaltern" speech is suspect. And as non-developed, un-developed, or under-developed bodies, adolescents are prime sites to be "colonized" by adult homiletic dispositions, content, and practices. Indeed, as Anna Carter Florence notes, youth "know the rules for sermons (no talking, fidgeting, pinching, fussing)."[17] As such, youth can and do become "docile bodies," disciplined to exercise a limited form of homiletic agency while they take up space in pews.[18] It is not shocking that many youth are anecdotally portrayed as "bored" with preaching since they have been disciplined to engage preaching in such limited ways.[19]

In postcolonial theory we find a matrix for understanding the constraints of young people's self-conception. Using the term "oppression" as a natural link to the term "liberation" serves as a way of marking some of the more severe experiences of other people and groups. The terms "oppression" and "marginalization" used for our purposes will focus more specifically on the ways youth are represented and are unable to represent themselves. "Oppression" and "marginalization" for our purposes are thus revised to mean *the systematic limitation of the possibilities for self-conception among youth.* This includes, but is certainly not limited to: limitations of speech, action, embodiment, ritual agency, and occupation of space(s). Most important for us are the ways young people's preaching agency is limited.

In light of postcolonialist analysis of these representations, it is no surprise that young people look and feel out of place in relation to the contemporary American pulpit (both as listeners and speakers). If, however, preaching could act as a site of youthful public, civic, and ecclesial

17. Florence, "Prodigal Preaching Story," 238. And as pointed out in chapter 2, Anna Carter Florence rehearses the model that young people do not speak the language of the church, its "mother tongue." In doing so, she reinforces a colonial narrative whereby the church's sophisticated and "true" language is not spoken by the exotic natives who do not know "the *art of listening,* of entering the world of a sermon." Florence, "Prodigal Preaching Story," 238. The notion of listening as an "art" should not be taken lightly as its language distinguishes between "high" and "low" cultures. See Kathryn Tanner's discussion of the history of "culture" in Tanner, *Theories of Culture,* 3–24.

18. The term "docile bodies" comes from the work of Michel Foucault. See especially Foucault and Rabinow, *Foucault Reader,* 179–87.

19. The phenomenon of boredom in relation to youth and preaching provides an opening for further research.

engagement, then the pulpit can also be a site for rehabilitation of both the ecclesial and cultural imaginary towards adolescents. With a language of critique and possibility, homileticians and preachers (Giroux would include them as "cultural workers"[20]), along with youth, can work together to create alternative representations while exposing false and harmful ones *through robust interaction with youth preaching.* I now turn to the ways in which recent homiletic theory has tried to correct the problems of various types of oppression with an eye toward their usefulness for addressing young people and preaching.

RECENT MODELS FOR PREACHING WHICH OFFER CORRECTION

Recent homiletic models have attempted to intervene in various so-called oppressive situations. The most recent generation of scholarship has programmatically explored various sources of theology and ethics in order to more properly define preaching practice and homiletic theory vis-à-vis the postmodern challenges of plurality, difference, and marginalization. Among these homiletic models, seeds for a new disposition toward adolescents can be found.

Conversation

Lucy Rose and Ronald Allen propose, in slightly different keys, the metaphor of "conversation" as an image of preaching that rightly responds to plurality within congregations.[21] Rose suggests a "form of preaching [which] aims to gather the community of faith around the Word where the central conversations of the people of God are fostered and refocused week after week."[22] For Rose, this kind of conversation is non-hierarchical on the part of the preacher whereby "the preacher is not the one-in-the-know but an equal colleague in matters of living and believing. Instead of impeding these conversations with a final or single answer, the preacher fosters them by explicitly acknowledging a variety of points of view, learning processes,

---

20. Giroux in Epstein, *Youth Culture*, 51–52.

21. John McClure's *Roundtable Pulpit* can also be grouped with Rose and Allen. Since his more recent work will be described below, and *Roundtable Pulpit* differs in some substantial ways from their work, I will not address it here. For McClure's own exploration of these differences, see McClure, *Other-Wise Preaching*.

22. Rose, *Sharing the Word*, 93.

interpretations, and life experiences."[23] This kind of preaching nurtures plurality within the congregation's preaching life as all of its members are "gathered" around each other, biblical texts, and the received resources of faith. Rose characterizes conversational preaching as having "an atmosphere of openness and mutual respect, as well as the willingness of the participants to acknowledge the particularity of their experiences based on their historical and social locations."[24] Rose seeks an integration of feminist inclinations of conversation and relationality alongside David Tracy's hermeneutic of conversation as outlined in his book *Plurality and Ambiguity: Hermeneutics, Religion, Hope.*[25]

Ronald Allen is more explicitly focused on David Tracy's conversational model of interpretation. He identifies "preaching as theological interpretation through conversation."[26] Allen consolidates more relational authority in the person of the preacher because "the church ordains the pastor to help make sure that certain voices are represented in the conversation and to help the church think its way through the pluralism of voices to theological conclusion."[27] This understanding of preaching "is mutual exploration of ideas, feelings, and behaviors with the goal of coming to as promising an understanding as is possible at a given moment. In the church, the conversation of preaching aims for an adequate interpretation of the significance of the gospel for the life of the ecclesial community and the world."[28] Allen's ethical disposition is a byproduct of this homiletical grounding in Tracy's theological hermeneutic. For Allen, preaching pursues the pertinent questions of the faith community's texts, with mutual respect for all the partners as "a complex phenomenon comprised of three elements: text, interpreters, and their interaction grounded in questioning itself."[29] The classic text(s) and its question(s) drive the process of interpretation through conversation.

23. Ibid., 96.

24. Ibid., 9.

25. Tracy, *Plurality and Ambiguity.* Rose believes her version of conversation is "more informal and personal than Tracy's" (9). Rose's language here also typifies the kind of "slippage" between homiletic theory and practice argued in the present work. By this I mean that Rose is simultaneously arguing for a particular mode of operation in homiletic discourse and preaching practice. This mode of operation casts the metaphor of "conversation" as a controlling metaphor which serves to open up theory and practice beyond dominant voices. This way of simultaneously talking about theory and practice is also present in the figures I highlight below.

26. Allen, *Interpreting the Gospel,* 66.

27. Ibid., 67.

28. Ibid.

29. Tracy, 28. See also Tracy's discussion of the conditions of conversation in chapter one.

All partners in the conversation are valued as potential dialogue partners on the way toward discovering truth.[30]

Testimony

Anna Carter Florence suggests that testimony "invites us . . . to rethink our ideas about freedom, power, and difference."[31] Florence attempts to retrieve a women's preaching tradition grounded through a multi-layered approach that includes historical narratives, hermeneutic theory, and feminist theology. Appropriating Paul Ricoeur's theory of testimony, Florence describes the power of "testimonial authority, [which] by definition, cannot be restricted to a select few. It is open and available to anyone willing to pattern herself after the testimony of Christ. Testimonial authority also compels listeners to focus on what the witness says and does, rather than her right to say it; the focus, in other words, shifts to the truth toward which she points."[32] Testimony is an act of interpretation by those who have had religious experience, and built upon the credibility of the witness. In this sense, Florence opens preaching up to those on the margins of authority structures for preaching.

Florence also incorporates ideas from feminist theologians Mary Mc-Clintock Fulkerson and Rebecca Chopp. In service of the accessibility of testimony as a working model for preaching, Florence uses Fulkerson's idea of "graf(ph)ting" as a component of women's (or marginal peoples') preaching. Florence explains "graf(ph)ting" in this way: "What we do, either quietly or publicly, is exercise our subjectivity: we take liberties with the text by making liberty with the text. We deliberately or unconsciously shift the way we interpret it. We redirect the flow of meaning until it is no longer oppressive or corrupt, either to us or others. And in so doing, we find new paths— new ways of reading and interpreting—that lead to value and wholeness."[33] "Graf(ph)ting," then, is a creative interpretive practice exercised by those who find traditional interpretations limiting.

From Chopp, Florence adopts a distinctive theological semiotics where the Word is "perfectly open sign."[34] By this, Florence understands

---

30. It is important to note "Conversation does not necessarily imply collaboration. We cannot assume that we are working together when we are having a conversation. Conversations can be dominated by certain parties and used to reinforce divisions or hierarchical power relations within congregations." McClure, *Roundtable Pulpit*, 50.

31. Florence, *Preaching as Testimony*, xxii.

32. Ibid., 67.

33. Ibid., 85. See also Fulkerson, *Changing the Subject*.

34. Ibid., 95. See also Chopp, *Power to Speak*.

the preached Word to be "a Word of power. It is a Word that creates and sustains all other words. It is a Word that opens up many voices, any of which can push and challenge and transform the present order. This Word is always open to new meaning; it is a perfectly open sign; it is God. It is also a bet against all odds that good news can still be proclaimed, even from the margins."[35] The "perfectly open sign" resists the closure of interpretation and thus subverts limitations on interpretive power. Florence's work offers a sweeping integration of theological resources in service of an ethic of preaching.

Other-wise Preaching

John McClure opts for the "ethics as first philosophy" of Emmanuel Levinas. Christian theologians who integrate Levinas' work into their own recognize a phenomenological account of being that, because of the infinity of the other, cannot support totalities (or the impulse toward sameness). For McClure, as preaching becomes "other-wise," "we will search for a form of preaching that is constantly interrupted by the proximity of the other, by an obligation to the other, and by what Levinas calls the 'glory of the Infinite' given in the face of the other."[36] In this short sentence, McClure captures several key ideas from Levinas: (1) the interruption of the freedom of the self by the real body of another person, (2) a real sense of responsibility or obligation to that other person, and (3) the nature of the other as an infinite being, fully exterior to the self and always transcendent. The kind of homiletic work funded by Levinas continually undergoes deconstruction as a result of both its proximity and openness to the face of the other. The result is a homiletic model that McClure has elsewhere called one of "hospitality" or preacher as simultaneously "host" and "guest."[37]

Gleaning from Recent Homiletic Models

There is much to learn from these most recent models. All propose ways of approaching self and other that honor the distinctive plurivocal nature of ecclesial gatherings for worship. Rose's account presents an open space for interpretation and preaching. Hierarchical power gives way to

35. Ibid.

36. McClure, *Other-Wise Preaching*, 9.

37. Which Lévinas also says is one of the goals of his work: "This book will present subjectivity as welcoming the Other, as hospitality; in it the idea of infinity is consummated." Lévinas, *Totality and Infinity*, 27. See also McClure, "Preacher as Host," 119–43.

relational solidarity in the church's week to week preaching. This insight can be instructive for seeing adolescents in a relationship of solidarity.[38] Allen's version of conversation focuses more on the hard work of the sermon preparation process within congregational life, and his more recent work seeks to merge the conversational hermeneutics of Tracy with the ethic of Levinas.[39] With Allen, adolescents can become a part of those incorporated into the sermon-writing process, particularly as part of the (Christian) tradition of interpretation Allen describes as the preaching process. Florence's historical framework provides a model for adolescents to claim their own historical narrative of preaching. As I have attempted to do earlier, claiming historical voices as a precedent for young people's homiletic voice is a powerful first step.[40]

Finally, McClure's use of Levinas adds a further layer of depth to the ethics of preaching. Indeed it offers a type of remedy to the problem of ontological adolescence as outlined earlier. In proximity to the "face" of adolescents, homiletics can no longer offer static renderings of young people. Nor can homiletics take a colonialist stance toward adolescents, since those movements toward sameness (totalities) are recognized as harmful actions. Hardened stereotypes of young people in preaching violate the infinite found in the particularity of each young person. Additionally, a homiletic informed by Levinas ensures listening to, and responsibility for, the one who is other.[41] If preachers are to reach beyond themselves, then they must listen to the absolutely foreign and expect to learn from her and to exhibit the utmost sensibility of care toward her. This culminates in the notion of asymmetry which "is not conditional upon a reciprocal agreement with the

38. See Rose's appropriation of feminist theory. It is important to point out, however, that Rose (and Florence) as an Anglo woman assumes a measure of voice and the potential for speaking that adolescents may not possess.

39. See Allen, "Preaching and the Other"; Allen, *Preaching and the Other*. It is unclear, however, how much credence Allen gives to Tracy's emphasis on the "classic text" as powerful agent who provides the questions for the conversation. Allen often advocates a conversational model characterized by mutual critical correlation, which while allowing "others" into the conversation, ultimately centers on biblical texts/traditions in the sermon preparation process (interpretation) rather than fully exploring an ethic of preaching.

40. Her use of Ricouer and Fulkerson, however, when applied to young people, still maintains an unhelpful center-margin dynamic. Whether it is Ricouer (and Brueggemann's) movement between testimony-counter-testimony or Fulkerson's graf(ph)ting, those dynamics reinforce young-old/youth-adult binary oppositions that continue the privileging of adult voices. Certainly there is a way to think and act past this toward a model where solidarity, responsibility toward one another, asymmetrical movements in homiletical power, and mutual critique all work together.

41. Lévinas, 73.

other that might lead me to voluntarily undertake such a commitment, to be for you if you will be for me."[42] McClure draws limits to what Hendley calls "conversational deference," through the image of the preacher as both "guest" and "host," explaining how that deference is disrupted because of the preacher's responsibility to limit others' voices and exercise more conversational power at times.[43]

Even as these most recent theological and ethical accounts of preaching are helpful in addressing plurality, difference, and otherness, these models all assume the potential for full participation in a congregation's homiletic processes. The listeners and speakers described by Rose, Allen, Florence, and McClure are all able to enter homiletic conversations and become active participants despite the limitations imposed by various "-isms." They all potentially incorporate young people into conversations about biblical interpretation and teach them what preaching is/does. What they do not account for, however, is age, and particularly youth, as a dimension of accounting for youthful preaching voices.

Even in the most generous of these preaching models, adolescents still do not find full incorporation as *speakers*.[44] The above models also assume that speakers and listeners in the postmodern situation, in many ways, have the resources (both internal and external) to participate fully as speakers and listeners. Even if young people did have the capacity for self-determination and representation in preaching, there is often still a significant need for various kinds of formation.

42. Hendley, *From Communicative Action*, 20. The notion of asymmetry is also explored in McClure, *Roundtable Pulpit*, 53–55.

43. See McClure, "Preacher as Guest and Host," 119–43. This limitation of "conversational deference" will also be important as we explore the pole of formation, below. McClure's work in this essay and in *The Roundtable Pulpit* help overcome Anselm Min's critiques of a Lévinasian-based theology and ethics in Min, *Solidarity of Others in a Divided World*. Min problematizes "an internal contradiction between Lévinas's intention, the defense of the other in her ethical transcendence, and his philosophical procedure, the denial of all historical mediation, which ironically reduces the human other to ahistorical, angelic existence elevated above all contingencies of history, above all vulnerabilities, and thus neither capable of issuing the categorical imperative 'Thou shalt not kill!' to devouring egos, nor indeed needing protection against such murder in the first place" (12–13). And also that "we murder the other not only by reducing the other to an object of violence in history but also by elevating and etherealizing the other beyond all history in thought" (14). This is also addressed in Farley, *Eros for the Other*.

44. For instance, even McClure's "guest/host" model, which might do the most to alleviate the difficulties young people face, and most closely approximates what I describe below, does not present specific guidelines for engaging the particular problems adolescence presents for homiletics. Most notably, we might be left wondering how preacher and young person know when to move in and out of roles as guest and host, and when/how young people are allowed to be host.

Adults are tempted to respond in two ways. The first is through indiscriminate approval, or redistribution of homiletic authority in the hopes of honoring the attempts of young people to come to voice through preaching. The second is through strictly disciplining young people into acceptable models of speaking/listening. Neither of these options is desirable. Instead, we will want to temper these impulses by a more balanced posture. The best parts of these models still need to be integrated into a more adequate theological and ethical disposition that attends to the particular situation of adolescents and carefully attends to young people as preachers. In order to offer a more appropriate model for the particular set of problems that adolescence presents, I offer an additional theoretical foundation that helps renew preaching as a component of the public sphere for adults and adolescents.

ENVISIONING A RENEWED PUBLIC SPHERE FOR PREACHING

In response to the need for a model that specifically attends to adolescents, I propose a model of mutual critique that moves between the poles of liberation and formation as adults and adolescents interact together around preaching. Rather than beginning with the assumed need for the formation of deficient adolescents, we will instead use liberation as the preliminary point of reference. In this way, we will see how theologies of liberation benefit both young people and preaching theories/practices without demanding culturally privileged competencies of the adult as seen in the postcolonial analysis above. The subsequent movement to formation serves to temper the liberative movement. This approach, as we will see in chapters 4 and 5, will not be so much a moment, but rather a reinvigorated public space of young people, adults, congregations, and preaching theories/practices.

What resources are available for imagining the kind of interaction in which this kind of relationship can take place? In describing a "critical homiletics" based on the work of Jürgen Habermas, John McClure hints at a possible source for theological and ethical homiletic models.[45] The potential for a "critical homiletics" based on Habermas's broad work remains relatively undeveloped. A model of homiletic interaction based in part on Habermas, and more recent appropriations of his work, in conjunction with the ethical impulses in contemporary homiletics explored above can revise preaching as a public sphere for young people.

45. McClure, *Other-Wise Preaching*, 102–11.

Habermas's belief that the public sphere is best renewed through "the critical exercise of reason"[46] serves as a useful point of departure in developing an environment for the adult-adolescent interaction in preaching.[47] Habermas believes that the process of communicative action works as a discursive process of reason-giving until a course of action is reached.[48] Here we see the dynamics of a kind of interactive process that might give shape to the adult-adolescent homiletic relationship. When adults and adolescents listen to one another about preaching, working to understand one another and learn from one another about preaching within a community, this functions as a type of reason-giving oriented toward renewed theories and practices of preaching.

This communicative process of reason-giving, or what we might call the public sphere of homiletic interaction, according to Habermas, is initially guided by a few conditions:

(3.1)   Every subject with the competence to speak and act is allowed to take part in a discourse.

(3.2)   a. Everyone is allowed to question any assertion whatever.

b. Everyone is allowed to introduce any assertion whatever into the discourse.

c. Everyone is allowed to express his attitudes, desires, and needs.

(3.3)   No speaker may be prevented, by internal or external coercion from exercising his rights as laid down in (3.1) and (3.2).[49]

---

46. Lakeland, *Theology and Critical Theory*, 43.

47. Parker Palmer also gives several dimensions of what happens in a best-case version of the public sphere that approximate what I am describing: "Strangers meet on common ground. . . . Fear of the stranger is faced and dealt with. . . . Scarce resources are shared and abundance is generated. . . . Conflict occurs and is resolved. . . . Life is given color, texture, drama, a festive air. . . . People are drawn out of themselves. . . . Mutual responsibility becomes evident, and mutual aid possible. . . . Opinions become audible and more accountable. . . . Vision is projected and projects are attempted. . . . People are empowered and protected against power." See Palmer, *Company of Strangers*, 45–51.

48. Habermas calls this "reaching agreement." See Habermas, *Theory of Communicative Action*, 286–87.

49. Habermas, *Moral Consciousness*, 89.

In this way, communicative action leads to lively and wide discussion among participants.

Habermas's version of interaction needs some revision to be of use for our purposes. In reality, not all parties in an interaction enjoy equality, nor is the public sphere a monolithic entity.[50] Nancy Fraser contends that Habermas's conception of the public sphere treats inequalities as if they did not exist and fails to account for the reality of "subaltern counterpublics," which are "parallel discursive arenas where members of subordinated social groups invent and circulate counter-discourses, which in turn permit them to formulate oppositional interpretations of their identities, interests, and needs."[51] This is an important correction as young people might compose a subaltern counterpublic, but are not formally organized as such. In some sense, adults will actually need to help organize and/or recognize such an adolescent homiletic counterpublic and bring it to the surface.[52]

Amidst this kind of differentiated public sphere where interaction about preaching takes place, we will seek to make "arrangements that permit contestation among a plurality of competing publics [rather] than by a single, comprehensive public sphere."[53] Instead of radical plurality allowing the free expression of all voices in the interaction, or some forced sense of equality (both of which are counterfactual according to Fraser), the public sphere is stratified with adults and young people, with both open to the possibilities of non-adversarial contestation.

We also need to carefully define "competence." Sharon Welch questions the basis for Habermas' understanding of competence/rationality. She highlights how "the insights of oral cultures [in Habermas' *Theory of Communicative Action*, vols. 1 and 2] are, however, summarily dismissed" when discussing an African tribe.[54] We will not want to dismiss the competencies young people display as "irrational," when and if they differ from adults. But we will also need to be discerning about the sufficiency of those competencies for reasoning in this contested public sphere on preaching. This is not to say that adults and adolescents approach each other "*as if*

50. Fraser, *Justice Interruptus*, 77–79.

51. Ibid., 81.

52. See, for example, a group such as the Academy of Preachers, which seeks to encourage young preachers. In the past, this kind of counterpublic might be described as the groups that authorized the published sermons of preachers in Puritan New England. As such, these counterpublics are not always oppositional, but do articulate identities, interests, and needs within their communicative practices, as we will see.

53. Fraser, *Justice Interruptus*, 82.

54. Welch, *Feminist Ethic of Risk*, 132. It is also important to point out that Habermas is not interested in religious discourse either, though this may be changing in his more recent work.

they were social peers in specially designated discursive arenas, when these discursive arenas are situated in a larger societal context that is pervaded by structural relations of dominance and subordination."[55] But it is possible that interaction about preaching can function as a rehabilitative microcosm of the public sphere.

Guided by these principles, homiletic communities are encouraged to engage in conversations about adequate homiletic theories/practices and test them out with the goal of transforming public spaces of preaching into an "ever-widening arena" enriched by competing claims.[56] The interaction, characterized by a continual movement between liberation and formation, will have a feel of mutual critique[57] through communicative practices aimed at refining the public space of homiletic theories/practices (synthesis). This kind of ethic includes adolescents as participants with valued (if different) rationalities, both as speakers and as reflective listeners. This ethic also exposes the liberative potential in their practices as well as the places where further formation would be beneficial. Adults and adolescents engage in a dynamic process of homiletic give-and-take, listening and speaking, with the result of refined homiletic theories/practices and an ecclesial public sphere that values adolescents in a way that it has not done on a large scale in the contemporary milieu.

LIBERATION: THE PRELIMINARY POLE

If the adult-adolescent relationship in homiletic communities is to move from silence and ontological adolescence to a more theologically and ethically grounded relationship of solidarity and mutual critique, then communities in which the issue of preaching and youth are important must first dispose themselves toward communicative practices that are liberative. The goal of a homiletic liberation for adolescents is not, as James Henry Harris states, "the ability to think and do for oneself."[58] While this first-wave liberation theology move to identify false-consciousness among those seeking liberation is valuable, Harris's goal of autonomous individuality is not our

---

55. Fraser, *Justice Interruptus*, 79.

56. Ibid., 82.

57. See Welch for this term. Alternatively, Fraser calls this accountability: "what institutional arrangements best ensure the accountability of democratic decision-making bodies (strong publics) to their (external, weak or, given the possibility of hybrid cases, weaker) publics?" Fraser, *Justice Interruptus*, 91.

58. Harris, *Preaching Liberation*, 9.

goal. Rather, the kind of liberation we seek will always reach toward mutual critique within the public sphere of homiletic interaction.

From another angle, Gustavo Gutiérrez reinterprets the phrase "preferential option for the poor" for multiple contexts, when he states that

> the poverty to which we allude here encompasses economic, social, and political dimensions, but it is undoubtedly more than all that. . . . What then does being poor mean? I believe that a good definition does not exist; but we can approximate it if we say that the poor are the non-persons, the "in-significant ones," the ones that don't count either for the rest of society, and—far too frequently—for the Christian churches.[59]

In contemporary preaching discourse, we have seen that adolescents are all too often "non-persons," rather than seeing how they attest to significant forms of homiletic identity. In this case, even though (especially suburban, Anglo-American) churches allocate significant resources towards young people, they still function as the *homiletic* poor. The liberative pole seeks to recognize the ways that young people can and do bring significant homiletic resources to the ecology of preaching, and in so doing, reshape the representations discussed earlier.

In speaking of the preferential option for the poor, Gutiérrez continues by using the image of the interaction between Jesus and the hemorrhaging woman:

> Such then is the preferential option: the dismantling of anonymity to give people a name and a face. In general Jesus has opted for the poor, but also, concretely, he has opted for people like the hemorrhagic woman. . . . When I affirm that Jesus favors the poor I know this woman is included, but one must value her as a person, make her assume an identity, she who thought of herself as worthless. To love is always to bring someone out of anonymity. Love helps give identity to others. When we speak of preferential love, and the love of God, preferably for the poor, we are speaking of giving the loved ones an identity, of making them feel like people.[60]

Liberation as it relates to preaching and youth takes the theological foundation of God's love for the marginalized, as demonstrated in the person of Jesus Christ, and seeks to rehabilitate the conditions for constructing identity. It is also grounded in the pneumatological: the Spirit gives voice

---

59. Gutierrez, "Renewing the Option," 71–72.
60. Ibid., 75.

to young people in significant ways.[61] Liberation theology sets the tone for this first moment, providing the foundation for at least two dimensions of liberative activity.

Liberation of Youth from Harmful Representations and Cultural Practices

An ethic of liberation confronts the conditions that make the homiletic identity of youth one of anonymity or render them as colonized bodies, so that those with privileged homiletic power and young people can occupy homiletic communities together in solidarity.[62] Those with privilege in homiletic communities have the responsibility to speak *with*, and then, as needed *for* adolescents in ways that strive toward liberation from harmful representations and limited/limiting cultural systems. If homiletic communities are committed to solidarity with young people, they will find themselves interested in protecting and empowering those with "vulnerable identities."[63] We have seen that young people in contemporary preaching discourse are vulnerable in terms of a homiletic identity. As young people and adults begin to engage one another in preaching, they can begin to help liberate, emancipate, and transform adolescents' homiletic identities.

Homiletic communities that work toward solidarity with adolescents realize their need to act on behalf of "vulnerable identities" and can respond in transformative ways. Congregations can begin to fashion themselves as "local support institutions" that combat broader cultural representations.[64] This can happen in three inter-related movements.

First, homiletic communities can identify representations of young people that are limited and limiting, and work toward the transformation of the various systems that promulgate them. If images of young people are produced by domineering cultural systems with far-reaching negative consequences, then homiletic communities can work to undo both the representations and the conditions that make them possible. Charles Campbell's

61. See Joel 2:28–32, Acts 2:17–22. See also White, *Dreamcare.*

62. I do not presuppose that adolescents have no homiletic power. That would deny the historical material and overlook what we will see particularly in the analysis of chapters 4 and 5. Much like Foucault, I believe that power is diffuse such that all people have power, though it is allocated and present in different forms.

63. Hendley, *From Communicative Action,* 41. Hendley takes this term from Habermas' understanding of selves formed in communicative networks.

64. For the term "local support institution," see Giroux, *Youth in a Suspect Society,* 30.

ethic of preaching, for instance, suggests a way that ecclesial communities can do this through preaching. Campbell describes preaching that

> exposes the powers of death. The preacher names the powers and unveils their reality. Like the cross of Jesus, this unveiling of the powers, which uncovers their false claims and deadly lies, marks the beginning of human freedom from the bondage of death. This exposing takes away the "mirrors" by which the powers delude us into thinking they are the divine, life-giving regents of the world. The powers are exposed as emperors without any clothes, a disarming humiliation for those who rely so heavily on their pretensions of dignity and control.[65]

If indeed "the complex machinery of pedagogy, media, and politics is now largely mobilized to demean and punish rather than protect and nurture children," then homiletic communities are responsible for exposing these representations with theological acumen.[66] In listening and preaching, we can ask, "What types of representations of adolescents exist within homiletical and congregational culture? How do they shape our perceptions, action, and ministry with youth?" In doing this kind of work, homiletic communities expose the representations at work in their midst, and the ways they are complicit in upholding them. This kind of exposing also moves homiletic communities' critique of adolescents forward (while standing in solidarity with them) as they hold young people responsible for their actions in light of the powers being unmasked.

Second, homiletic communities can offer up new representations of young people—representations that disentangle them from the "complex machinery" and present positive images that "protect and nurture." Campbell pairs identifying oppressive representations with offering new representations for homiletic and cultural imaginaries:

> Simply exposing the principalities and powers and unveiling their ways of death in the world is not sufficient for preachers. If preachers stopped with exposing, they would deny the good news of the gospel that the new creation has, in fact, broken into the world in Jesus' life, death, and resurrection and will be brought to completion in the fullness of time. If all preachers do is expose the principalities and powers, congregations might be left in despair, overwhelmed by the enormity of the powers'

65. Campbell, *Word before the Powers*, 106.

66. Giroux, *Youth in a Suspect Society*, 28.

work, without the hope that is essential to sustain the life of resistance.[67]

This kind of envisioning looks at adolescents in the homiletic community and beyond as more than consumers or part of the disposable class (using Giroux's terms). New homiletic imagery presents representations that are life-giving and that grant youth possibilities for self-conception beyond commodification and disposability. Envisioning new representations in homiletic communities fuels the work toward renewed futures for those with vulnerable identities.

Third, in challenging representations and offering up new ones, homiletic communities begin to present a new kind of public religious space which can prove to be liberative for young people. Homiletic communities can offer languages of critique and possibility in regard to adolescent representations. Giroux points toward a number of non-religious advocates who imagine their work as this kind of public space. "The point," he says,

> is that art, education and cultural work need to reinvent spaces for ethical, political, and pedagogical practices through which diverse cultural workers might create alliances and produce social practices and policies that rewrite the importance of what it means to treat youth with dignity. Unlike cultural workers such as Calvin Klein and [filmmaker] Larry Clark, who offer children either the cheap satisfactions of stylized bodies and commodified pleasures, or the sensationalism of decadent sexuality, progressive educators and other cultural workers need to challenge such limited representations of youth through an 'integrative critical language in which values, ethics, and social responsibility can be discussed in terms' of how youth are constructed within such images.[68]

Homiletic communities are certainly among those whom Giroux deems "cultural workers," capable of re-invigorating public spaces that treat youth with dignity. Striving to make an impact on the larger cultural imaginary by creating public spaces in which re-imagination can occur, Giroux offers a challenge to congregations, seminaries, and non-profits to do this hard work in a way that impacts entire communities, if not the larger public arena.[69]

67. Campbell, *Word before the Powers*, 119–20.

68. Giroux, *Youth Culture*, 51–52.

69. Giroux believes that education (in the vein of John Dewey) is a way to ensure a more democratic future. Similarly, I believe that critical homiletic communities that work toward solidarity and mutual critique with adolescents can work towards transformation of other spheres of public life when they move between the poles of

Liberation of Privileged Homiletic Knowledge

As a type of public space complicit in harmful representations, homiletic discourse stands alongside congregations as an area in need of liberation. Liberation, as a process of recognizing the worth and identity of the marginalized, also means coming to terms with the homiletic wisdom of adolescents. This commitment means de-centering privileged homiletic rationalities/competencies and taking the position of a listener/learner in dialogue who receives insight. Within the liberative pole, those with privileged control over homiletic discourse recognize that the values, categories, terms, and modes of thinking at work in contemporary homiletics are not superlative and final. Homiletic knowledge is largely controlled by a specific type of literature disseminated through formal theological education, immersed in academic rationalities (largely set by elite white males) that have been recognized as more and more tentative in recent years. The more recent influx of pluralistic accounts of homiletic knowledge (i.e., feminist, Latino/a, African American, LGBTQ, etc.) have called into question the certainty of prevalent rationalities.

Yet even as the emerging accounts of homiletic knowledge value difference along the lines of gender, sexuality, and ethnicity, they leave little room to be informed by adolescents. Within the liberative pole, homileticians and preachers reflect on these types of questions: What are the definitions of homiletic competencies and rationalities in my homiletic community? How are homiletic competencies produced and acquired? How are they mediated and controlled?

This de-centering of privileged homiletic knowledge has some implications. Scholars must reassess the boundaries of homiletic research and what counts as valid forms of knowledge. For instance, while homiletic theories built on philosophy and academic theology have much to offer, their origination in the academy does not automatically grant them superior status as homiletic knowledge. Henry Giroux suggests that it is possible to peel back layers of hegemony within educational institutions and discover "fugitive forms of knowledge."[70] In order to do this, Giroux invites committed parties to begin "questioning the very conditions under which knowledge, values, and social identities are produced, appropriated, and often challenged."[71] Giroux understands the link between power and knowledge at work in cultural practices. Moreover, Giroux observes that "critical pedagogical

---

liberation and formation.

70. Giroux, *Fugitive Cultures*, 19.

71. Ibid.

practices also allow students to produce and appropriate space for the production of fugitive knowledge forms, those forms of knowledge that often
exist either outside the mainstream curriculum or are seen as unworthy of
serious attention."[72] When scholars of preaching seek to transform (and be
transformed by) alternate definitions of homiletic rationality, they will position themselves as listeners and begin to identify "fugitive forms of knowledge" at work within homiletic communities, particularly those operating
among adolescents. This process can de-center assumptions about homiletic competency and rationality, thereby allowing serious public space for
adolescent critique of entrenched homiletic theories/practices, and reach
toward solidarity and more communal forms of homiletic practice.

The kind of public homiletic space of which I seek to foster in chapters
4 and 5 is a first step toward giving an example of how participants in homiletic communities can speak to one another in solidarity about homiletic
theories and practices. This can prove to be liberative for both youth and
adults, and transformative of the public spaces of congregations, seminaries, and academic homiletics. Preaching by youth constitutes a place where
liberation might take place. When young people assume preaching roles
in ecclesial settings, the kinds of liberation we have explored above can
emerge. Although we can expect that such preaching will contain traces of
hegemonic influences, forms of "fugitive knowledge" will also be present.
In freeing this "adults-only" space, adults listen to young people preach and
take them seriously—not as trivial or viewing young people as capable of
significant preaching only in their adult futures. Subsequently, adults enter
into dialogue with young people about that preaching, and look for the ways
that together we might formulate significant ethical and religious resources
for transforming representations, de-colonizing the lifeworld, suggesting
new theories/practices of preaching, as well as rethinking what it means to
be people of faith. But this does not happen without another moment in this
interaction, which we will call the formative pole. This moment will seek
to understand how adolescents are still in need of formation and what that
process of formation might look like.

FORMATION: A COMPLEMENTARY POLE

One of the questions in the wake of the homiletic model proposed above is
about the nature of mutual critique, particularly in the adult-adolescent relationship. Not every communicative practice by adolescents will be worthy

72. Ibid., 19–20. It is worth noting here that Giroux is an intellectual heir to Paulo
Freire.

of lifting up as liberative. In fact, many will be characterized by pedagogies of commodification and/or disposability. Without dismissing adolescent homiletic insight, moving too quickly toward an authoritative posture, or uncritically validating adolescent voice, how do we critique the "homiletic competencies" of adolescents? I propose formation as the other side of the disposition, which paves the way for a constructive mutual critique in this renewed public space of preaching. Formation, properly conceived, serves to add depth and complexity to the developing homiletic and Christian identities of young people. The formative pole asks, "After speaking and listening *with* and *for* youth, and listening for "fugitive forms of knowledge" *among* youth, in what ways can adults speak *to* youth?"

Inasmuch as homiletic communities work toward recognizing the "being" of adolescents, they are also obligated to recognize the "becoming" of adolescents. I have not used the resources of developmental psychological models in order to focus on the liberation of "being" rather than formation of "becoming." Adolescents are, however, engaged in significant processes of development in a wide array of arenas: physical, social, psychological, religious, and emotional. And as young people go through these processes of change faith communities are responsible for helping them manage change. Preaching communities that embody the formation side of the disposition should be open to adolescents as listeners and communicators, yet recognize the spaces where adolescents need assistance becoming people who can "interpret lived situations in light of Gospel."[73]

One of the hallmarks of Christian faith is formation of varied kinds, and particularly for the young. There are temptations, however, to articulate formation in ways that are reminiscent of the kind of colonialist impulses described above. Valerie Walkerdine notes the subtle ways that pedagogical practices, overly dependent upon developmental psychology, "are normalizing in that they constitute a mode of observation and surveillance and production of children. . . . It is important to point out that the processes of normalization are not the product of some repressive superpower hellbent on keeping people in their place. That is, disciplinary power does not function through overt repression but through the covert reproduction of ourselves."[74] Walkerdine's healthy suspicion of the deployment of developmental psychology as a definitive, ideologically-neutral interpretive key for the development of children is instructive. Attempts at formation with preaching in mind should avoid "covert reproduction of ourselves." As scholars, teachers, and congregations live more fully into the liberative

73. Farley, *Practicing Gospel.*
74. Walkerdine, "Developmental Psychology," 195–96.

pole of the approach, adolescents, freed from oppressive representations, are better able to work in solidarity with others on their own developmental processes. When homiletic communities engage in the formation pole of the disposition, they do so intent on helping shape two forms of identity among young people: Christian identity and homiletic identity.

Formation of Christian and Homiletic Identities

As preaching communities attend to the speaking and listening practices of adolescents, they will find latent theories and practices of what it means to be a person of faith, as well as what it means to preach and listen to sermons as one in need of formation. Conceding young people's contributions to homiletic communities does not automatically and uncritically validate all their contributions. We must discern together if the theories and practices that emerge through careful listening are in need of further formation.

If, as Giroux points out, young people are subject to pedagogies of commodification or disposability, then they are just as likely to have internalized those pedagogies. Their operative theories, practices, and content are subsequently just as likely to be mired in false consciousness, contradictions, or injustice. In this case, the homiletic community has a responsibility to help young people critically reflect on their faith and homiletic practices, encouraging them in the kind of formation that develops healthy Christian and preaching identities.

Thomas Groome states that "there is a maintaining, conserving, and transmitting of our Christian tradition that is part of the task of Christian religious education. For that, 'intentional socialization' is essential. But there is also a creating, liberating, and transforming activity that must take place as we come to appropriate the tradition and become creative members of the community to which it gives rise."[75] Groome's idea applied to this situation means that as homiletic communities engage in mutual critique between adults and youth, passing on traditions that are integral to the Christian tradition as a local community understands them is a *sine qua non*. Identity formation, however, is always in service of transforming the homiletic community (or in other words, always tempered by the liberative moment of the approach), helping young people become "creative members of the community," not "docile bodies" or replications of particular members of the community. This goal should be the greatest hope of homiletic communities as they seek to help form identities among young people.

75. Groome, *Christian Religious Education*, 124–25.

The list of those things that might be in need of formation could be extensive. Pedagogies of commodification can incite young people toward the ethereal and vapid at the expense of venerable long-lasting traditions that have served to sustain faith communities. In addition, traditional forms of theological and homiletical reasoning have long made the work of preaching intelligible, both within congregations and in relation to wider publics. Young people may need to be formed in these modes of reasoning in ways they have not yet understood *critically*. This is not just a task relegated to young people who will later choose forms of theological education as a way to understand their homiletic communities, but for all young people engaged in the homiletic community. We should attend to formation not only in terms of traditions and reasoning, but also through body, voice, space, and other material aspects such as dress, furniture, and technology use. Pedagogies of commodification and disposability can treat the body, voice, and space as well as other materials in ways that dishonor their inherent worth as created by or in the image of God. Those interested in the Christian and homiletic identities of young people would do well to help them think about bodies and materials beyond the lessons of commodification and toward more theologically appropriate forms. This short list is, in many ways, abstract. Chapters 4 and 5 will formulate concrete ways to think about and enact this kind of formation by looking at sermons from young people.

Two Arenas of Formative Activity

As stated above, homiletic communities interested in formation are seeking to add depth and complexity so that, as young people's homiletic wisdom is liberated, it can also be formed in step with the gospel and with faithful preaching. As a result, those with privilege within homiletic communities offer formative critique within two different arenas.

(1) Providing Narrative Complexity

Undoubtedly one of the primary functions of preaching in the first five centuries of the church was catechesis. Through preaching, local priests and bishops passed on the mysteries of the faith in preparation for, and in response to baptism. Local homiletic traditions arose that provided interpretations of the faith including explanations of baptism and other rites, the content and meaning of the creed, moral suasion, community-building, exegesis of Scriptures, and mediation between faith and culture. This kind of preaching assisted neophytes in living into a catholic, yet contextual

Christian identity. Craig Satterlee contends that catechetical/mystagogical preaching is especially suited for the formation of Christians in a pluralistic religious and social marketplace.[76] It is a fitting genre of preaching when thinking about the relationship between adults and adolescents.

The catechetical function of preaching rarely receives attention in the contemporary US context. Early mystagogical catechesis is mined for reclamation of liturgical forms rather than for preaching wisdom. The situation is doubly complex in regard to adolescents. Christian education, rather than preaching, has largely assumed the function of catechesis among traditions diverse in baptismal understanding and practice. And, as seen in the development of a historical perspective earlier, Christian religious education has taken over homiletics' voice concerning adolescents. As such, homiletics has abdicated (as of the late nineteenth and early twentieth centuries) some of the fundamental qualities that had been integral features through its history.

In light of this situation, formation funds reclamation of the catechetical nature of preaching, particularly as adolescents are concerned. Adolescents should be able to find in the pulpit intentionally structured rhetoric that helps form them as individuals who can "interpret lived situations in light of Gospel" by assimilating the Christian narrative into their lives. Local communities have an obligation to responsibly pass on the contours of the Christian faith in context.

This does not mean, however, that a catechetical homiletic stance toward adolescents is merely what Thomas Groome calls "socialization."[77] Groome highlights that socialization is an insufficient term because it (1) denies that Christians are part of more than one social grouping than just the church (i.e., creates an us vs. them mentality), (2) focuses on maintenance of the Christian community when reform and transformation are part of its calling, and (3) it overestimates the power of socialization to "sponsor them toward Christian faith lived with human freedom in response to the Kingdom of God."[78] Preaching and religious education in these modes operate with much the same function: bringing people into the narrative framework of the church or enculturation into the church's own specific culture or grammar. We previously saw these versions in the work of Anna Carter

76. Satterlee, *Ambrose of Milan's Method.*

77. Groome, *Christian Religious Education,* 109–27. Groome points to Bushnell as the pioneer of socialization under Bushnell's preferred term "nurture."

78. Ibid., 124–25. In many ways, Groome's response to socialization in religious education (written in 1980) anticipates responses to what would later become articulated in homiletics as expressions of the cultural-linguistic or postliberal versions of theology. See Campbell, *Preaching Jesus*; Willimon, *Peculiar Speech*; Willimon, *Intrusive Word.*

Florence and Sarah Arthur. While these versions of preaching provide a powerful account of the function of so-called Christian narratives/cultures that are of some use, socialization and cultural-linguistic/postliberal models of preaching fail to recognize and respond to the narrative complexity that exists between church and world.[79]

Catechetical preaching does not automatically default to the narrow narratizing claims of cultural-linguistic/postliberal models. Instead, catechetical preaching focuses on formation of young people through the three dimensions Groome raises. First, it helps young people discern ways of simultaneously being part of the social fabric of the church *and* wider culture. Second, this kind of preaching practice invites young people into the full life of the community for its ongoing reformation and transformation *in the present*, not delayed until they are able to fulfill institutional ecclesial roles (as important as those are). Third, this kind of preaching helps give contextual appropriations of Christian faith that are characterized by response to the good news of the Kingdom of God.

This kind of formation toward Christian identity certainly includes not only passing on the content of the faith but moreover the encouragement to embody a habitus of *theologia*, as Edward Farley describes it, a sapiential wisdom or reflective way of living the Christian faith.[80] This reflective way of living promotes discernment between the various narratives available to young people, not as a simple either-or choice.

While modeling a particular way of thinking and acting, catechetical preaching is also an act of speaking for/to/with adolescents that offers up representations of young people within the narrative tradition of the church. Tertullian, for instance, offers Christians the image of the fish for neophytes: "But we, little fishes, after the example of our ΙΧΘΥΣ Jesus Christ, are born in water, nor have we safety in any other way than by permanently abiding in water; so that most monstrous creature, who had no right to teach even sound doctrine, knew full well how to kill the little fishes, by taking them away from the water!"[81] Catechetical preaching for/to/with adolescents offers narrative complexity while sponsoring contextually appropriate representations of young people.

---

79. Again, for the specific shortcomings of postliberal theology as they relate to the concerns of this project, I refer to Tanner.

80. Farley, *Theologia*.

81. Tertullian, *On Baptism*, I.

(2) Engaging in Processes of Conscientization and Empowerment

As narrative complexity gives depth and dimension to young people, formation also takes the shape of what Paulo Freire calls "conscientization." According to Daniel Schipani, who follows Freire's thought toward Christian education practices, "conscientization is a process of cultural action in which women and men are awakened to their sociocultural reality, move beyond the constraints and alienations to which they are subjected, and affirm themselves as conscious subjects and co-creators of their historical future."[82] In this we see a two-step process of reflection and action, which we will divide into (1) conscientization and (2) empowerment. First, homiletic communities are responsible for formation that brings to consciousness the ways that adolescents are being led into representations of commodification and disposability, and the myriad ways that colonization of the lifeworld of adolescents is taking place (we also named this as a function of the liberation, above). This involves discernment about the social, cultural, and economic forces at work within communities and subsequently equipping young people—through preaching practices—to recognize how those forces are at work to oppress them.

Second, the church continues the formative work begun in conscientization through actions of empowerment. Schipani observes of Freire that "he believes that modern society does not encourage authentic freedom and does not promote the development of critical consciousness. Further, he claims that people must liberate themselves in order to fulfill their human potential in light of the ontological vocation as history makers."[83] Applied here, formative practices do not stop with consciousness-raising (reflection), but also necessarily includes empowering others (action). Rather than ontological adolescence and silence, or commodification and disposability, Freire provides youth with an "ontological vocation as history makers."

Freire articulates the foundations of an education that is liberative for the oppressed. He believes "revolutionary praxis is a unity, and the leaders cannot treat the oppressed as their possession. Manipulation, sloganizing, 'depositing,' regimentation, and prescription cannot be components of revolutionary praxis, precisely because they are components of the praxis of domination."[84] Freire's description approximates the kind of relationship needed for the pole of formation. Those with homiletic privilege cannot treat adolescents as their possession, nor can they resort to the practices

---

82. Schipani, *Religious Education*, 13.

83. Ibid., 15.

84 Freire, *Pedagogy of the Oppressed*, 121.

which Freire describes as constitutive of "the praxis of domination." Adults who engage in homiletic relationships of formation with adolescents do so not to dominate, nor to validate homiletical norms or exercise power over, but rather are interested in exercising "power with" adolescents. This kind of "power with" in homiletic communities maintains that formation of adolescent identities are always disposed toward critical reflection on Christian faith and preaching.

With these arenas of formation in mind, homiletic communities must articulate a strategy for how formation takes place.

Shared Praxis as a Model for Formation

In order to give more specificity to the tasks of formation of identifying narrative complexity, engaging in conscientization, and working toward empowerment, homiletic communities can move toward formation in a way similar to what Thomas Groome calls "shared Christian praxis."[85]

Groome's model of shared Christian praxis shares affinities with what we have explored through the liberative model above, as well as the kind of pedagogy described by Paulo Freire and Daniel Schipani. Groome believes that "Christian religious education by shared praxis can be described as a group of Christians sharing in dialogue their critical reflection on present action in light of the Christian Story and its Vision toward the end of lived Christian faith."[86] This process integrates the three arenas of formation we have outlined above (narrative complexity, conscientization, empowerment). For Groome, the practice consists of five components and five corresponding movements. Groome summarizes them as such:

1. The participants are invited to name their own activity concerning the topic for attention (present action).

2. They are invited to reflect on why they do what they do, and what the likely or intended consequences of their actions are (critical reflection).

3. The educator makes present to the group the Christian community Story concerning the topic at hand and the faith response it invites (Story and its Vision).

4. The participants are invited to appropriate the Story to their lives in a dialectic with their own stories (dialectic between Story and stories).

---

85. Groome, *Christian Religious Education*, 184–231.
86. Ibid., 184.

5. There is an opportunity to choose a personal faith response for the future (dialectic between Vision and visions).[87]

The process is fairly straightforward. Participants engage in a dialogue about a particular topic or course of action within human life. They reflect on the reasoning and consequences for that action. The educator intervenes to provide a recollection of "the whole faith tradition of our people however that is expressed or embodied" (Story) and "a comprehensive representation of the lived response which the Christian Story invites and of the promise God makes in that Story."[88] This moment does not provide the final answer. Instead, participants reflect on how their experiences might appropriate the vision expressed by the educator (with room for acceptance, critique, amendment, and/or rejection). Finally, the participants choose how they will respond in light of the preceding moments.

This is easily adapted to the formation of youth within preaching communities, whether considering faith practices or preaching practices. Here adults invite adolescents as participants into a dialogue about ideas and practices associated with preaching. This dialogue can include, but is not limited to: the meaning of preaching, the role of the preacher, the nature and claims of sermons, the role of Scripture, the goals and purposes of sermons, and sermon design/delivery. Then together they critically reflect on those practices, listen to the normative stories and their invited responses, think about the stories and visions in relation to present experience, and voice a course of action for the future.[89]

In the same way that young people are invited into pulpits in the interest of liberation, they are also invited into pulpits in the interest of formation. When young people preach and adults engage them in feedback, they become involved in the kind of processes that are formative of both their Christian and homiletic identities. Through the kind of listening and feedback I carry out in chapters 4 and 5, young people are provided with the resources of traditions that can bring them along to greater maturity as Christians and as preachers. By preaching and engaging with adults about that preaching, young people's agency is more fully exercised, not just as those who reflect on biblical texts or on sermons (i.e., collaborative models), but as voiced preachers who exercise critical engagement with Christian and homiletic traditions. Adults then enter into feedback *first as listeners,* and then subsequently as those who help young people in identifying formative

87. Ibid., 207–8.
88. Ibid., 192–93.
89. See, for instance, Parker, *Trouble Don't Last Always.*

resources/tasks, while simultaneously holding out the likelihood that they will receive the benefit of formation as well.[90]

CONCLUSION

This chapter proposes a theologically and ethically grounded norm for renewing the relationship between adults and adolescents in homiletic communities. Through a theological and ethical vision of liberation and formation which uses postcolonial analysis to revise the concept of oppression, an exploration of recent proposals for the ethics of preaching, and the introduction of homiletic versions of communicative action and mutual critique, I have articulated a foundation for renewing the adolescent-adult public sphere of preaching. With that foundation in mind, chapters 4 and 5 will move to enact the model of liberation and formation by closely listening to adolescents' preaching.

90. This is the benefit and best hope of apprenticeship models of preaching pedagogy, prominent in African American and Latino/a traditions.

4

Youthful Preaching

Listening to Young Preachers on Christian Identity

The disposition articulated in chapter 3 encourages us to engage in some intentional listening practices. To this point, I have suggested that those with homiletic privilege have been doing the bulk of the speaking without attending to the ways that adolescents are speaking back to homiletics and/ or are in need of formation. This chapter and the next seek to put into practices forms of interpretive and evaluative listening by fashioning a method of rhetorical analysis that takes seriously adolescents' sermons.

LISTENING THROUGH RHETORICAL ANALYSIS

Rhetorical analysis "can provide some important clues about the role of preaching in congregational life."[1] In the case of adolescents' sermons it can account for the ways that young people are functioning as rhetorical actors in given situations. As such, methods of rhetorical criticism provide multi-faceted interpretive schemes for understanding adolescents preachers as rhetors—symbol-wielding actors attempting to "gain adherence," "form attitudes," or "induce action," in their communities.[2]

1. McClure, *Four Codes*, xii.
2. Burke, *Rhetoric of Motives*, 41–43; Perelman and Olbrechts-Tyteca, *New Rhetoric*,

One of the major foci in the liberation-formation disposition is identifying the representations of adolescents at work in a homiletic community, as well as the ways that self-representation is constrained. As such, rhetorical analysis takes a prominent role here because it helps identify the representations of adolescent identity at work in religious speech. Recent studies in communication and rhetoric suggest that identities are performed, rather than merely something one possesses. Donal Carbaugh wants to shift attention away from three idioms of identity at work in wider cultural accounts of identity: biological identity, psychological traits, and cultural/social identity. These three idioms often overlap or form hybrid accounts of identity. Carbaugh critiques these accounts of identity because they are generally regarded as internal to the self—either possessed or acquired.

Contrary to these passive accounts of identity, Carbaugh proposes that identities are communicative. He says,

> [T]he basic site of identity, in this view, could be formulated in this way: What exactly one is being, or saying, or doing, by being such a person as a worker, or a woman, or a man, or an environmentalist, or a German, is largely contingent upon the scene in which one is acting, and the way that scene is set, cast, and communicatively improvised. Focusing on this performative mode of identity, or selves, as in social interactions in actual scenes, in a particular somewhere and not just an abstract anywhere, leads me . . . to add a fourth "cultural pragmatic idiom" to the [idioms] above.[3]

This approach leads Carbaugh to the following statement as a framing device for communicative identities: "[I, We, You, They] [know, show, constitute] who [I, we, you, they] [am, are] in part, by the way [I, we, you, they] [symbolize, perform, participate] in situated social scenes."[4] He places this understanding to the test through different social scenes: a fan at college basketball games, differentiation of roles in the workplace, the married self, the gendered self, and political identities, among others. Dan Handelmann explores this concept in terms of ritual. By the process of "autopoiesis" or self-organization, "a ritual produces the persons that will produce the ritual as that ritual produces them."[5] The self is organized and re-organized by participation in ritual, even as the ritual is (re-)organized by one's participation.

4

3. Carbaugh, *Situating Selves*, 23.

4. Ibid., 33.

5. Handelman, *Ritual in its Own Right*, 11.

Similarly, Thomas Nakayama and Robert Krizek approach "whiteness" or what it means to be white through a rhetorical/communicative lens. For Nakayama and Krizek, "we should not search for what whiteness really means; instead, we should seek out its rhetorical character. . . . [W]e seek an understanding of the ways that this rhetorical construction makes itself visible and invisible, eluding analysis yet exerting influence over everyday life."[6] With a more critical objective of exposing the way rhetorical identities marginalize some and normalize others, Nakayama and Krizek adopt the same approach as Carbaugh.

This perspective helps to cast light on the way we will approach adolescents' preaching practices. If young people and their religious speech practices are to be the object of rhetorical criticism, and we want to discern the dynamics of their self-representation, then it is imperative to attend to the ways that they are performing two major types of identities: Christian identity and homiletic identity.[7] A method of rhetorical analysis will help us to interpret the identities adolescents perform which can subsequently be evaluated through the lens of liberation-formation.

A CONSTRUCTIVE METHOD
OF RHETORICAL CRITICISM

Sonja Foss outlines the process of rhetorical criticism as unfolding this general way: "(1) selecting an artifact; (2) analyzing the artifact; (3) formulating a research question; and (4) writing the essay."[8] Adolescents' sermons will be the artifacts analyzed and the question has already been formulated: "How do adolescents perform Christian and homiletic identities through sermons?" Below is a method by which I propose adolescents' sermons should be analyzed. In outlining these methods of criticism, I will address the following: (1) what the method hopes to accomplish and (2) how the method operates as an analytical tool for the sermons of adolesecents.

6. Nakayama and Krizek, "Whiteness as a Strategic Rhetoric," 91.

7. Undoubtedly, these identities, and their rhetorical performance by young people are also shaped by factors of race and class, as Giroux suggests in almost all of his analyses. While we will pay attention to factors of race and class and how they condition these kinds of identities, they will not be the *primary* factors in defining homiletic and Christian identities.

8. Foss, *Rhetorical Criticism*, 12.

DISCERNING CHRISTIAN IDENTITY THROUGH PENTADIC AND METAPHOR CRITICISMS

When young people preach (as with all sermons), they advocate a specific kind of Christian identity for themselves and for their listeners. Can the Christian identity they espouse open up possibilities for the homiletic community that it has not considered? Or, conversely, does it need to go through additional formation to be adequate for the homiletic community? Rhetorical criticism provides the kind of interpretive devices that can frame the Christian identity performed by adolescents in their religious speech. In the interest of discerning this identity, I propose using two forms of rhetorical criticism that help answer the question "What does it mean for young people to identify themselves as Christians and promote that identification in others through preaching?" In order to see how adolescents' religious speech answers this question, I use a mixture of (1) Kenneth Burke's pentadic criticism and (2) metaphor criticism.

Pentadic/Dramatistic Criticism

Kenneth Burke's pentadic criticism, or dramatism, operates under the premise that

> humans develop and present messages in much the same way that a play is presented. We use rhetoric to constitute and present a particular view of our situation, just as a play creates and presents a certain world or situation inhabited by characters in the play. Through rhetoric, we size up a situation and name its structure and outstanding ingredients. How we describe a situation indicates how we are perceiving it, the choices we see available to us, and the action we are likely to take in that situation.[9]

Burke's pursuit of motives through rhetoric emerges here by discerning a speaker's attempts to communicate a course of action. In order to identify the dramatic structure and elements of an artifact, pentadic criticism analyzes a rhetor's use of five basic elements of drama: agent, act, agency, scene, and purpose.[10] These terms are defined as follows:

9. Ibid., 384.

10. Alternatively, we could also use narrative criticism, which Foss explores in Ibid., 333–82. Also helpful in identifying "theological worldview" is the structuralist theological narrative that John McClure calls the "theosymbolic code" detailed in McClure, *Four Codes*. All assume the dominance of a rhetorically-communicated worldview, but Burke's pentad is slightly less complicated than the two alternatives mentioned above.

1. Agent: the group or individual who is the main character or protago-
   nist. This could be the rhetor or another person or group.

2. Act: the action taken by the agent

3. Agency: the means by which the action is taken by the agent

4. Scene: the stage set by the speaker which describes the conditions, influence, and/or causes of the rhetorical situation

5. Purpose: what the agent hopes or intends to accomplish by performing the act and the agent's feelings or intentions[11]

The rhetorical critic analyzes the artifact, identifying these elements
and subsequently looks for the ways they interact. In order to do this, the
elements of the pentad are placed in ratios in order to answer these questions: "(1) Which factor dominates the discourse generally? And (2) When
two factors are discussed simultaneously, which predominates and why?"[12]
Placing the pentadic elements in ratios and then assessing the dominant
term(s) and relationships builds a more complex picture of the dramatic
framework latent in the artifact. For instance, Foss begins a ratio pairing
"by putting together scene and act in a scene-act ratio. This ratio involves
asking whether the nature of the scene, as described by the rhetor, affects
the nature of the act the rhetor describes. . . . An act-scene ratio, in contrast,
would explore whether the nature of the act dominates—whether the act, as
it is described, directs, determines, or shapes the nature of the scene."[13] Hart
and Daughton suggest that through examining these ratios, the dominant
terms prove to "feature" the dominant element and its characteristics while
the lesser element in the ratio is "muted."[14] Additionally, each privileged
term may serve either a "eulogistic," laudatory purpose or a "dyslogistic,"
uncomplimentary purpose.[15]

In terms of discerning Christian identity in adolescents' religious
speech, pentadic or dramatistic criticism identifies a *dramatic* structure of
Christian identity within sermons. Identifying these elements and their ratios exposes the ways that the speaker construes relationships between contexts, motivations, actions, and traditional theological symbols (e.g., God,
Jesus, Holy Spirit, church, Scripture, etc.). As such, the dramatistic picture

---

In the interest of portability for the method, I opt for Burke's dramatism.

11. Foss, *Rhetorical Criticism*, 386.

12. Hart and Daughton, *Modern Rhetorical Criticism*, 277.

13. Foss, *Rhetorical Criticism*, 387.

14. See Fig. 12.1 in Hart and Daughton, 279–80.

15. Ibid.

within a rhetorical act provides a contoured picture of the way(s) a speaker negotiates, champions, or silences key players which construct a picture of Christian identity. Figure 4.1 shows the workflow of pentadic/dramatistic criticism for discerning Christian identity in adolescent religious speech. An additional framing device should help compose a more richly textured picture of Christian identity.

Metaphor Criticism

Metaphor criticism supplies another way to frame Christian identity among young people's sermons. In this case, the critic seeks to identify the dominant metaphors the speaker uses to describe Christian identity. Rather than "mere ornamentation," metaphor works as an integral way that communicators frame reality.[16] Metaphors attempt to capture the understanding and experience of a concept or phenomenon and put it into terms that relate it in terms of another system of understanding or experience. For instance, Lakoff and Johnson use the sentence "You're wasting my time" as an example of a metaphor that suggests the concept "time is money." Rather than a simple concept of measuring the length of a moment, time functions as a commodity.[17] This metaphor reflects and structures the way that time functions in North American culture if not in many parts of the globe today. If this is true, then the metaphors that young people use to describe Christian identity impact the nature of Christian action as they see it. As pentadic analysis analyzes a dramatic structure for Christian identity and charts a narratival path for expected action, analyzing metaphors helps to identify the ways that young people construct a conceptual system for Christian identity built out of key words and phrases.

Metaphor criticism proceeds by identifying metaphors, then examining the ways metaphor functions within a particular rhetorical artifact. Since metaphors are built upon concepts, called tenors, and are expressed in terms called vehicles, metaphor criticism looks at the way vehicles express tenors. Philip Wheelwright defines vehicle and tenor as "the one for the imagery or concrete situation described [vehicle], the other for the significance that this suggests to the responsive imagination [tenor]."[18] In this case, we will be looking at metaphors that express the tenor of Christian faith or Christian identity. As Foss suggests, the tenor may only be implied, but the

16. See Lakoff and Johnson, *Metaphors We Live By*; Soskice, *Metaphor and Religious Language*.

17. Lakoff and Johnson, *Metaphors We Live By*, 7.

18. Wheelwright, *Metaphor & Reality*, 55.

vehicle will always be present.[19] For example, one young preacher named Katie says about the life of faith (tenor), "God however, does not give me a scroll—not for my sermon and not for my future. Instead, God has given me a pen and a blank piece of paper [vehicle]. But He hasn't left me alone to write it myself." The preacher proceeds to build a theological system about the life of faith through this metaphor, both implicitly and explicitly.

Finding the "entailments," or logical implications of the metaphor is a necessary next step, and in this case attempts to identify the theological system implied in the way the preacher employs the metaphor. In this case, the metaphor used for Christian identity (tenor) is "faith is a composition" (vehicle) and the entailments are all the implications (again, implicit or explicit) about theological anthropology, theology, Christology, pneumatology, ecclesiology, etc. The critic draws out the way that the metaphors used by adolescents construct conceptual systems of Christian identity.

Metaphor criticism looks for the metaphors used in a manner of intensity in a rhetorical artifact and attempts to explain their use. Combined with pentadic/dramatistic analysis, a rich picture of Christian identity begins to emerge. Figure 4.1 shows the workflow of this part of the analysis. Later, in the evaluative stage, the pentadic and metaphor analyses will be placed into the evaluative framework of liberation-formation in order to appraise their viability for the homiletic community.

EVALUATION IN THE LIBERATION-FORMATION DISPOSITION

After having interpreted artifacts through the rhetorical analyses outlined above, we will have an opportunity to filter those interpretations through the poles of liberation-formation. When we enact the theological and ethical disposition of listening outlined in chapter 3, we should expect to find places where the faith commitments and practices of a community might need revision (liberation). We should also expect to find places where adolescents' Christian identities are in need of formation, in the vein of "shared Christian praxis."

For example, if the Christian identity heard within an adolescent's sermon "transgresses" a community's confession of faith, then there will be a moment where we decide together if that theological transgression can be beneficial or is in need of further formation. Does the transgression help further or correct the narrative arc of the historic tradition and

19. Foss, *Rhetorical Criticism*, 303.

contemporary theological families with which I identify? Or, does the narrative arc provide helpful boundaries that suggest the transgression be reigned in for formation?

Those particular commitments and norms of Christian identity will, of course, vary from community to community. Of utmost importance is that homiletic communities begin to live into the disposition. Careful listening and interpretation should lead to respectful, critical evaluation of adolescents' religious speech. This kind of evaluative process makes use of the rhetorical analyses for the purposes of refining a homiletic community's Christian identity as well as its theories and practices of preaching.

The process of interpretation and evaluation could (and hopefully will) take shape in a number of different ways besides what I present here. For example, in order to integrate Christian education and homiletics more fully, a homiletic community might develop an interactive strategy of teaching and preaching whereby preaching, listening, interpretation, and evaluation lead the way to a curriculum of Christian education where both the liberative and formative elements are integrated into the content of learning together (rather than vice versa). Or, homiletic communities might find places in their calendars for "seasons of preaching" that embody the ethic of listening, opening their pulpits to young people beyond limited "youth Sundays" with intergenerational feedback groups designed to evaluate young people's preaching for the purposes of liberation-formation. In order to more fully instantiate the process of interpretation and evaluation, I will now place the method I have developed into practice.

ANALYZING ADOLESCENTS' SERMONS FOR CHRISTIAN IDENTITY

Preliminary Remarks on the Sermons

Having established a method for analyzing the religious speech of adolescents, I use thirteen sermons from high school students. The thirteen sermons examined were acquired from YouTube, which allows any free account holder to upload digital video content. YouTube contained the greatest number of sermons by young people in one public resource. In the past, using video recorded sermons which were uploaded to the internet might have limited the range of available sermons to individuals and congregations because of the expense of video recording and editing. Current video recording technology is much more affordable and accessible now, as are the means to transfer that content to the internet.

Sermons were selected by entering search phrases such as "youth preacher(s)," "young preacher(s)," and "youth sermon(s)." As a result of the "tags," similar or related videos on the website became available. In order to limit the field and establish a diverse group of preachers, sermons were chosen from young preachers who preached in multi-generational settings, mostly for weekly worship gatherings.[20] This is true for every sermon but one (Sam N), who preached in a youth-only setting. Only preachers who were identified as "youth" or "student" were chosen (either by self-identification, by the accompanying details on the web page, or by someone else in the video) and, when apparent, identified as high school students. Only sermons that were complete from beginning to end were selected.[21] Length was not a part of the criteria and, in fact, the sermons vary greatly in length. In addition, only recordings that were of sufficient quality to be transcribed with relative ease were chosen.

An almost equal number of sermons by male (seven) and female (six) preachers were selected.[22] Eight come from preachers of European American descent (though all of these preached sermons less than ten minutes long), three from African American preachers, one Latina preacher (who preaches in Spanish and uses a translator), and one Asian American preacher. Denominational diversity was also a factor in selection. Denominations represented are as follows: Vietnamese Assembly of God, Episcopal (four), Missionary Baptist, Baptist (three—unidentified in terms of specific type of Baptist), Seventh Day Adventist, Pentecostal Holiness, Presbyterian Church (USA), and Lutheran (presumably Evangelical Lutheran Church in Amer-

20. There is presently a group called the Academy of Preachers, which is funded by a grant from the Lily Endowment and seeks to encourage young preachers (ages sixteen to thirty) as they begin to preach. This group, with which I have had extended contact, has its own YouTube "channel" through which they post sermons preached at their National Festival of Young Preachers. I chose not to use these sermons, though numerous, (1) because they were dislocated from congregational contexts and intended more for audiences comprised of preachers and (2) because of my contact with a number of the preachers through the Lilly Endowment funded National Festival of Young Preachers, as well as their "preaching camp."

21. A surprising number of sermons available from young people on YouTube are only available as clips, or edited to two or three minutes, and serve as advertisements— either for their services as a supply preacher or for the viewer to purchase the sermon in its entirety. This is a fascinating phenomenon, but one that is beyond the scope of the present project.

22. There are certainly more male preachers available on YouTube than female preachers. Whether this is an indication of the ratio of male to female young preachers actually preaching or an indication about the nature of digital media, gender, and preaching agency is also a fascinating question, but beyond the scope of the present project.

ica). At the time of selection, there appeared to be no Roman Catholic or Orthodox sermons available. Other denominations were available (both so-called Mainline and Evangelical), but may not have met the other criteria.

One other caveat is necessary. Integrating preaching into a media outlet like YouTube generates considerable questions for preaching. Any sermon found on YouTube shows the number of times the sermon has been viewed, hosts a space for other users to comment on the sermon, decontextualizes the sermon from its original performance, and acquires other accouterment indicative of the internet (titles, usage statistics, advertisements, suggestions for other videos, a specific URL address, etc.). Furthermore, the intent for publishing the sermon, and by whom, significantly changes the questions surrounding the agency and authority of the preacher as well as the purpose(s) for preaching. In short, the internet sermon takes on a digital life of its own apart from the context in which it was first preached. All of these factors and the new digital lives for these sermons construct a different atmosphere for receiving these sermons.[23] Rather than seeing decontextualization, digital accoutrement, etc. as *limitations* of this particular data pool, we might instead see this format, along with its accompanying cultural artifacts, as a new type of homiletic space with unique potentiality for constituting what I have been calling "homiletic communities," albeit with different modes of interaction and with differing definitions of relationality and space.

CHRISTIAN IDENTITY

As we begin the work of listening to sermons, I will first examine how a few of these young preachers mediate Christian identity through pentadic/dramatic structures with dominant elements, then how they construct metaphors that conceptualize Christian identity. As we will see, rhetorical constructions of Christian identity emerge in these sermons.

---

23. I do not address the preaching of young people on YouTube as a phenomenon unto itself. While these are important questions that warrant significant attention, they are beyond the scope of this project. Other than information on the web page that may have helped identify a particular preacher by name, age, race/ethnicity, or denomination, I do not address the ways that digital media may affect these sermons (or vice versa). Ronald L. Grimes's recent work on ritual and media places begins to discuss some of the trajectories this new space for ritual and religious practice takes in Grimes, *Rite out of Place*.

Pentads/Dramatistic Structures

Among the thirteen preachers, none of the pentadic structures were replicated, though as we will see, there are some similarities between pentads. Each of the preachers implicitly assigns a variety of elements to pentadic roles, with different elements rising to the fore as dominant.

For Katie, God is the dominant element in the pentad as the agent. Her pentad also heavily features the act, which for Katie is God's act of giving. God gives the pen and paper, Bible, Holy Spirit, Jesus, comfort, guidance, and help. She describes Christian identity as a relationship between God, who gives out of God's concern for humanity in the form of love and forgiveness (God's agency), and humanity. God's action takes place on the scene of the lives of believers, who experience difficulty in knowing what they are supposed to do with their lives. Katie's sermon serves the rhetorical purpose of voicing a human problem and speaking God's assurances of presence in the midst of that difficulty. As the speaker, Katie acts as a representative of both the congregation's vocational (and here the fullest sense of that word is intended) confusion and God's assurance of presence.

In Minister Keith J.'s sermon, God is also clearly the agent who acts by speaking and showing through the authority given to Keith (agency). While the agent is the most dominant, act, agency, and purpose are highly integrated as Keith hopes to convince the congregation to live in the way of holiness. While the scene is not a dominant factor, it is the place of a highly stratified view of social activity. There is a clear demarcation by God through Keith that there are acts that are in keeping with the call to holiness, and some that are unclean which violates the church's call to holiness. The scene is the place where the church accepts God's call to holiness. In terms of Christian identity, Keith presents a picture where God clearly speaks to the church, commanding holiness in a world that is not holy. With God as the strong agent, the faithful can continue to count on God to present a clear message to the world through the Bible and the preacher.

For Emily B., God is also the agent who acts by allowing preaching to take place, who speaks through preachers and who "knows me," "never makes mistakes," "loves me," "is in control," "has my back," "protects me," "has a plan," surrounds, and is always with Emily. All this happens on a few scenes: Emily's tumultuous growing up, the life of Moses, and the experience of the Psalmist. God is the dominant, eulogized agent, but God's agency is undeveloped and implied rather than stated outright. God conceivably acts out of the resources of God's own power and foreknowledge, but again, this is unstated. The purpose is muted as well. Emily speaks largely in a testimonial fashion, and thus implies that the truth that God is a consistent presence in her life will also be true for others. She does pray to God to "Let everyone here leave changed because of your impact on our lives." Christian identity in Emily's pentad is entirely dependent upon God's activity in the lives of human beings, even amidst confusion about God's activity and God's plan for individuals.

Unlike the previous preachers, the scene dominates Jessi's pentad, where change is a constant in the world. Some of this change as a part of the human condition is good and some of it is bad, but the nature of change desired in the Christian life is that of "extreme change," which is typified by Nicodemus. The kind of change Jessi advocates is "a reform or a new lifestyle" which is offered by a rather weak-acting (in terms of the pentad) picture of two agents: God and human beings. As Jessi says, "God's way is . . . a commitment realized between God and man." As Jessi advocates for extreme change (purpose), she continues by saying "extreme change is only possible when our weakness and our will unites with the powerful will of God." The purpose is accomplished (1) by the agency of a unification of wills and (2) by more fully understanding the example set by someone like Nicodemus. As the scene of change is ubiquitous, the agent(s) are left with a rather open choice: allow normal changes to occur in one's life or choose a more extreme change, which characterizes the identity of Christians. Christian identity is dependent upon choosing to unite with God for the purpose of extreme change.

Metaphors

Though treated separately, the pentadic elements each preacher constructs are not unrelated to the metaphors they develop. Within the pentadic structures, each preacher develops metaphors that help them conceive symbol systems that describe the members of the Trinity, the Bible, the church, the self, the Christian life, sin, and/or the relationships among all of these. Because some of the metaphors are highly integrative of a number of those components, we will treat them on a preacher-by-preacher basis in the same order as the pentadic/dramatistic analysis.

Trevor's main use of figures of speech comes by way of using his congregation "All Saints" as metonymy.[24] As he recalls the instance of his father's illness he says, "We went straight from the hospital to the church and it was so great to have All Saints here for comfort when there was no other forms of it around." Here Trevor clearly does not refer to every member of

24. Although metonymy is not metaphor, it does function in a similar way: conceiving of one thing in terms of another.

the congregation or the building, but most likely refers to certain members, groups, or clergy as representatives of All Saints as a collective whole. In the same way that Trevor uses All Saints to describe his experience of a place of comfort, he also uses it as a benefactor when he says, "All Saints has truly been the greatest example of God and one of his miracles in action" and "All Saints is the greatest miracle God has ever given me." Again, Trevor uses All Saints to refer to certain programs, particular groups, and members of the clergy staff to talk about how he perceives God to have gifted him through his time at the church.

He transitions in and out of the metonymy by using metaphor when he says, "When a home was broken, I was given a new one here with the most welcoming inhabitants I have ever known." Here Trevor refers to the congregation as a family system where he feels welcome. By using metonymy and metaphor to describe the church, Trevor forms a picture of Christian identity where the church acts as a benevolent caregiver. Trevor finds a new home in All Saints, which is viewed with increasing importance through his life. The congregation acts as an anthropomorphized giver of psychic/emotional consolation and opportunities that have equipped him to help cause change. As God's miracle given to Trevor, the church testifies to God's presence in the midst of his life. Christian identity is formed by a strong local ecclesiology for Trevor. The church does not just provide an environment with the right conditions as it does for Jane Doe; it functions as a powerful, active agent.

Giving a defense of what God means to her, Jane develops a number of metaphors around the concept of a relationship with God. Jane speaks about her relationship with God as one of measurable proximity. She says, "there were two outstanding events that really helped me *get close to God*"; "I really had to figure out *where I was at with God*"; and "God will be *in my rearview mirror.*" The last statement combines the metaphor of relationship with God as one of measurable proximity with the metaphor of relationship with God as exploratory journey/expedition. She identifies a beginning to her "journey of faith"; recounts "the first time I was able to really *explore* what God was and how he was affecting my life"; says of her confirmation that "I was promising *to continue with my journey of faith no matter where it takes me.*" God operates in this metaphor as a travel companion on a trip that is in new territory and has no certain or known destination. She also inserts the proximity and journey metaphors into a metaphor where she envisions her relationship with God as one of a simultaneous gamble and safe bet, saying "The most important thing I learned on that retreat was that with God, *you have to take chances.* You have to take that *leap of faith in order to get anywhere.* But don't worry, because *God will always catch you.* He may let you fall for a bit, but *he will always catch you* before you go splat on the side-walk." As someone admittedly new to Christian faith, Jane identifies herself in a relationship with God that takes on a number of different metaphorical descriptors. As she narrates her journey in the life of the church, she is able to communicate the various ways that her doctrine of God has changed. For Jane, Christian identity is an open process of a developing relationship with God and the church provides the environment for that relationship.

While Jessi's pentad functions in a weak fashion when compared to some of the others, she does develop some strong metaphors around Christian identity. Most notably, she develops "extreme change" as a metaphor of a contract or business transaction. Jessi compares "the way man (sic) *offers* extreme change and the way God *offers* extreme change." Change first comes to humans as a kind of sales pitch from a representative. Characterizing God's offer, she says, "God's way is *always free*. It's always *simple* and it's always *easy*. But even though it's simple, easy, and free, they have *conditions that are non-negotiable*." Jessi's metaphor begins with the Christian life as a choice between two "sales pitches," but the metaphor intensifies as she describes choosing God's way as simultaneously undemanding and accepted on inflexible terms. Jessi develops Christian identity as a contractual choice between two ways with the conditions of the agreement set by God.

Jessi also explores metaphors for Christian spirituality through her analysis of Nicodemus. She says of Nicodemus, "Observing Jesus and the way that he talked and walked *opened up* and *woke up* the curiosity of Nicodemus." In using Nicodemus as an example for Christian spirituality, she proposes two quick metaphors for appropriate Christian spirituality. First, Nicodemus' curiosity operates much like a container, as it was "opened up" by proximity to Jesus. By this Jessi indicates that Nicodemus' capacity to be filled by what Jesus has to offer is made more accessible. Secondly, Jessi proposes the metaphor of spirituality as a condition of sleep. While Nicodemus was ostensibly once asleep, observation of Jesus' actions supplies the necessary action to bring Nicodemus to a situation of spiritual wakefulness. Openness and being awake quickly supply Jessi with two metaphors for lifting up Nicodemus as a paragon of Christian spirituality.

Liberating Representations

All of these preachers exhibit organizing pentads that help communicate their operative theologies. Whether the preachers organize their rhetoric by highlighting themselves, the Bible, God, Jesus, church, or any other element, they all form dramas that demonstrate how they conceive Christian identity in its ideal form. They also develop highly functional metaphors for Christian identity. Some of these metaphors are familiar, while others wholly unfamiliar, but they are coherently employed in service of the overarching purposes of their sermons. Having listened to these young preachers, and examined the ways that they conceive Christian identities, it is now appropriate to view these interpretations of their preaching in light of liberation and formation.

Before moving to this process, however, it is important to note that by close analysis of these young people's sermons, we have already begun to "liberate" representations of youth. The contemporary literatures examined in chapter 3 depict the ontological adolescent as absent, as deficient listeners, as unable to exercise facility with the church's language (exilic), in need of entertainment, taking part in a universalized experience, and without capacity for difficult theological reasoning. With these sermons in view, however, we begin to form a specifically *homiletic* picture that de-essentializes the representations of young people and begin to present a different type of public homiletic space. More specifically, we can see liberation of these representations in the following dimensions:

1. Liberation from "absence."

This is perhaps overly-simplistic, but it must be noted youth *are* present, undertaking preaching in significant ways. If we are to take the instances of these young people preaching at any level of seriousness, then we must admit that young people are not invisible or absent from the preaching moment.

2. Liberation from "the non-critical."

These young people demonstrate a capacity for critical thinking about their own Christian and homiletic identities, about their places within their own social location, and about how biblical texts are interpreted within/for congregational life.

3. Liberation from "the non-ecclesiastical," "extra-ecclesiastical," or "para-church."

The preachers do not exhibit an amorphous religious commitment, but show a fairly sophisticated (if sometimes implicit) knowledge of their ecclesial traditions.

4. Liberation from the realm of de-centered, non-authoritative "cultural" Christianity.

This is related to number three, above, in that these youth are eager to claim various forms of spiritual authority and voice, whether through implicit theologies of preaching, use of self, the creation of ethos, or measured use of material devices (considered in the next chapter). In this way, they are not guilty of Smith and Lundquist Denton's "moral therapeutic deism," but confess fidelity to, take ownership of, and claim authority within their respective traditions (and the broader Christian tradition at large).

5. Liberation from the "non-theological."

The pentadic analysis demonstrates a range of approaches to the Christian drama. These include the ability to identify spiritual agents, and construct elaborate forms of spiritual agency, theological scenes, theological acts, and purposes. Even if these accounts are unsophisticated (read: not conversant with academic theology), they show the ability to be fairly precise, coherent, and consistent.

6. Liberation from cultural stereotypes and the need for entertainment.

Rather than the young person who can only engage in communication through limited, stereotypical cultural idioms (i.e., Mitchell's "lingo"), the preachers here demonstrate the ability to make use of a wide range of metaphors for God, engage in a variety of patterns for communicational design, and are able to manage cultural models that are outside the typical purveyance of "youth." As speakers, they also work past the depiction that young people must be entertained to gain a homiletic hearing.

CHRISTIAN IDENTITY: MUTUAL CRITIQUE THROUGH LIBERATION AND FORMATION

The process of listening and interpretation are only the first steps toward a more appropriate homiletic relationship with young people. The homiletic relationship takes another step forward by placing the analysis of these sermons into a moment of mutual critique through liberation and formation. By evaluating these preachers and their sermons through the category of Christian identity, we find ways that the preaching of young people can offer challenge to constructions of Christian identities, as well as the places where young people are still in need of formation. This section will proceed thematically by using some of the larger strands that emerge in the sermons as a group. The themes discussed here are suggestive of my own reflections, rather than exhaustive or definitive, and are intended to show the beginning edges of what the process of listening and mutual critique can look like.

Nature and Presence of God

In terms of Christian identity, one of the major features of these preachers' theological themes is the nature and presence of God, and more specifically, how God acts in relationship to human beings. Repeatedly, their sermons express how they conceive of themselves and others in relationship to God.

One of the most recognizable ways these preachers talk about their relationship with God is through metaphors of proximity, measurable distance, attention, and visual focus. The metaphors of proximity and measurable distance in particular are rooted in biblical language. All of the metaphors describe a sense of theological anthropology expressed in terms of evaluating the state of a relationship. In describing the contours of a systematic theologian's theological anthropology, Daniel Migliore states,

> [H]uman beings are created for life in relationships that mirror or correspond to God's own life in relationship. In light of the history of Jesus Christ, Christian faith and theology are led to interpret the *imago Dei* as an *imago Christi* and an *imago trinitatis*. Just as the incarnate Lord lived in utmost solidarity with and for sinners and the poor, and just as the eternal life of God is in communion, a triune "society of love" that is open to the world, so humanity in its coexistence with other is intended to be a creaturely reflection of the living, triune God made known to us in Jesus Christ and at work among us in the Holy Spirit.[25]

The preachers express Migliore's thought in an encapsulated form by assessing the status of their respective relationships with God through metaphorical language. As a result, their language reflects their commitment to a historical doctrine: God exists in relationship with creation and human beings experience varying degrees of the status of that relationship.

This relationship is expressed through other dimensions. Minister Keith J. and Chloe in particular envision God as an active speaker to humans. While Keith portrays God as engaging in literal back and forth conversation, Chloe's depiction of God shows God talking to the church in a non-descript manner. For these preachers, God is actively engaged in the life of the community of faith, directing its life.

25. Migliore, *Faith Seeking Understanding*, 141–42.

Sam and Katie envision God acting in relationship as a helper for the human condition. God provides the primary psychic, emotional, and spiritual resources out of which humans are able to live in faithful relationship with God and humanity. Rather than God speaking directives as with Keith and Chloe, God resources the Christian life with a support system including the community of faith, the presence of Jesus and the Holy Spirit, and the Bible. These are all positive dimensions to portraying the nature and presence of God. Although they all differ in various ways, these preachers possess an active theological imagination by which they strive to live more faithfully. They encourage faith communities to conceive of God and God's activity in imaginative ways.

Not all the depictions display a positive use of the theological imagination as it relates to the nature of God, however. For Emily, God acts as the divine planner who acts with unmistakable precision. God's plan somehow includes a reversal in her social status as portrayed when "the same kids that hung me up by my overalls in middle school also voted for me as Memorial's homecoming queen. It's true. I know—I now know that God is surrounding me, he's always with me, and there is nothing in the world for me to fear." Emily indicates that her election as homecoming queen is the sign of God's presence and protection for her. God's salvific activity and providential care for human beings certainly extends to the repair of human relationships. But God, even as creator and savior "is the God, not of unrestricted and static powerful 'god almightiness,' which resulted in empire's worship of 'power itself,' but the social and relational God, the Trinitarian narrative God, the vulnerable God, the God of covenantal invitation and participation—in short, the God of the power of love."[26] Emily mistakes God's love for God's involvement in the processes of social status and as a result, Emily's election reflects the powers of social status rather than reflecting divine care. Emily's operative theology of God's presence and activity needs further shaping in such a way that it can account for those who do not achieve the social successes she does.

Jessi's contractual/business language as she formulates a partial soteriology is also of concern. If her metaphors are followed through with their entailments, then God becomes a shrewd contract maker characterized by inflexibility rather than grace. Jessi's metaphors show how the forces of a market economy and a cultural imaginary filled with litigious language impinge upon God-language in a way that should be offered up for further formation.

---

26. Hunter, "Creation," in Heltzel, *Chalice Introduction*, 127.

Suffering

Related to Emily's depiction of God's presence and activity, she, along with Matthew and Chloe talk about the nature of suffering as a part of Christian identity. Emily's suffering is at the direction of God's plan. Matthew's depiction of suffering extends to a wide array of social sources and subjects (both Christian and non-Christian), but believes suffering to be essential to Christian identity and redemptive in nature. Chloe pinpoints specific instances of suffering in her community: parental neglect, sexual abuse, economics, and health problems. All three versions of suffering develop significant theological systems, and invite our interaction.

In the same way that Emily's picture of social success does not align with a broad picture of God's activity in the world, the same is true of her picture of her own suffering. God's action as the agent in her pentad corresponds to this view. Emily expresses a theory of theodicy that Migliore categorizes as "the incomprehensibility of God," which "may tend to suppress all questions and to encourage the unchallenged acceptance of all suffering."[27] Emily's uncritical perspective fails to account for her own participation in the natural order which is subject to disease, decay, and death. To disallow humanity's subjection to the natural order distorts what it means to be human in the midst of God's creation.

Matthew's picture of suffering, made apparent through the pentadic element of purpose, approximates what Migliore calls "person-making theodicy" in which "God desires not puppets [as Emily's version might be characterized] but persons who freely render their worship and adoration. Hence human beings are created incomplete and must freely participate in the process by which they come to be what God intends them to be."[28] The point of suffering in this view is for humans to emerge on the other side as having grown into more mature and God-like human beings. Matthew states that the suffering of Christians is a conscious decision that people of faith enter freely for the benefit of eternal life and closer relationship with God: "when we are persecuted, we are brought closer to God." Migliore points out that the weakness of this model is its relative lack of emphasis on Christian social ethics.[29] As a result, when Matthew points to the suffering of the world in the dimensions of economy, family, politics/war, and technology, he fails to address social responsibility in suffering. Instead he focuses on suffering incurred because of a non-descript Christian wit-

27. Migliore, *Faith Seeking Understanding*, 123.
28. Ibid., 130.
29. Ibid.

ness. This too is inadequate because Matthew fails to take into account (1) humanity's participation in causing suffering and (2) the victimization of many who will not find flourishing through suffering (and the silence of many Christians on their behalf).

Chloe's approach to suffering, corresponding to her pentadic elements of act and agent, provides a more palatable model of suffering. While suffering happens as a result of lack of power to make choices on behalf of oneself because of age, Chloe believes that there are choices that individuals can make that give individuals some sense of self-determination. Chloe's approach to suffering here approximates what Migliore calls "liberation theodicy."[30] Rather than passivity to suffering or expecting growth through suffering, Chloe advocates pursuing available avenues of action in order to make life better. Rather than admitting to absolute powerlessness, Chloe pushes young and old to identify the places where they are able to take action to pursue a godly life. Here Chloe admits to the specific death-dealing forces that cause suffering in her faith community and calls her listeners to greater faithfulness in the midst of situations of powerlessness. While her approach to suffering invites active engagement and names the forces of suffering, she could also to call attention to the ways that those forces might be called to conformity with the way of Christ. Of the three, however, Chloe's demonstrates a commitment to social engagement and helps the Christian community formulate a response to oppression as an integral part of its identity.

Sin and Grace

Sin and grace are related, in part, to suffering. My tradition, the Christian Church (Disciples of Christ) assert a few guiding principles around sin and grace. Most broadly, the statement of identity recognizes that we "are a movement for wholeness in a fragmented world."[31] This statement proposes that an underlying nature of sin is the divisions among humanity. Disciples theologian Joe R. Jones suggests that salvation "becomes an ethics of grace: given what God has done in Jesus Christ, Christians live under the summons to be peacemakers and forgivers, lovers of neighbors, strangers, and enemies."[32] And it is in baptism and weekly celebration at the eucharistic table that Disciples identify with what God has done in Jesus Christ, provid-

30. Ibid., 131.

31. "About the Disciples." http://disciples.org/our-identity/.

32. Jones, "Salvation: Mapping the Salvific Themes in Christian Faith," in Heltzel, *Chalice Introduction*, 200.

ing experiences of grace that empower believers to live out what Jones calls an "ethics of grace." These preliminary statements provide some evaluative guidelines for how a few of the preachers construct Christian identity in their sermons

Christine M., in connection with the pentadic element of purpose, discusses the "little" sins. While the acts she lists might be classified as mere violations of white middle class social conventions, rather than sins, she demonstrates in parts of her list the knowledge that sin consists of being complicit in the fragmented state of the world (not inviting an outsider to social activities, placing self and busyness before friends and family). She is right to acknowledge that none of the acts she lists "will spell the end of the world," but she does acknowledge that these little acts are in need of God's grace. Grace is embodied in the community through acts of love and a process of recognizing mistakes, asking for forgiveness, and trying to live in ways that correct sin. Even in an unspecific way, Christine suggests a way that the "ethics of grace" operates in her community of faith. This is commendable, even as her understanding of what constitutes sin needs formation.

As with suffering, Chloe recognizes that sin takes the form of violations of the integrity of, and relationships with young people. For Chloe, sin also carries the misguided perception that "God cannot call you our use you because of your past." Though she does not call it grace, Chloe identifies God's salvific activity as God's acting to "clean you up" and, more importantly, the incorporation into the company of those chosen by God for service to the world. This is similar to the gift language found in the Preamble to the *Design of the Christian Church (Disciples of Christ)*, which says, "within the universal church we receive the gift of ministry. . . . In the bonds of Christian faith we yield ourselves to God that we may serve the One whose kingdom has no end."[33] In this language, the corresponding gift of grace is vocation of ministry to the world. She is not specific as to what the call and service entails. It would be more desirable for her to name that service as forming a community of resistance and working to right the situations of brokenness she identifies early in her sermon. As it stands, however, she gives a helpful identification of what sin and grace look like in her community.

For Trevor, the strong pentadic agent of All Saints church provides a picture of an ecclesiology that functions as a model of grace. As he experiences the dissolution of his family structure (fragmentation), the church functions as a means by which he encounters God's grace. He also learns

---

33. "The Design of the Christian Church (Disciples of Christ)." http://disciples.org/our-identity/the-design/.

what it means to spin that grace outward through his work on immigration and his sister's work in New Orleans. Sharon Watkins expresses this as the ideal function of the church, a "sacrament of human wholeness," whereby "God's intention expressed in the prophetic search for shalom, Jesus' proclamation and the apostles' teaching, is that the human community, indeed the cosmos, though broken and dying, can and should live in peace, in wholeness."[34] Trevor identifies God's activity in the world through the activity of the church, which provides a strong structure for Christian identity.

Minister Keith J.'s version of sin operates as a byproduct of the pentadic element of purpose, which is to convince listeners to live in holiness. Keith identifies holiness as "God's standard" repeatedly and those who do not "go forth in the beauty of holiness" are "unclean." For Keith, sin is violation of standards of holiness clearly outlined in biblical texts. Specifically he points to fornication, lying, cheating, homosexuality, and "whatever falls under the category of sin." Keith's internal homiletic logic supplies only the oppositional categories of holiness and sin, and does so in a rather circular manner. It is difficult to discern how one achieves holiness. Is it bestowed by God, achieved by human will, or both? Keith does not supply a sufficient framework to discern how sin and grace operate in Christian identity other than by repeating the mandate for holiness and pointing out clean/unclean practices.

In terms of experiencing grace, none of the preachers discuss eucharistic practice and only one of these preachers (Jessi) discusses Christian identity with reference to baptism. Even though none of the preachers are inheritors of my tradition, the Christian Church (Disciples of Christ), all Christian traditions lay some emphasis on baptism and Eucharist as places where we encounter, or at the very least, remember God's work for humanity in the person of Jesus. That only one out of the thirteen preachers references baptism and/or eucharist is lamentable in my estimation. On the other hand, their failure to identify these practices as significant moments of grace might indicate that they function as what Gordon Lathrop via Paul Tillich calls "broken myths," in which "the terms of the myth and its power to evoke our own experience of the world remain, but the coherent language of the myth is seen as insufficient and its power to hold and create as equivocal."[35] As such, baptism and eucharist are not rendered obsolete in the communities of faith, but they may have lost a sense of vitality for young people in homiletic speech. As a result, the young preachers do not know

34. Watkins and Watkins, "Church as Sacrament of Human Wholeness," in Heltzel, *Chalice Introduction*, 137.

35. Lathrop, *Holy Things*, 27.

how to speak of these ritual practices in significant ways. If this is the case, then the relative absence of water and table language requires of Christian and homiletic communities the hard work of ensuring that the foundational myths of baptism and eucharist remain "juxtaposed"[36] to vibrant rhetoric that can nourish Christian identity and come to meaningful expression in homiletic practice.

CONCLUSION

We have seen in this chapter that adolescents demonstrate the ability to piece together rhetorically coherent and theologically significant Christian identities. By carefully listening to their communicative practices, we become more attentive to the ways that their preaching liberates representations of ontological adolescence and possibly liberates privileged, adult-centered Christian identities. By moving back and forth between the poles of liberation and formation, with attention to our own rhetorically performed Christian identities, we participate in a process that moves us toward a renewed public sphere of homiletic interaction. We acknowledge their voices as potentially powerful participants in our faith communities while voicing the ways in which we might offer correctives to young people's faith.

36. This is Lathrop's language.

5

Youthful Preaching

Listening to Young Preachers on Homiletic Identity

Having seen some of the ways that young people articulate Christian identity in preaching, we will now examine how young people formulate homiletic identity through preaching. As was the case with Christian identity,
speakers mediate homiletic identity through what Hart and Daughton call
"rhetorical role, a regularized set of verbal strategies resulting in a distinctive personal image."[1] In this chapter, I will outline how we might construct
a picture of the homiletic identity of adolescents and then engage in the
kind of careful, critical listening as we did in chapter 4.

HOMILETIC IDENTITY
IN CONTEMPORARY HOMILETICS

Homiletic identity has become an important category for contemporary
homiletic discourse. Recent discussions around this topic have centered on
"images of the preacher." Homiletic identity, or the image of the preacher,
includes a number of key homiletic ideas: ethics of preaching, theology of
preaching, relationship to the congregation, relationship to the Word, authority of the preacher, voice, etc. Robert Reid identifies these identities as

1. Hart and Daughton, *Modern Rhetorical Criticism*, 272.

the imaginative figure of thought which best captures what they believe they are "up to" in preaching. This kind of reflection can speak to preachers and students of preaching who struggle in the effort to realize some of the assumptions they bring into the pulpit when they preach. . . . While the concept of agency may be new language for some readers, the question about the relationship between the human and the divine in preaching is not. . . .There are a variety of perspectives that explore how a preacher views scripture, revelation, and his or her own identity in preaching. Each perspective implies something about how that preacher would view agency—the relationship between the work of God, the work of the preacher, and what can occur efficaciously as a result of the act of preaching.[2]

Reid's edited volume juxtaposes eight varying images of the preacher as completing the phrase "preacher as": messenger of hope, lover, God's mystery steward, ridiculous person, fisher, host and guest, one "out of your mind," and one entrusted. These images supplement Thomas Long's list: the herald, the pastor, the storyteller/poet, and the witness.[3] Whether these disparate images emerge from biblical texts, biblical theology, systematic theology, philosophical theology, or other realms, they have much to offer. Pedagogically, these metaphors give preachers language to help them explore how they view themselves as homiletic agents. From the standpoint of academic homiletics, the discussion of images has fostered generative conversations about the nature of preaching. As preaching changes in the wake of pluralism and questions about the authority of the preacher, the development of relevant images has been important work.

What they do not do, however, is account for the ways that homiletic identity emerges in performed communicative scenes. And while the group of authors who offer these images would be charitable enough to recognize the images are not exhaustive, they do not begin with actual sermons. Theory precedes practice. This is not a criticism; indeed this is helpful work. But it is unidirectional, and there is another way to go about discerning homiletic identity. Within the framework of theories of communicative identity, we will determine how homiletic identity emerges in actual sermons. We can expect to see in adolescents' sermons the formation of distinct homiletic identities. These latent homiletic identities may prove to be useful as critique in homiletic communities, or uncritically mimetic in character, and/ or prove themselves to be mired in false consciousness and thus in need of significant formation.

2. Reid, *Slow of Speech and Tongue*, 2–3.
3. Long, *Witness of Preaching*.

A CONSTRUCTIVE METHOD FOR DISCERNING HOMILETIC IDENTITY

Preliminary Sources of Rhetorical Role

Hart and Daughton outline three preliminary sources from which a person produces "rhetorical personae, that complex of verbal features that makes one person sound different from another."[4] The first is a personal rhetorical history, which is determined by a combination of socialized features that *might* typify the ways one speaks (geography, class, education, etc.). Here we are searching for the factors that constitute the context from which adolescents speak which help determine, in part, what we might expect these preachers to talk about. In terms of establishing a rhetorical history of adolescents, this calls for identifying the basic components of the situations in which their homiletic identities might be formed.

Second is identifying ideological influences. Here Hart and Daughton suggest looking at educational history, generational characteristics, philosophical leanings, and social groupings. These factors are particularly suggestive around self-selected social groupings or "subcultures." For instance, Ross Haenfler's description of "straight edge" subculture has a highly differentiated ideology than what Bakari Kitwana describes of "wigger" subculture.[5] We might expect highly different homiletic identities from preachers who self-identify with these, or any other subculture. Inasmuch as these kinds of ideological influences can be determined, they help present some of the factors that help determine a rhetorical role.

Finally, Hart and Daughton suggest that institutional affiliations contribute to the emergence of rhetorical role. In analyzing speech acts of religious communication among adolescents, it is important to discern (again, as much as possible) if they take place in ecclesial environments that are commonly characterized (or self-described) as conservative, liberal, moderate, or with other markers such as denomination. In those terms, does the speaker's role seem to support or argue against the predominant ideology? And how does that seem to build a role for the speaker?

4. Hart and Daughton, *Modern Rhetorical Criticism*, 212.

5. For more on these subcultures, see Haenfler, *Straight Edge*; Bakari Kitwana, *Why White Kids Love Hip-Hop*.

Credibility Devices

Moving from preliminary sources, another dimension of discerning identity is the use of credibility devices. What makes a preacher worthy of the audience's attention and how does she speak in ways that indicate that she is a competent speaker? In determining how an adolescent speaker attempts to establish credibility, we are also looking for how a speaker makes appeals to authority and in what the speaker locates his/her authority. In order to determine this, Hart and Daughton propose seven dimensions of credibility:

1. Power — Rhetor can provide significant rewards and punishments (either material or psychological) for audience.

2. Competence — Rhetor has knowledge and experience the audience does not have.

3. Trustworthiness — Rhetor can be relied on beyond this one moment in time

4. Good will — Rhetor had the best interest of the audience in mind.

5. Idealism — Rhetor possesses qualities to which the audience aspires.

6. Similarity — Rhetor is seen as resembling the audience in some ways.

7. Dynamism — Rhetor presents credibility through bodily and vocal activity.[6]

When analyzing adolescents' sermons, as those who do not preach regularly in week-to-week settings (more often than not), there will be verbal and non-verbal cues by which the speaker will indicate that she is worthy of the audience's attention. This may be particularly acute among a group with little social/symbolic/homiletic capital.

Another category should be added to these: material. Within this category, we look for the preachers' use of materials beyond voice and body. In other words, we will look for how the preacher dresses, how the preacher makes use of a pulpit or preaching space, and any other items accompany the preacher in order to establish credibility. In terms of homiletic identity, adolescents will obviously not rely on discrete forms of homiletic knowledge gained through seminary training or many years of focused mentorship. Appeals to credibility will often be different from those we might expect from adult preachers. Careful attention to these credibility markers in sermons will indicate something about how young people understand and appropriate authority in the pulpit.

6. Hart and Daughton, *Modern Rhetorical Criticism*, 223–24.

Self-References

In determining the preacher's self-conception, it is also useful to track his/her self-references. Hart and Daughton advocate "look[ing] with special care at I-statements since they make special claims on the audience's attention. . . . A useful critical procedure is to extract from a text any phrase or clause containing an 'I' and then to lay out these statements one after another (paraphrased, if necessary)."[7] By examining these "I-statements," we can show how the preacher creates a nexus for self-identity through expressing emotion, directing action, sharing personal experiences, and expressing the importance of self-involvement/self-revelation in preaching. Conversely, a preacher who makes no I-statements suggests something about limiting the role of self-expression in preaching.

The issue of the self in preaching has proven to be a topic of some discussion. Is the preacher's own experience important or do preachers function, in Karl Barth's words, as those "who simply have the role of announcing what God himself wants to say" and where preaching is "the involuntary lip movement of one who is reading with great care, attention, and surprise, more following the letters than reading in the usual sense, all eyes, totally claimed, aware that 'I have not written the text'"?[8] Barth's issue is a theological one, challenged by contemporary theological accounts of homiletics (i.e., feminist, racial/ethnic accounts which appeal to the theological importance of personal experience and testimony). J. Randall Nichols, on the other hand, raises the issue of pastoral integrity when he contrasts "self-disclosure" with "self-display."[9] While self-disclosure is an appropriate use of the self that "risk[s] a certain vulnerability in order to reach a purpose that has fundamentally to do with their [the listeners'] well-being."[10] Self-display, on the other hand is narcissistic use of the self. Finally, David Buttrick is concerned with use of the self in preaching because it violates the communicative function of sermons. Personal references "split consciousness," directing the attention of the sermon towards the preacher, rather than toward the listeners as a communicative group.[11] While adolescents are not likely to be aware of these arguments, they are likely to use self-references for particular theological, pastoral, or communicative purposes that can converse with those academic accounts from a distinct point of

7. Ibid., 226.
8. Barth, *Homiletics*, 46, 76.
9. Nichols, *Restoring Word*, 121.
10. Ibid.
11. Buttrick, *Homiletic*, 141–43.

view. Through analyzing the kinds of I-statements used by adolescents in sermons, we should be able to further the conversation about the use of self in preaching.

Cluster Criticism and Homiletic Identity

A final element in the analytical matrix for discerning homiletic identity is cluster criticism. Cluster criticism provides an additional form of rhetorical criticism that investigates the way adolescents' sermons "are revealing the worldview or what [Kenneth] Burke calls the terministic screens of the rhetors who created them. The terms we select to describe the world constitute a kind of screen that directs attention to particular aspects of reality rather than others. Our particular vocabularies constitute a reflection, selection, and deflection of reality."[12] In sermons, adolescents, like any other group, constitute a particular frame of reality as they see it. This includes homiletic identity. This allows us to see how the vocabulary choices of young preachers describe their self-understanding as participants in homiletic communities. Cluster criticism helps in that "the meanings that key symbols have for a rhetor are discovered by charting the symbols that cluster around those key symbols in an artifact."[13] By investigating key words and what clusters around them, we can expect to see (1) the meanings that young people invest in homiletic identity and (2) how those meanings are constructed rhetorically.

Foss provides three basic steps for cluster criticism: "(1) identifying key terms, (2) charting the terms that cluster around the key terms, and (3) discovering an explanation for the artifact."[14] She advocates choosing terms in an artifact by their "frequency" or "intensity," and no more than five or six terms. Since we are centering on homiletic identity, then the terms up for analysis in adolescent sermons are fairly straightforward, though they may not appear with any uniformity between preachers nor with either frequency or intensity. The terms we are after rise from each preacher's language about the nature and task(s) of preaching. After locating the occurrences of these terms, the words and phrases that cluster around them are charted. Foss suggests that what we are looking for in these clusters are relationships. She says that "terms may cluster around the key terms in various ways. They simply may appear in close proximity to the term, or a conjunction such as "and" may connect a term to a key term. A rhetor also may develop a cause-

12. Foss, *Rhetorical Criticism*, 71.
13. Ibid.
14. Ibid., 72.

and-effect relationship between the key term and another term, suggesting that one depends on the other or that one is the cause of the other."[15] By examining the cluster terms and the ways they form relationship to the key terms, a more textured picture of how the preacher understands her/his homiletic identity should begin to emerge.

By listening to sermons and carefully analyzing them, we hope to point to how adolescents are establishing a homiletic identity in the midst of a homiletic community. Figure 5.1 shows a sample worksheet of how this analysis might proceed on paper. After these moments in analysis, we can begin formulating a hypothesis of the preacher's operative homiletic identity. Statements such as "The preacher sees himself/herself as . . . " or "The preacher seems to identify preaching's role/function as . . . " or "The preacher develops the image of x in order to describe his/her understanding of homiletic identity" begin the process of interpreting the nature of homiletic identity among adolescents. Formulating these kinds of statements is explanatory and interpretive, rather than evaluative. This part of the analysis is performed without yet placing the emerging identity through the evaluative emphases on liberation-formation.

HOMILETIC IDENTITY AMONG ADOLESCENTS

Remembering that the first movement in analyzing these sermons is an exploration of how these preachers perform (or self-organize) homiletic identity, this section will highlight some of the ways that the preachers articulate homiletic identity.

Preliminary Sources of Rhetorical Role

Of the three categories constituting preliminary rhetorical role, institutional affiliations are the most heavily identifiable within these sermons. Overwhelmingly, these preachers identify as "students." This is chosen over other options such as the son/daughter of X, a member of a specific subculture, or perhaps an employee. For Matthew S., his status as a student provides the opening for the introduction to his sermon: "I am a senior at Decatur High School. And actually as a graduating senior I've been assigned a good number of books to read." Katie places the sermon-writing process within her life as a busy high school student: "So to start off, I wrote this on the bus ride

15. Ibid., 73.

back from my basketball game on Wednesday, so my intro is a bit lacking."[16] Similarly, Christine M. also uses the end of school as a way of commenting on the sermon-writing process: "first off, let me just say that ever since AP exams were finished for us seniors way back in May, um, we've been done. And I mean totally done. I haven't written anything or been particularly creative or insightful since then, so you'll have to forgive me if this sermon is a bit boring or unrefined." Emily B., like most of the others, uses her status as a student as a primary identifier for herself and a way to introduce herself to the congregation: "My name is Emily, also known as Mustang Sally by my peers at Memorial High School. Yes, that's right, I'm the mascot. I think it's perfect for my personality." Emily's identifier also serves as a way of entering into her sermon content.

When the identifier of student is used it functions to build the preacher's homiletic identity. It is used as an important device to identify oneself to the congregation (always early in the sermon), for the development of content within the sermon, for the form of the sermon (i.e., as part of an introduction), or as a complex device to accomplish a combination of these tasks. This also manages expectations for the listening audience. As a high school student, the preacher's rhetorical persona and the congregation's expectations of that persona will necessarily be different from that of a bishop or denominational leader, for example. This does not mean that these preachers portray themselves as incompetent to preach, but the use of the self as student does establish boundaries and expectation. For instance, the preacher who establishes the rhetorical role of "high school student" will likely not talk about their experiences as a parent or seminary student. If they did, this would violate the expectations they have established through rhetorical role.

Of the thirteen sermons, six do not mention school or their status as a student, though they do use other strong institutional affiliations to build their homiletic identity. Jane Doe and Trevor, who preach back-to-back sermons, establish rhetorical personae through using language common to the Episcopal church, and specifically All Saints Episcopal church. Jane Doe says, "Fast relief is a fundraiser in which we fast for thirty hours to help raise money for Episcopal relief and development. It was an amazing experience. Then I attended the diocesan senior high dance bishop's ball." Trevor exhibits knowledge of the sacraments and the congregation's clergy: "Shannon Ferguson came to the hospital and performed the sacrament of unction." Minister Keith J. establishes a rhetorical persona as one who is able to comment on the state of the Pentecostal Holiness church at large: "There's so

---

16. I will discuss the use of negative references to the sermon below.

many people, even though they realize they're not Holiness, they're professing to be Holiness because, because it brings on some type of—there's an
attraction behind that name Holiness." These uses of institutional affiliation
establish the preacher as an "insider" and, as such, one who can speak to
insiders about the state of, or experiences within, the institution.

Sometimes religious institutional rhetorical roles are combined with
that of "student." Katie states, "My name is Katie Whiteman and I'm a junior at Bettendorf [high school] and I've been going to Redeemer since I
was about seven years old." This compound institutional affiliation establishes two rhetorical roles at once, with the second serving to identify her as
someone who has attended Redeemer (Lutheran) since she was a child. As a
longtime member of that community, Katie is able to establish herself with
a homiletic/rhetorical persona that is trustworthy and familiar.

The preachers' ideological influences are more limited. They reveal
a small amount of rhetoric about social groupings, but also some about
categories of class and knowledge of political/social issues. Emily identifies herself through the social groupings present in her school community.
Pointing out that she has an outgoing personality and serves as her high
school's mascot, she recalls that this was not always the case: "In middle
school though, I would have loved to have a mascot suit to hide in. I was
kind of self-conscious, I felt overweight and nerdy. I also felt like all the
other girls were more fashionable and more attractive. In fact my idea of
fashion was wearing overalls every single day. In fact I even got hung up by
my overalls one day. It was pretty bad. Also I had the red hair, freckles, braces—it was just not a pretty picture." Emily's use and connection of the words
"overweight," "nerdy," "fashionable," "more attractive," and the descriptors
"red hair, freckles, braces" are culturally loaded terms that help establish
Emily's former place within her community's social groupings. Her more
recent loss of weight and increasingly outgoing personality have now placed
her in a different social grouping, even to the point of being voted the homecoming queen. These rhetorical cues about social groupings identify them
as knowledgeable about their own identity as it relates to part of an overall
homiletic identity, namely being able to speak authoritatively on situations
that occur in the Christian life, and especially the Christian lives of youth.

In terms of class, the preachers that do establish rhetorical markers
around class do so in ways that identify them as middle class. Alex D. comments on the historical distance between the time of Jesus and contemporary
times by reminding listeners that "They didn't have anti-perspirants back
then, so he would have probably carried a rather foul odor." This comment
suggests middle class expectations about hygiene. Likewise, Jessi's opening
story contrasts professionals with an alcoholic, drug-addicted beggar. Many

of the rhetorical markers around class have to do with free time, discretionary spending, and/or the importance of the nuclear family. Christine M. says, "I feel bad if I'm out every night of the week and haven't seen my family in ages. I feel bad if I always show up late just because I try to do one more thing before I hop in the car." Katie lists her activities, which cost considerable amounts of money: "I've been taking piano lessons since I was ten and art lessons since I was seven." In addition, she voices the assumption that she will go to college.

Political and social issues also help define a rhetorical context in which these preachers form their homiletic identities. Matthew S. knows that "the car companies are suffering, this economy, the stock market is suffering, the divorce rates is on the rise because of this, and children are suffering. The internet has provided new ways for bullies to harass people and youth through cyberspace. Civil wars are going on around the world and nations are also suffering." Chloe outlines the challenges facing the young people in her community:

> [We have] no choice in having a momma or a daddy that are
> strung out on drugs, alcohol, or gambling so bad that they can't
> even take care of us. We have no control or no choice having a
> momma or a daddy that chooses the street life over parent life.
> We have no control over parents who choose not to spend time
> with us and love us the way a parent should. We have no control
> over having a father who wants nothing to do with the children
> he helped to make. We have no choice in having a father who
> thinks it's alright to have sex with his son or daughter. (80–86)

Jane Doe displays a particular political knowledge when she admits that she "first started coming to All Saints because of Desmond Tutu. My mother heard from her union that he was speaking." Trevor also talks about his knowledge of issues about immigration and health care.

Rhetorical history proves to be a more difficult category to analyze. Admittedly, these sermons are dislocated from their original contexts, which would help establish a longer rhetorical history (particularly over long periods of time within each congregation). This task is even more difficult in the contemporary homiletic atmosphere because it is virtually impossible to say that a particular homiletic style is congruent with "a particular locale (say, the Midwest) . . . a particular style of speech (directness) . . . [or] a particular group of people (the middle class)."[17] In other words, it is not always appropriate to point to a region or group of people and assume that they will preach in ways that approximate homiletic stereotypes that may

17. Hart and Daughton, *Modern Rhetorical Criticism*, 213.

have once been largely true in the history of preaching in North America. For example, it may be unexpected that Matthew S., an African American in metro Atlanta, Georgia, does not exhibit the cadences, rhythms, and rhetorical flourish found among many African American preachers from the American South. But this does not help isolate his rhetorical persona or build a narrative of his rhetorical history. We dare not assume that these preachers preach in a certain way by virtue of their gender, ethnic/racial identity, or denomination alone. There simply is not enough information in these isolated sermons to conduct a complete rhetorical history.

Credibility Devices

These young preachers create credible homiletic identities by a variety of rhetorical methods. Perhaps the most significant of these is through the category of "competence." The ways that some of these preachers establish credibility is fairly typical: giving background knowledge for the biblical text under consideration. For instance, Alex D. counters a perceived faulty assumption by saying, "And lest we should think that Jesus was being conceited by expecting these things, it is important to remember the time in which he lived. He was probably walking around all day in sandals, so his feet would have been covered in dirt and grime."[18] Similarly, Joshua L. narrates the story of David and Goliath by commenting on the fundamentals of swords, using a prop: "Now a man's sword is generally proportional to his body. Kind of like this one is proportional to me. . . . Now, I'm like about five feet tall, or so, and Goliath is ten feet tall so twice the size of this sword." Jessi even develops a type of dramatic delay by giving information about a biblical character, but waiting to name him specifically. Their special knowledge about the background of the biblical story not only grounds the claims of the message; it helps to establish them as authoritative voices.

Others, like Chloe, establish competence by narrating the results of spiritual practices, like her family's prayers; or by expressing knowledge of martyrdom in the early church like Matthew S.; or even more dramatically, by stating God's direct activity in the sermon writing process as with Minister Keith J., who passes on what God has told him.

Another rhetorical phenomenon combines the categories of "competence," "good will," "trustworthiness," and "dynamism" in a negative fashion when preachers construct a diminished view of the preacher's preparation, sermon writing skill, and/or pulpit presence. Sam N. prays before his sermon that he would not stutter, then does: "Ok, and Mark 16:15, ok . . . yeah,

---

18. This is also an example of a "contrapuntal," which is explored in Buttrick.

if you could all turn at all . . . up . . . to me . . . with me. Like I said, stuttering my words." As stated above, Katie identifies her sermon by saying, "I wrote this on the bus ride back from my basketball game on Wednesday, so my intro is a bit lacking. But everyone bear with me and Andy, don't fall asleep this time." Christine M. also portrays her sermon as potentially faulty for her hearers when she says, "you'll have to forgive me if this sermon is a bit boring or unrefined. I'm a bit off stride with that whole doing work thing." It is uncertain exactly what these preachers hope to accomplish by using this rhetorical convention, but there are a few possibilities: (1) the device functions to win a sympathetic hearing as the preacher acknowledges that she is not performing a rhetorical role within the regular rhetorical roles she performs (perhaps as a way to acknowledge anxiety about taking up this role), (2) the device functions as a type of false humility, (3) the device functions to differentiate the young preacher's particular style from that which is experienced within the congregation on a regular basis and signals the preacher's awareness of congregational expectations (and thus a preparatory device for transgression of rhetorical conventions), and/or (4) the device functions as a way for the preacher to establish this homiletic instance as one that is authentic.[19] Whatever its more discrete function might be, these rhetorical disclaimers appear at the beginning of the sermons, before the preacher enters into major sections of preaching, and contributes to an overall sense of how listeners should perceive the preacher.

These preachers also use a variety of materials to establish credibility. All the preachers use the physical devices of a pulpit/lectern and some type of written materials. Many use voice amplification through pulpit microphones, seemingly dependent upon the regular practices of their respective congregations. Trevor and Jane Doe use Caucasian flesh-colored headset microphones. Joshua and Alex B. both use PowerPoint presentations along with their preaching. Alex D. is the only preacher who wears a clerical garment, choosing an alb for his preaching attire. Sam N. piles books and papers up high on the pulpit which serve as a material contrast of authority to his self-deprecating words about his stuttering. He also brings up volunteers to demonstrate his "Christmas" sign, which signifies authority and credibility. When illustrating the story about David and Goliath, Joshua holds up a plastic sword to demonstrate his knowledge about swords. The most conspicuous material credibility device is Jessi's use of a translator. In what seems to be a bi-lingual congregation, Jessi preaches in Spanish while an older male (perhaps the pastor) translates Jessi's words into English. While Jessi's preaching voice and mannerisms are subdued and she stays within

19. For this final possibility, see Smith, *New Measures*.

the pulpit space, her translator is mobile and animated as he translates Jessi's sermon. As a result, Jessi's sermon inhabits two distinct states of embodiment and she is able to communicate with a broader audience.

Self-References

The key question in terms of self-references at this point is if these young preachers are talking about themselves and if so, how those self-references function. Out of the thirteen sermons, ten of the preachers talk about themselves in what I call "substantive" ways. By this I mean that the preachers refer to themselves and use their personal stories in highly developed ways within the sermon. Entire units of thought within the sermons are dependent upon the preachers' use of self (or, in some cases, the entire sermon). Two of the preachers (Joshua L. and Alex B.) refer to themselves in what I will call "minimal" ways. By this I mean that the preachers do refer to themselves, but their self-references have little impact upon the sermon as a whole. Only one preacher, Jessi, does not talk about herself, other than very brief moments where she includes herself with the congregation—and always in the first person plural. She engages in what I will call "negligible" use of self-references. Beyond directing action twice in the sermon and her opening and closing prayers, she exhibits an extremely limited role for herself.

Despite how we might categorize the ways these preachers incorporate themselves into their sermons, all of them make theological claims in regard to homiletic identity by the ways that they do so. For those in the substantive category, they all seem to engage the self as a significant site of theological and homiletic reflection and thus a natural partner to the sermon. For those in the minimal category, the self is a part of theological and homiletic reflection, but in ways that are only tangentially related to the theological conceptualization of the sermon. Personal stories and use of the self are present, but not for any significant purpose. For the negligible category, as is true for Jessi, the self is only present (if at all) to direct the action of the sermon; the authority of theological concepts or the authority of the Bible function in such a way that the self is an insignificant source of theological and homiletic reflection. The predominance of the substantive category will be an important feature for the evaluative process, below.

Clusters

In terms of rhetorical clusters, some significant traditional homiletic categories emerge which serve to help form a picture of these preachers' unique
homiletic identities. First, however, an admission is needed. At the outset of
finding and listening to these sermons, I expected to find that these preachers would often refer to their age in direct relationship to their homiletic
identity. I assumed that many of these preachers would feel compelled to
offer an apology for their role as preachers—that their relatively young age
did not in any way diminish their authority or competence. Much to my
surprise, only one of the thirteen preachers (Chloe) makes a case for her
identity based on age. Her defense is pronounced as she identifies herself in
the following ways: "I come before you with no titles. Not Reverend Chloe,
no Preacher Chloe, not Evangelist Chloe, just Chloe. A vessel. A young vessel, a chosen instrument of God being used as a messenger for Christ. That's
it" (9–11). She is more pointed when she says in relation to King Josiah in 2
Chronicles 34 that

> Now I'm sure that there was (sic) a lot of gossipers or haters or
> some church folk who were questiononing how an eight year
> old boy could rule over a nation. And right now I bet there are
> someone (sic) sitting here saying that I am too young to get be-
> hind this pulpit and give a message. But the people who were
> bothered by this and asked these type of questions were not only
> questioning Josiah, but questioning God. God does not need
> our help or guidance or our permission on a decision he is going
> to make or who he chooses to use.

Chloe articulates both a highly developed biblical typology and theology
about God's call which she uses to defend her preaching. This, however, is
not typical of the preachers, contrary to what I had expected.[20]

While Chloe was the only example among these sermons who focused
on age, there were a number of clusters about the honor it brought some of
the preachers to be preaching. The language of gratitude about preaching
somewhere during the sermon comprises a primary cluster. Emily Baird
opens her sermon by saying, "We're very thankful to be here with you this
morning. It's an honor to be involved in the weekend in such a huge way."
Likewise, Trevor opens by saying, "It is my honor to be speaking here before
you today." He also ends his sermon by saying "thank you," as do Katie,

---

20. This may be (consciously or unconsciously) because the preachers make use of
other types of credibility devices within the rhetoric of their sermons or because they
feel confident enough in their settings so that such a defense is not necessary.

Matthew S., and Jane Doe. Matthew S. thanks the congregation for their attendance on youth Sunday. These rhetorical conventions portray speakers that either (1) are not accustomed to having the attention of such public (adult) audiences, (2) unreflectively affix "thank you" to the end of public discourse, (3) have a minimal sense of homiletic authority, and/or (4) feel compelled to gloss the significance they perceive to be in the homiletic moment. Others (Christine M, Alex D, Jessi) conclude their sermons by saying "Amen," which suggests that they either perceive their respective homiletic moments differently than the others or that they engage in an equally uncritical rhetorical convention as a way of concluding their sermon. The differences in these comments may connote different senses of authority within homiletic identity. For those who say "thank you," they may derive some part of their homiletic authority from the perceived attention of the listeners while those who say "amen" may view themselves as having more implicit homiletic authority.

Other rhetorical clusters that help construct homiletic identity were present. The most significant of these clusters reveal what is variously called "purposes of preaching," "images of the preacher," or "images of preaching identity" which reveal the purpose(s) of preaching and an operative theology of preaching.[21] Revisiting Chloe's cluster, we find that Chloe views herself with a minimal sense of agency, as she claims "no titles" for herself and prays for a homiletic transparency in order for the congregation to "see" God. Additionally, she sees herself as a "vessel" who delivers God's "message." With only a few indicators Chloe develops an unambiguous conception of preaching where she is chosen by God to deliver a message to the congregation.[22] It is curious, however, that Chloe makes use of a number of personal stories and testimonial moments, despite her prayerful request to be transparent. Chloe either does not believe that these two types of theological rhetoric are mutually exclusive, or she violates her principle of transparency (being a "vessel") for the more rhetorically and theologically powerful stories about herself.

Emily B. makes a similar claim, though rather than transparency, she hopes to act as a conduit as demonstrated by her prayer, "Please speak through my peers and myself today" (13). In fact, she depicts God's role as highly active in the gathering of the people, in giving the preachers permission to preach, and by attributing to God the capacity for people to leave the

21. See Childers, *Purposes of Preaching*; Long, *Witness of Preaching*; Reid, *Slow of Speech and Tongue*.

22. It is curious, however, that Chloe makes use of a number of personal stories/ testimonial moments. It will be necessary to ask if these two are mutually exclusive or contradictory in the evaluative section below.

church service as different than how they arrived. She prays, "Dear Lord, thank you for bringing everyone here today and allowing us to preach your word. . . . Let everyone here leave changed because of your impact on our lives." God performs a dynamic role in the homiletic event, from beginning to end, but God is invited to use Emily and her peers for preaching as they engage in "speaking about Psalm 139."

Minister Keith J. has a more highly developed sense of God's agency within the pre-delivery sermon process—one that likely has roots in his Pentecostal Holiness tradition. Keith depicts the pre-delivery process as a dynamic conversation between himself and God. God is clearly the source of the sermon, as Keith says, "I give you what the Lord has given me" (8) and "And the subject that the Lord gave me on today—he said—going forth in the beauty of holiness." In fact the phrase, "He said," (referring to God's speaking to Keith) appears numerous times. But Keith is not solely an ec-static receiver of God's message. In a manner reminiscent of characters of the Hebrew Bible, Keith asks questions of clarification of the message, such as "And, and as I was before the Lord, before I came to preach, the Lord was just speaking to me then and he said, 'This message—he said, I want you to go and preach on the battlefront.' So I said, 'Lord, what does that mean?' He said . . . " In addition to serving as a credibility device, Keith establishes this pattern of dialogue with God as a firm sense of homiletic identity. Keith is the messenger of God, but his preaching also engages in a cosmic struggle with the powers of evil as when he says, "There's something else that the Lord shared with me. And the enemy is trying to snatch it from my mind, trying to make me forget it. But, but, the Lord was speaking to me. The Lord was speaking to me. And the enemy, he's trying to take it, he's trying to take. But it's there, and I thank God for it." As the preacher, Keith stands in the midst of a homiletic moment where God and "the enemy" are engaged in a struggle for the preacher's message.

In contradistinction to Chloe and Minister Keith J., Katie expresses God's relative distance from the pre-delivery sermon process as part of her preaching identity. As she collapses the sermon-writing event with knowl-edge about her personal future she says, "God, however, did not give me a scroll—not for my sermon or for my future. Instead, God has given me a pen and a blank piece of paper. But he hasn't left me alone to write it myself." Here Katie describes a partnership with God in the sermon-writing process. Katie is neither the recipient of God's completed message filtered through her experience (Chloe) nor the ecstatic recipient of God's message (Keith). Instead, she engages in a type of compositional partnership between her-self, God, the Bible, the Holy Spirit, and Jesus. Katie admits a significant amount of human involvement in the sermon. And if we are to follow her construction to its logical conclusion, the sermon and its writer will inevitably make mistakes, though God's presence will be a constant.

Matthew S. mediates a double sense of agency. After the lector reads the Gospel reading for the day from the book of Matthew, Matthew says "I'm glad she said that the word comes from Matthew because I didn't know whether she was talking about me or the Lord. Either one is accurate." Although Matthew intends the statement as a humorous opening statement, he provides an entrée into his homiletic identity as a co-producer of "the word." Not only is the biblical text derived from God as "the word," but Matthew also believes that "the word" is present within his preaching.

Joshua L. asserts his homiletic identity in specific relation to the biblical text, rather than God, as he says to his congregation, "So what I want to convey to you guys tonight is pretty much, 'We must win spiritual victories for the glory of God.'" Joshua sees his function as preacher as one who "conveys" a propositional truth. Like his preaching partner, Alex Beals does not differ from Joshua. In fact, he sees himself in continuity with him: "Josh has already given the reason why we must win spiritual victories for the glory of God, but I have a couple more." Additionally, Alex repeatedly describes the relationship between sermon ideas, text, and congregation as a process of "seeing." For instance, Alex says, "We see that we must win spiritual victories . . . because of the effect it will have"; "We see that in verse ten . . . "; "So generations later after David's victories we can see that those victories . . ."; "Here's a profound way to see how important this is"; "So you see that there are many effects to the decisions . . ." Alex conceives of his function as preacher to help the congregation come to new realizations and new courses of action through exposing the truths of the text. For both Joshua and Alex, the biblical text functions almost autonomously. The preacher's job is to help relay the text's truths (reason-giving) to the congregation so that they will frame the text correctly, comprehend the force of the text, and subsequently live it out.

Sam N. sees himself in a similar way to Joshua and Alex B., but rather than reason-giving, he understands himself as a teacher by way of his role as conduit. For Sam, "it's not by me that this lesson's being produced, it's by you God. And I pray that you would speak through me . . . " He concludes his sermon by praying that "everyone in the teen group and me myself has learned something from this, uh, sermon, O God." Sam includes himself as a potential recipient of the lessons provided by God through the sermon, along with the rest of the listeners. An additional facet of Sam's self-concept in preaching is his attempt to summarize near the conclusion of his sermon: "I know we're growing short on time so these are my main points. Ok?" After this declaration, Sam does not deliver one or even a series of "main points," but rather continues speaking in a dialogical form. How do we account for Sam's homiletic (self-) violation? While Sam's sermon organization or conceptual process may have broken down, or Sam's nervousness or sense of time may have interfered with his ability to name his main points, it is equally plausible that Sam never intended to communicate "main points" in the first place. While Sam may come from a homiletic community that expects points, Sam's communication style within the entire sermon never suggests that "points" will be verbalized. It is likely that Sam knows the rules of his homiletic community, and even acknowledges this one particular expectation, but violates it because it is not integrated with his own homiletic logic. Instead of preaching with points, Sam exhibits a conversational communication style throughout the sermon.

Trevor views his homiletic identity as even more relational with the congregation than the others analyzed thus far. He understands his task to be "sharing with you my journey at All Saints." While his comments about homiletic identity are limited to this one statement, Trevor understand his role as one who is sharing his religious experience rather than "speaking," or "giving a message," "preaching," or even characterizing himself as a "vessel" or conduit. While this statement does not draw out a theology of the word, it does show that Trevor conceives of his authority as symmetrical: he is not delivering a message from God, but engaging in the act of "sharing." This image connotes images of preaching as giving out of one's possessions for the benefit of others.[23]

Finally, as identified in the section on self-references above, Jessi seems to develop the least sense of homiletic identity through clusters in her sermon. Aside from her opening statement where she names the sermon, Jessi only makes two references to her homiletic activity. First, she indicates sermonic movement when she says, "Now we're going to talk about the experience of the man of extreme change." Second, she says, "We're going to analyze a little bit the way man offers extreme change and then the way God offers extreme change." Though sparse, Jessi's two comments suggest that she conceives of her role as leading the congregation through a process of analysis with discernible moments along the way.

The analytical tools here begin to give a picture of how these preachers perform homiletic identity. The facets of preliminary rhetorical role, self-references, and clusters provide tools for understanding the various ways in which they self-identify as participants within a homiletic community.

---

23. Trevor's homiletic identity seems to share affinities with testimonial approaches to homiletics. See Florence, *Preaching as Testimony*; Rose, *Sharing the Word*.

HOMILETIC IDENTITY: MUTUAL CRITIQUE THROUGH LIBERATION AND FORMATION

Use of Self

The overwhelming amount of self-references among these young preachers demonstrates that the use of self in the rhetoric of the sermon is an important category. Is it a practice that needs to be refined in or does it offer a helpful corrective to established homiletic concepts? As briefly reviewed above, the question of whether this practice is a best practice has been raised by homiletic communities on the levels of theology of the word (Barth), pastoral integrity (Nichols), and theories of communication (Buttrick). All three of these levels caution against use of the self (or, in Nichols case the kind of use of self results in self-display). According to Barth, Nichols, and Buttrick, the use of self by these young preachers might be characterized as violations of homiletic theology, pastoral integrity, and communication theory. They might also be labeled as "self-centered" filtered through either a malformed concept of Freud and Erikson's theories of development, cultural stereotype, or both.[24] All of these options would thus conceive of adolescent preaching as deficient in some sense because of this practice.

Rather than seeing their rhetorical use of the self as some type of homiletic violation or egotistical rhetoric, the use of the self demonstrates a beneficial example of theological and homiletical reasoning. The self is intentionally used as a site of theological reflection and deemed useful for others in the public role of the pulpit. In a sense, these homiletic expressions by young people are processes of becoming "voiced" when the cultural expectations about the voice of young people is quite low. As Mary Donovan Turner and Mary Lin Hudson write, "Voice reflects a valuing of the self in relation to particular contexts, allowing authentic dimensions of the self to arise to expression rather than be submerged in a sea of competing expectations and roles."[25] Rather than being "submerged in a sea of competing expectations and roles," young people come to voice in new ways through the pulpit, and their sermons allow them the opportunity to express a theological-homiletical self. This self sees that God's activity happens in the present, not just in the world of the biblical text or the world of adults, and that their lives are also useful homiletic material in a variety of ways.

24. Anecdotal evidence bears this out. In conversing with a group of pastors about my observations, on the topic of use of self, some questioned whether this use of self was simply because "teenagers think the world revolves around them."

25. Turner and Hudson, *Saved from Silence*, 11.

Additionally, through the pentadic analysis of Christian identity, we see that the preachers always convey a strategic picture of relationships to God, Jesus, Holy Spirit, Bible, church, social structures, etc. They do not use self to the neglect of other indispensible theological partners. Though we should continue to caution against dangerous uses of the self, these young preachers' use of themselves in their sermons help displace Barth's and Buttrick's rigorous homiletic rules. They add their distinctive voices to the conversation about how self-references voice young people beyond cultural expectation (ontological adolescence) and how self-references can serve as authoritative, effective homiletic devices. Katie, for example, builds *ethos* with the congregation by giving biographical information which leads to her contemplation of the future. Trevor does likewise as he recounts his personal experiences with the church as a place of comfort. Alex D. establishes authority when he tells the story about the woman from his childhood who seemed as if she had been at the feet of Jesus. In the same way, Chloe's personal experiences with prayer establish her as an authority on its effects. Jane Doe exhibits a participatory role within her denomination as she lists the ways that her experiences with the distinctly Episcopal ministries of her church have helped her faith. Emily B. uses herself in order to establish a theological account of God's activity and care in the midst of difficult times. All of these examples show that the use of self is a strategic decision (though this is not necessarily the case in every instance), incorporated into the preaching moment in order to further the purposes of the sermon.

Purposes of Preaching/Images of Preaching

A variety of models of the purposes of preaching and images of preaching emerge from these young preachers' sermons. Chloe, Emily, and Sam all exhibit tendencies toward the image of the conduit as they hope that God will speak through them or that listeners will see God rather than the preacher. This is consistent with their respective preaching traditions (Baptist and Assembly of God). But in each case, this hoped-for invisibility is undone by their significant uses of the self (see discussion above). Since they are not internally consistent, we should ask if the image they articulate is a desirable image, or if the image they develop needs formation. Since each of these preachers lift up their own lives as beneficial sites for theological reflection, it seems that their remarks genuinely serve to invite God into the process and rhetorically serve to indicate authority and competence (credibility devices), rather than render the preachers invisible. Indeed, we have already explored the ways that young people are rendered invisible both inside and outside homiletic discourse! As a convention of homiletic speech learned from adult sources, we should be careful of language about invisibility encroaching upon young people's speech. In these cases, the preachers could be encouraged to shift their image of preaching (and accompanying homiletic spirituality) to that of Tom Long's "witness" or another image in order to more carefully integrate the roles of God and self within the preaching identity they already develop.[26] In this case, the adult homiletic community can offer correction to an internal inconsistency around the image of preaching, as well as issue a caution to itself about what kinds of images it offers young people.

Although I believe Minister Keith J.'s development of Christian identity needs formation, parts of the image of preaching that he develops represents a strength of his own tradition (Pentecostal Holiness), which is instructive. Keith envisions preaching as a dynamic conversation between preacher, God, Bible, congregation, and context. By this, Keith demonstrates a homiletic identity that exists as a conversational relationship between all the parties associated with preaching, even the forces of evil. This is a helpful dynamic for conceiving the preaching task, and shapes sermonic form in ways which some academic homiletic authorities do not take account.[27]

On the other hand, Keith's conviction that God tells the preacher exactly what to say, even as that takes place within a preparatory conversation, lacks a nuance found in his own tradition. Cheryl Bridges Johns, in speaking about the impact of Pentecost on Pentecostal worship, says "The meaning of scripture is made known by the power of Pentecost. Because of the ongoing ministry of the Holy Spirit, the text of scripture, as written word, is alive and powerful. Spirit and word are fused into a gestalt which reveals the mysteries of God. It is more than a revelation of meaning, it is a revelation of God whose presence is actualized by the Holy Spirit."[28] Bridges Johns points to a crucial component missing in Keith's operative theology of preaching: the Holy Spirit and its activity in worship practices. Rather than direct, privileged dialogue with the first person of the Trinity, homiletic revelation takes place through the Holy Spirit, "which supersedes any form of human critical reflection, [and] makes known those things which are masked, repressed, and denied."[29]

Trevor's conception of the purpose of preaching as one who shares presents a mixed model for evaluation as well. On the one hand, Trevor

26. Long, *Witness of Preaching*, 45–51.

27. Allen, *Interpreting the Gospel*; Campbell, *Word before the Powers*.

28. Johns, "What Can the Mainline Learn," 5.

29. Ibid.

articulates a relational homiletic identity where he conceives of preaching as an act of sharing out of his own experience. This is the strength of the more recent testimonial models found in homiletics. But as seen in the pentadic analysis for Christian identity, while he develops a strong and compelling local ecclesiology, purpose takes on a very weak role. Trevor makes no claim for a change in listeners' mindset or behavior, nor does he outline what Brad Braxton calls "gospel conduct."[30] To simply "share" out of one's own experience, while claiming and developing voice, neglects preaching's proper use of authority to call listeners to more faithful conformity to the shape of the good news in one's context. The image of preacher as one who shares limits the authority of the preacher and the weight of the preaching moment in the community of faith. Trevor could have been more explicit in this regard, perhaps by encouraging the congregation to continue their efforts to create and sustain the kind of congregational culture that provides comfort to the hurting.

Matthew S.'s almost flippant opening comment, "I'm glad she said that the word comes from Matthew because I didn't know whether she was talking about me or the Lord," expresses the idea of the threefold form of the word of God as a dominant image for Matthew's preaching identity. Matthew simultaneously identifies preaching and the biblical text as Word. Although Matthew's comment arises out of a coincidence between his name and the biblical text from which he preaches, his comment also suggests that he has considered how his preaching functions as an aspect of the Word of God. As Matthew works out his own theology of preaching and sense of authority, he suggests that speaking aloud one's theology of the Word on occasion is a meaningful rhetorical task. Most introductory preaching texts encourage preachers to take stock of their own conception of what God is doing during preaching and to what degree preaching functions as Word, but beyond this introductory pedagogical exercise or occasional prayers for illumination in the liturgy, they do not advocate for the preacher to make a case for how the Word arrives during the preaching moment. In order for congregations to develop their own sense of how the Word arrives, it would be good practice to insert rhetorical indicators of the preacher's conception of how Bible and preacher function as Word of God, as Matthew does. In this way, Matthew encourages listeners to, at the very least, be aware that these kinds of considerations take place and at the most, consider how they can function in a highly significant way. The Listening to Listeners project shows that God's

---

30. Braxton also follows in the line of Henry Mitchell, who calls this a "behavioral purpose" and Tom Long who more broadly calls this the "function" of the sermon.

role in the sermon is a concern for many listeners. [31] Matthew serves as an example, perhaps unintentionally, that preachers' speech on this topic can help listeners make sense of God's involvement in preaching.

Privilege of Preaching

Also among these themes is that of the privilege of preaching. On the one hand, these preachers comments indicate that they know that the pulpit is a space normally restricted to those of their age. Their comments show that their speech is often so limited, and silence so often the norm, that they must profusely thank those who have allowed them to speak. Contemporary homileticians marvel at the lowly estate of preaching[32] and wonder at the low enthusiasm for preaching by young people. When pulpits across the United States restrict access to young people in so many ways, the aversion to preaching later in life makes sense. Those who do enter pulpits at such a young age do so, as seen in many of the sermons examined here, heaping thanks on those who have bestowed the honor of preaching on them. These remarks by young people encourage us to open homiletic space to young people in increasingly significant ways. Here I must admit my commitment to my denomination's relatively "low" theology and ordering of ministry, especially as it relates to those who are allowed to preach. Almost all denominations, however, make provisions to preach for those not yet ordained.

On the other hand, these preachers' comments offer a distinctive reminder that preaching occurs by different types of authorization, and that charge is not to be taken lightly. Preaching is both an honor and a privilege for all who enter the pulpit. As a result, these preachers' comments suggest to all who enter the pulpit, young and old, that they do so with a responsibility to preach with integrity. Preaching occurs for the benefit of those who listen and on behalf of God's desire to draw people into a resurrected community. To handle sacred texts and messages demands much of the preacher and these young preachers offer a reminder to those who have forgotten the weightiness of the call to preach. This is a risky and important concept to admit in the pulpit and these young people model a type of (public) homiletic humility that seems rare among many contemporary preachers. Those of us who are older would do well to learn from them in this regard.

These preliminary categories begin to show the ways that the preaching of young people is liberative for entrenched homiletic theory/practice, as well as the ways that young people's homiletic theories/practices remain

31. See Mulligan, *Believing in Preaching*, 152–68.
32. See Graves, *What's the Matter.*

in need of formation. The relationship between young people and preaching is not nearly as simplistic as we might think. Rather, this relationship is highly complex: historically, theologically, ethically, and theoretically. And by no means has this study been exhaustive. The lives of the church, youth, adults, and the public sphere benefit from engaging in significant reflection for and with young people on this enduring practice of the church's ministry.

Sermon Analysis Worksheet (Figure 4.1)

<u>**Christian Identity**</u>
Pentadic/Dramatistic Criticism

Pentadic Elements:
Agent:

Act:

Agency:

Scene:

Purpose:

Ratios:
Agent-scene:
Agent-act:
Agent-agency:
Agent-purpose:

Act-scene:
Act-agent:
Act-agency:
Act-purpose:

Agency-scene:
Agency-act:
Agency-agent:
Agency-purpose:

Scene-act:
Scene-agent:
Scene-agency:
Scene-purpose:

Purpose-scene:
Purpose-act:
Purpose-agent:
Purpose-agency:

Dominant element and its effects (Featured? Muted? Eulogistic? Dyslogistic?):

Metaphor Criticism
Metaphors (vehicle, tenor, and entailments):

Conclusions regarding Christian identity:

Sermon Analysis Worksheet (Figure 5.1)

Homiletic Identity

Preliminary Sources of Rhetorical Role:

Use of Credibility Devices:

- Power
- Competence
- Trustworthiness
- Idealism
- Similarity
- Dynamism
- Material

Self-references:

Clusters:

Conclusions regarding homiletic identity:

Sermon Transcripts

6.1

ALEX B.

http://www.youtube.com/watch?v=jQ89bzD2bLU

Baptist
White Male

Hi, my name is Alex Beals. I am in 10th grade at Northpoint High School. And Josh has already given the reason why we must win spiritual victories for the glory of God, but I have a couple more. The second point is that we . . . ah . . . The second reason why we should win spiritual victories for the glory of God is because of the effect it will have on the lives of those around us. Each spiritual victory that we win will affect at least someone around us. Let's go back and think about how much David's victories affected the lives of those around him. Turn in your Bibles to 1 Samuel chapter 17 verses 8 and 9. It says, "And he stood and cried unto the armies of Israel and said unto them, 'Why come out and . . . am I not a Philistine and ye servants to Saul? Choose you a man . . . choose a man for you and let him come down too. If he be able to fight me and kill me then will we be your slave . . . servants. But if you prevail against him . . . but if I prevail against him and kill him, then ye shall be our servants and serve us.

If David had not come along with his strong faith in God, then the Philistines probably would have beaten Israel and the Israelites would have become slaves to them. Think about that. One man, one victory changed the entire history of the Old Testament as we know it. Each victory that we have does not go without a ripple effect.

There was a man in Jacksonville, FL named Paul Woods. He is the youth pastor at Trinity Bible College and Paul was called into the ministry when he was in high school. So he went to Bible college and became the youth pastor there and one night when he was having a sermon or something, Pastor Lee (laughs), Pastor Lee was called into the service and because of Paul Wood's victories pretty much, Pastor Lee was able to share his victories with us and now me and Josh are out here preaching today.

It's really neat if you sit back and think about how much another person's life has affected yours. And how much they influence you to win more victories. What victories have you accomplished lately that you will (stumbles) . . . What victories have you accomplished lately for the glory of God so that other people can see and reach their own? We see that we must win spiritual victories for the glory of God because of the effect it will have on our own lives and the lives of those around us, but there's also the effect that it will have on the lives of future generations.

Turn in your Bibles to 2 Kings chapter 11 verses 10–12. I'm not going to read the passage yet because I want to explain the background of the story first. So you have the people of God, years later, hanging out, when you see the house of Ahab is ruling over the throne. And the house of Ahab does not want to lose their throne at all so Ahab's daughters sent out men to kill everyone in the royal family. And they think that they've succeeded except that there's one boy who survives and he lives in the Temple of the Lord for seven years. And after those seven years, the priests in that temple decided to bring the little boy back to the throne. Verses 10–12 say, "And to the captains over hundreds did the priest give king David's spears and shields, that were in the temple of the LORD. And the guard stood, every man with his weapons in his hand, round about the king, from the right corner of the temple to the left corner of the temple, along the altar and the temple. And he brought forth the king's son, and put the crown upon him, and gave him the testimony; and they made him king, and anointed him; and they clapped their hands, and said, God save the king.

We see that in verse 10 that David's swords and shields were used years later to give these people their victories. What if David had never even fought those battles or if he had never brought those swords or shields as testimonies to the great things he's done for God. We would probably assume that those wicked people in the story would still have control over the throne. So generations later after David's victories we can see that those victories have brought about even more victories. Here's a profound way to see how important this is. In 1492, you all know Columbus sailed the ocean blue. And because of his victory of finding the United States of America, we are sitting in here today. The decisions that each one of you are making today and tomorrow will affect future generations to come if the rapture hasn't occurred yet. So you see that there are many effects to the decisions that you make may they be good decisions or bad decisions. It doesn't matter the severity of your victory either. It could be something simple like inviting your buddy to church or something fantastic like getting that buddy saved. I recommend that tonight and every night for the next couple of weeks, you tally up your victories for that day and see how many you have whether it be a lot, a little, or at least one. Because at the end of the day when you look back and see that during your lunch break you helped a complete stranger get to know Christ as their savior, you will never have a greater feeling. So I'm telling you tonight that we must win spiritual victories for the glory of God.

6.2

ALEX D.

Youth Sunday Sermon
http://www.youtube.com/watch?v=_bGCYo3jg48&feature=related

Episcopal
White Male

Although this section of the gospel is often used to point out Jesus' forgiveness for the unsaved, I believe it speaks even more to those who already
follow him. Note that although Luke never tells us of how the woman knew
of Jesus, she did in some way believe he had the power to forgive her sins.
The very action of going to his feet and humbling herself as she did suggests
that she had quite a strong faith in him indeed. In fact Jesus says that it is her
faith which has saved her. This understanding that the woman was . . . that
someone with faith in Jesus, very much like ourselves, that I would suggest
that we may garner two brief lessons.

The first lesson has to do with humility. We are shown a woman who approaches Jesus in tears. She anoints his feet and dries them with her hair.
Even among some who do not accept him as the messiah. Imagine the effect
that such an intimate gesture might produce. Although it would surely be an
uncomfortable moment for the observer, it would also open up a great many
doors for conversation. In fact, it is only after this woman approaches him
that Jesus is able to point out that the Pharisee did not neglect to greet him
in a proper manner, but he also neglected to provide him water for his feet
and oil for his head. And lest we should think that Jesus was being conceited
by expecting these things, it is important to remember the time in which he
lived. He was probably walking around all day in sandals, so his feet would
have been covered in dirt and grime. They didn't have anti-perspirants back
then, so he probably carried a rather foul odor. So the Pharisee's apparent
oversight was, in fact, an insulting gesture.

But immediately after Jesus rebukes the Pharisee for his judgment of the
woman, he forgives the woman's sins, thereby inviting the Pharisee into

forgiveness as well. So too, we are shown how our humility, uncomfortable though it may be, can serve to draw others to Christ.

For me, the strongest point that I can identify with this lesson is from when I was very young—about seven or eight. At that time, my family and I attended a Bible study every Friday night. Through the years I grew very close with one of the women who attended. And in some ways she become almost like a young aunt or an older cousin. I thought of her as very nearly perfect. She went on nursing missions to Africa, she was always there for you and she truly reflected the love of Christ. So it was hard for me to see why she would ever need to be sorry for anything. But then, one Friday as she was leaving was leading worship, she sang us a song that she had written that described coming to the feet of Jesus, repenting and finding comfort. It did not strike me consciously then, but looking back now I know it made an impression on me. It seemed as if she had dwelled at the feet of Jesus and I thought of her as nearly perfect, then everyone must need to.

The second lesson is based on the word "faith." Even though it may seem like a matter of mere semantics, it struck me that Jesus did not say that love saved the woman, or even her repentance, but faith. This tells me that though she did love him and though she did repent, she knew deep down that he would not abandon her. I must admit that in my own life, I often find this faith difficult to achieve. When I was little, I think I must have asked Jesus to save me at least a hundred times just to ensure that I was going to heaven. But here we are challenged to try to have that faith. We are challenged to continue to approach Jesus in a genuine manner, contrite and humble, and to also remain confident in him. Despite the fact that I do not read my Bible as much as I should and I don't really have any semblance of a regular quiet time, I try and live these lessons. One way that I have found very helpful is to start the day off with a prayer. It's simple and short, no more than a minute. But it puts God before me at the start of every day. And though I do not flaunt the fact that I am praying, I don't try to hide it either. This practice might not work for everyone. It might not be practical for everyone. But there are many small ways that we can continually come to Jesus, repent, and show our faith to others.

It is easy for us to be like the Pharisee and frown upon the sinner, asking why Jesus demands that we love, all the while forgetting that we ourselves are sinners. But perhaps that despite looking to the woman in this passage, who is labeled as a sinner, that we can grow closer to Christ ourselves. So may we remain humble and faithful and always remember that in some ways, we are exactly like that woman. Amen.

6.3

CHLOE

Youth Message From A Youth, Part 1 and 2
http://www.youtube.com/watch?v=io6CyCNmpo4
http://www.youtube.com/watch?v=pabCWS14WDA&NR=1

Missionary Baptist
African American Female

I come before you with no titles. Not Reverend Chloe, not Preacher Chloe, not Evangelist Chloe, just Chloe. A vessel. A young vessel, a chosen instrument of God being used as a messenger for Christ. That's it. Will you please go before the throne of grace with me?

Dear Lord, I wanna thank you for this day that wasn't promised to me. I ask you to let your people see you through me and none of me. In Jesus' name, Amen.

If you have your Bibles, please turn to 2 Chronicles chapter 34. We will be reading verses 1 through 3. Everyone who is able, please stand and honor the word. Josiah was eight years old when he began to reign. And he reigned in Jerusalem one and thirty years. And he did that which was right in the sight of the LORD, and walked in the ways of David his father, and declined neither to the right hand, nor to the left. For in the eighth year of his reign, while he was yet young, he began to seek after the God of David his father: and in the twelfth year he began to purge Judah and Jerusalem from the high places, and the groves, and the carved images, and the molten images. Amen. Be seated.

Now Josiah became king at the age of eight. God saw something in him that a normal person would never see in an eight-year-old. Josiah reigned in Jerusalem for thirty-one years doing what was right in God's eyes. King Josiah was getting older and was beginning to see the things his people were doing. He saw that his people were worshipping false gods and idols in the temple. Josiah began revivals and started burning down all the false idols and gods that his people were worshipping. One day his servants had found the book of law or Bible as they were digging in the ground. Josiah told his servants to read it to him. When they were done Josiah was struck with guilt and reformed his nation, having his people pledge to the covenant. The subject of this message is to the youth: you are not too young. And to the older generation: it is not too late to do the right thing.

Now God saw that Josiah was the one to reign over the people in Jerusalem. Now I'm sure that there was a lot of gossipers or haters or some church folk who were questioning how an eight-year-old boy could rule over a nation. And right now I bet there are someone sitting here saying that I am too young to get behind this pulpit and give a message. But the people who were bothered by this and asked these type of questions were not only questioning Josiah, but questioning God. God does not need our help or guidance or our permission on a decision he is going to make or who he chooses to use. God is god all by himself and he can do whatever he chooses to do and will not run it by us to see if we are ok with it.

But don't we have these problems in the church? When certain people or persons placed in a position at church there is always that group of people that meet up and discuss how they feel about the decision. Because they think that whoever made the decision should have ran it by them or perhaps considered them first to be the one over that certain position. For example, if the pastor places a woman over the women's ministry, maybe it's because he feels that woman has the gift to lead, connect and reach out to women. Now don't be mad or be a hater because it's not you over the ministry, maybe it's not your time. Or maybe it's just not meant to be. Women, we have so many gifts and talents. We must do the right thing. Stand together and work together to build up the kingdom of God and not tear each other down.

To the men, first let me say, I'm glad to see some of the few men we have here today. But I've noticed that the women outnumber the men. And I know there are some men who are struggling with committing to the things of God. For example, I'm learning that some men have problems with having another man having authority over them—like the pastor. Do the right thing for some of those who (sings) got a big ego. Drop your ego. Stop ego-trippin'. Don't think of him as the boss. Think of him as a tour guide. A sheep leader, giving you directions to get to the (inaudible).

Now to the young people—those of us who are still being raised by our parents, aunt, uncles, or grandmothers—or still just under the responsibility of someone. Being our age there are choices that are made for us. Some of them good and some of them bad. Now all the good things may not seem so good to us right now, but as my momma always says to me, "You may not understand right now, but one day when you become older, you will see that I'm doing this for your good." Some of the decisions that are made for us when it comes to what we can and cannot wear, where we can and cannot go, who we can and cannot hang with, what time to be on and off the telephone or cell phone, all the way to maybe what we eat, or what they will or will not spend they money on when they're buying us things. These good choices may not always be what we need . . . I mean . . . may not always be what we want, but in the long run we will see it is what we need.

And then there are the bad choices, the ones we have no control over because we are not yet accountable for ourselves. We have no control or no choice in choosing what kind of mother or father we have here on earth. No choice in having a momma or a daddy that are strung out on drugs, alcohol, or gambling so bad that they can't even take care of us. We have no control or no choice having a momma or a daddy that chooses the street life over parent life. We have no control over parents who choose not to spend time with us and love us the way a parent should. We have no control over having a father who wants nothing to do with the children he helped to make. We have no choice in having a father who thinks it's alright to have sex with his son or his daughter.

But in the midst of all the choices we cannot make, there are some that we can make. We have the choice to either dwell on the fact that we don't have a mother or father to take care of us, but if God has blessed you with someone to step in and take care of you, and keep you safe, whether it be your grandmother or your grandfather, your aunt, your uncle—you have a choice to either rebel because your parents aren't the ones raising you or you can show respect and love them because they are there for you.

And youth, we also have a choice on who we will serve. Matthew 10:32 and 33 says that, "whosoever shall confess me before men, him will I also confess before my father who is in heaven. But whosoever will deny me before men, him will I also deny before my father who is in heaven." To confess simply means that you are not ashamed to say that you believe that you know Jesus and are willing to do his work. To deny is another way of saying that you don't know Jesus and you are not willing to do his work. I want to encourage the youth and everyone here on today that whenever you are asked to pray, read the Scripture, or give service and effort to build God's kingdom or to do anything for the Lord, stop saying you cannot or you are scared or that you don't want to. Instead, ask and choose to be used by God and know that he will bless you for doing his work in his name.

Now let's spend a little time on prayer. This is something I'm learning the power of very early in life. You see it started with me hearing my mother pray over some situations and some circumstances that we were facing in my family. I remember her praying out loud either by herself or just asking me to pray with her. I was almost six years old, I remember her thanking God for the gift of motherhood and for blessing her with me. And then she went on to say, "but if it be your will, would you please allow me to experience motherhood again" by blessing her with another child. Sometimes she would pray so hard that she would start to cry. You see the doctors told her that she couldn't have any more children without the assistance of fertility drugs. Now I did not understand any of that at that time, the one thing that was clear to me was that my mom was asking God for another baby. Shortly after that, my daddy was struck with diabetes, so bad that he was sick for almost a year, practically bedridden. I remember hearing my mother praying around the house and pulling me aside to pray with her. This time she was praying for the healing of my father. Then one day she told me to go lay on my daddy and pray for him out loud and to make sure that I prayed loud enough for him to hear me. And I did without hesitation. She told me to do that several times while he was sick. Again I did not understand all that was going on, but I know [break in clip]

[Part 2]

(inaudible) you know, the rest is history. Now here I stand the day before my birthday, and I can tell you that I understand the power of prayer. You see I know the same God who answered the prayers of my mother and me is the same God who can hear my prayers and can hear your prayers. Even now I'm praying for and asking the Lord to do a mighty work on my daddy once again. See I believe that if he did it before he can do it again. To the youth of the church you are not too young to pray to God, to talk to him, and for him to hear your prayers.

Now to the older generation in the house. It's not too late for you to choose to let God use you. If you've been putting of doing God's work, getting close to him, letting him use you, and just doing what is right in his sight. See God told Noah to build an ark and load up (inaudible) two by two of every clean species and seven unclean species along with his family. Noah was six hundred years old of age when the flood came upon the earth after building the ark. Noah was obedient. When God called him, he answered. Noah did the right thing. Now . . . now don't wait until you're six hundred years of age to decide that you want God to be in your life because you don't have all that time to wait. Tommorow's not promised to you. There is somebody that's here today that God has chosen and he's calling you right now and you are choosing not to answer. Joshua 24 and 15 says, "to choose you this day who you will serve. Will it be God or man?" Joshua goes on to say "that for me and my house, I choose to serve the Lord." Maybe there is someone here today that thinks that God cannot call you or use you because of your past. You think he can't use you because of all the wrong things you have done. But I'm here to tell you that God can still use you if you ask him to. He can clean you up. Don't let your past interfere with your future. Romans 3 and 23 says, "For all have sinned and fallen short of God's glory."

Look at Saul in the book of Acts. Saul was known for hustlin', cussin', and gang bangin'. He stole, tortured, and killed people who believed in God. But one day God struck him and asked Saul, "Saul, why do you persecute me?" God took away his sight for three days. You see for some of us this is what we need in order to hear what God is trying to tell us. Sometimes he has to blind us or take some things away in order to get our attention. Now I don't know what your blind spot is but maybe God has to take something away that's distracting us in order for us to see what he's trying to tell us. See Saul was living a thug life. He was known as Saul the persecutor or the gang banger. But when God changed him so that he could use him, he also changed his name to Paul. God gave Saul a new name when he changed him and when he cleaned him up. That same God wants to give somebody else a new name. He wants to clean your name up and make it something . . . known for something good as an instrument for him.

If you are here today, know that God is . . . know that it is God's way of giving you another chance to do the right thing. And the right thing is to stand up to God's call today while we are still young or while we still have the time. The time is now. There is no more time that we have to be wasted. Because like I said, tomorrow is not promised today. You can wake up and realize there is no more time left for you to make this decision. Remember God called Josiah at the age of eight and he answered the call. Some of us are wondering how and why did he become king at such a young age. I don't know why, but one thing I do know is that he did what was right in God's eyes. And whatever is right in God's eyes is the only approval that matters. If God can call an eight-year-old to be king, he can call each and every one of us to do great things if we are willing to answer the call and choose to be used by God. Amen.

6.4

CHRISTINE M.

Youth Sunday Sermon
http://www.youtube.com/watch?v=2jNWWStOudw&feature=related

Episcopal
White Female

Hey guys! How y'all doin'? Um, so, a bunch of people told me that since my dad's been preaching sermons about me, I should, you know, since it's Father's Day and all, I should take this opportunity to (inaudible) him. But, unfortunately by the time that was suggested to me, it was a great idea, and I really wish I would have thought of it, I had already finished the sermon, so I know you're all disappointed. Sorry.

Anyway . . . get you later . . . first off, let me just say that ever since AP exams were finished for us seniors way back in May, um, we've been done. And I mean totally done. I haven't written anything or been particularly creative or insightful since then, so you'll have to forgive me if this sermon is a bit boring or unrefined. I'm a bit off my stride with that whole doing work thing.

So today's sermon is based on a pretty well-known story—a simple woman washing Jesus' feet with her hair. I've gotta say, this woman is a lot braver than I'd ever be. She's a known sinner—probably been sleeping around and prostitutin' and such and she just waltzes into this room with all these priests and religious higher-ups, all of whom have probably berated her or openly spoken ill of her. It might have taken some doing just to get into the place and I'm sure the atmosphere really wasn't that welcoming. I mean it takes some guts to crash a party. So to go to all that trouble must have meant that she was pretty dedicated. And she was certainly pretty gutsy.

Now at first glance in this gospel it might seem like Jesus is saying that those who sin more need to be forgiven more and thus they love more. So if you really want to love Christ, you should go out and sin as much as possible. Except, that isn't true at all, as we all know. Truth be told, the Pharisees in that room were just as sinful as that woman. Their sin might not have been as blatant or apparent, but we all know there's more than one way to sin. They just didn't realize their own sin or choose to ask for forgiveness. They could not be forgiven much because they didn't ask to be forgiven.

Now this might seem pretty easy, but honestly, this is one of the things I have most trouble with. A lot of times I consider myself to be a pretty good person who's doing pretty well in life. I mean, I have a few flaws here and there, but who doesn't? And most of the time I'm doing better than the rest, right? I mean, I have friends who go out and drink on weekends, who lie to their friends and family, who mess around with sex and drugs. I look at them and I look at me and I don't think I really need to make that many changes. I tend to focus more on helping others fix themselves than focusing on fixing my own life. And I tend to fell as if I don't really need to ask for that much grace.

Of course, that's just what the Pharisees thought too. But our souls don't just suffer from the big sins—those sins the whole world sees and looks down upon. I know I often times suffer more from the little things—the things most people don't hold against me. I feel bad when a bunch of friends and I are hanging out and I don't take the time to call and invite another friend who doesn't often get invited to things. I feel bad if I'm always too busy to spend time with old friends or new ones. I feel bad if I'm out every night of the week and haven't seen my family in ages. I feel bad if I always show up late just because I try to do one more thing before I hop in the car. I feel bad if I procrastinate on really important things like scholarships or this sermon for example. None of these things are huge or disastrous and none of them will spell the end of the world, but as humans we all make so many little mistakes and we all just need so much grace.

Allowing God to smooth over so many of these little mistakes we are also bound to make, no matter how hard we try not to does allow us to love more deeply and fully. And the Jesus of this passage is only too willing to forgive. As long as we just ask, he's more than willing to do, or at least help with all the rest. The more we realize our own shortcomings the more we can forgive others' flaws and not take it so hard when our friends arrive late or our families can't spend time with us. When we ask for grace, we understand that we are no better than anyone else.

I have been shown so much of this grace and love at St. Matthews through-out my six years here. And I honestly can say that I would not be here today if it were not for all of you. The love and dedication of my church family and friends has helped me so much over the years and shown me so much grace when the world is so often been unwilling to. It is one of the things I love most about St. Matthews. We tend not to judge people. We would much rather show them that they are loved and I cannot tell you how beautiful that is. I think this is in part because you are not afraid to realize your mistakes, ask for forgiveness, and try to correct them as best as we are able.

This simple woman was brave enough to crash a party full of people who hated her. And she was brave enough to recognize her own sin and brave enough to ask for grace. It is not exactly the courage of the dragon-slaying knight, but perhaps it is far more relevant to us all here today. I pray that we may all have such bravery. Amen.

6.5

EMILY B.

My Sermon
http://www.youtube.com/watch?v=jX4IeKxuiME

Baptist
White Female

We're very thankful to be here with you this morning. It's an honor to be involved in the weekend in such a huge way. I'm glad y'all came. Today we'll be speaking about Psalm 139. Please pray with me.

Dear Lord, thank you for bringing everyone here today and allowing us to preach your word. Please speak through my peers and myself today. Let everyone here leave changed because of your impact on our lives. In Jesus' name I pray, Amen.

My name is Emily, also known as Mustang Sally by my peers at Memorial High School. Yes, that's right, I'm the mascot. I think it's perfect for my personality. I mean, I love attention and making people laugh and I love hugging little kids at all the football games.

In middle school though, I would have loved to have a mascot suit to hide in. I was kind of self-conscious, I felt overweight and nerdy. I also felt like all the other girls were more fashionable than me and more attractive. In fact to my idea of fashion was wearing overalls every single day. In fact I even got hung up by my overalls one day. It was pretty bad. Also I had the red hair, freckles, braces—it was just not a pretty picture. I got called Pippi Longstockings every day I wore pigtails. But things began to change in 7th grade. I started losing weight. And not just losing baby fat, growing up kind of weight. It was a lot of weight. I would be hungry non-stop and I would eat whatever I wanted. And I would still be losing weight. I also couldn't sleep at night. My heart would just be pounding and I would just sit up in bed wondering what was going on. Well I told my parents and they knew something was wrong too. So we went to the doctor. We ran some tests and after the results came back in I found out I had a disease. This disease is called

Grave's Disease and it affects your thyroid. I was immediately put on beta-blockers to slow down my heart rate so I wouldn't have a heart attack. It was a terrible point in my life. I was at my worst. I didn't feel good, I was always hungry, and I still couldn't sleep. Also it was confusing because I was really, really thin and I didn't feel good and teachers and parents and kids would say, "Emily you look so great. You're becoming such a beautiful young lady. You're so skinny." And I was confused thinking this . . . my doctor says this isn't a healthy weight, why are you telling me I look great? And it just taught me a lot about the hypocrisy of trying to please the world and how people view others. It just, it really was hard to learn at such a young age.

And God knows me, even when I'm angry or trying to run away from him. To be honest I was mad. I felt like I didn't deserve this. I mean, I was only 13 years old in the 7th grade. I was just beginning to meet my new friends in middle school and it just, it was just a bad time for me. I also was angry because I couldn't do the things I wanted to do anymore. I couldn't play sports anymore. I had to sit on the sidelines. I had to get blood drawn all the time for tests and I had to take really bad tasting medicine. I tried to run away from God because I was mad and I also tried to fight this disease thinking that God had made a mistake. Well, God never makes mistakes.

But this is the same kind of situation with Moses and God. In Exodus 3:11, Moses said to God, "Who am I that I should go to Pharaoh and bring the Israelites out of Egypt?" God had told him to go save the Israelites from Pharaoh but Moses was saying to God, "what are you doing? You're making a mistake." He was basically telling God, "I'm right, you're wrong." And that's kind of the thing. God you made a mistake I'm not supposed to [video skips] this disease, maybe that's somebody else, maybe you made a mistake but God basically showed me that I had to make a choice between dwelling on this illness or moving on and letting him give me a bigger plan like the one he gave for Moses.

Please open your Bibles to Psalm 139 verse 1 through 5. It reads, "O Lord, you have searched me and you know me. You know when I sit and when I rise; you perceive my thoughts from afar. You discern my going out and my lying down; you are familiar with all my ways. Before a word is on my tongue you know it completely, O Lord. You hem me in-behind and before; you have laid your hand upon me."

God does know me. He knew how much I could handle and even though he gave me this disease, I never hit my breaking point. And right now I'm stable with the medicine I'm on. He loves me and he is in control. He has my back. He protects me. Knowing that God's in control of my life has really allowed me to be free. I can be free with God knowing that he's got the plan and I don't know . . . have to know everything every second of every day. Also it just allows me to trust others and love them for who God has made them to be now that I love myself for who God has made me to be. God definitely has a plan, because this fall the same kids that hung me up by my overalls in middle school also voted for me as Memorial's homecoming queen. It's true. I know . . . I now know that God is surrounding me, he's always with me, and there is nothing in the world for me to fear.

6.6

JANE DOE

Youth Sunday Preachers at All Saints Pasadena, Part 1
http://www.youtube.com/watch?v=W2IPpCRXxEE

Episcopal
White Female

What God means to me. What a question. About two years ago, I would
have said nothing. But now, God means everything. I first starting coming
to All Saints because of Desmond Tutu. My mother heard from her union
that he was speaking, and she came to listen and told me that I just had to
come see this place. Well, my mother is agnostic, so for her to be telling me
to go to church—I knew I had to go. I came one Sunday and was amazed. I
felt so comfortable here. I wasn't being told that I had to believe anything.
I wasn't being forced to say anything. I was allowed to just be. Then, I filled
out one of the newcomer information cards from the pew rack in front of
me, and so began my journey of faith.

My first year at All Saints was a hectic one. My very first youth group, I
signed up for fast relief. Fast relief is a fundraiser in which we fast for thirty
hours to help raise money for Episcopal relief and development. It was an
amazing experience. Then I attended the diocesan senior high dance bishop's
ball. One of the most fun dances I have ever been to. Trevor was there too.
And then I was an angel in the Easter vigil. That is where I met Wilma and
MaryAnn. It was amazing and so are they. Well that was how it all began.

I started to develop relationships with all the kids in youth group and all
the volunteers. But more importantly, I started to develop my relationship
with God. For me, there were two outstanding events that really helped me
get close to God. The first was the winter retreat I went on to Camp Stevens.
We were only there for a weekend, but it changed my life. I remember it
was the first time that I truly felt like a child of God. For one thing, it was
my first weekend away from home. Secondly, it was the first time I was able
to really explore what God was and how he was affecting my life. The most
important thing that I learned on that retreat was that with God, you have

to take chances. You have to take that leap of faith in order to get anywhere. But don't worry, because God will always catch you. He may let you fall for a bit, but he will always catch you before you go splat on the sidewalk. The other thing that happened on that retreat was that I got really close to Dave Erickson. It was the first time I got to have a serious conversation with him and ever since then, he has been the person that I could go to for anything.

The second event that changed my faith was "Seekers." For anyone that doesn't know, "Seekers" is the confirmation class here at All Saints. "Seekers" was the first time that I really had to figure out where I was at with God and if I was ready to make a major commitment to him. There were a few things I knew for sure. There is a God. I do believe in Jesus. I am forever loved. And God will always be there for me. Now this may sound like a firm basis on which to get confirmed, but I changed my mind more than anyone else in my class. There was and is a lot of pressure from my relatives to be a Lutheran. But, after my mother stopped going to church altogether, they figured a different church was better than no church.

Another hurdle in deciding to get confirmed was dealing with the idea of forgiveness. It just seems too easy. But that is an entirely different subject. But because my mother supported me every time I changed my mind, I continued to question. So what I finally decided with "Seekers" was that I was ready to make a commitment to God to stay committed. I decided that by being confirmed, I was promising to continue with my journey of faith no matter where it takes me. I realize that I don't have to agree with everything the church says and I am forever allowed to change my mind, but I do have to continue to question. I must continue to pray and listen. I will never get all the answers I want, but I will always get all the answers I need. And as long as I continue to pray, God will provide. As long as I work on our relationship, so will he. Every time I look up, God will be in my rearview mirror. All I have to do is try and I will be rewarded with more than I could ever imagine. And the best part, so will you. Thank you.

6.7

JESSI

Youth Sermon Part 1 and 2
http://www.youtube.com/watch?v=_2eQ5w4dXVg&feature=related

Seventh Day Adventist
Latina Female

The title of tonight's sermon is extreme change. In a convention of barbers, they wanted to show that their profession was able to change a person's life. After running through some streets in the city, they found the perfect person. An alcoholic. He stunk. And dirty and a beggar. Well, before, two days after, they found this guy in the streets. But before they took the man and they bathed him, they shaved him, they cut his hair, and they clothed him in a very elegant and professional way. His appearance, his odor, his (inaudible) was all different. Like how I said before, two days later he was in the streets again. He had torn his clothes and had wasted all the money on alcohol and drugs. The barbers were able to change the man's outside, but he couldn't change his nature. The constant change. Let us pray.

Heavenly father, which art in heaven. Help us to be better Christians. And to have the presence of your Holy Spirit inside of us. Because we ask these things in your sweet name, through your son Jesus Christ. Amen.

Extreme change are transformations produced by circumstances that can either be external or internal. Things that you saw coming or things that came by surprise. Nowadays the industries that are most lucrative are the ones that deal with plastic surgery or aesthetic surgery. People will pay whatever they need to pay to make certain changes in their bodies so they can look a little bit more beautiful. To be a little more attractive or to be in the new, in the new fashion mode. In Columbia for example, a person, one of the people that experienced an external, uh, aesthetic change, was a football star that played in the national football team of Columbia. Renee Egita. He entered into a surgical procedure that helped him look physically more handsome. And even though they could change him physically, he says "I am still the same inside." Now through communication and commercials, everybody is really big into plastic surgery and all sorts of aesthetic procedures. Changes are constant in our world. We have the society is changing. Economics are changing, nature is changing. Scientific breakthroughs. A spiritual revival and physical change, babies are growing up into adults. Changes will affect a human being in one way or another. We will either respond with rebellion or peaceably. We will either become addicted or abstinent. We will either refuse to believe and doubt or to believe and have faith. We'll either wind up poor or we'll wind up rich. Healthy or sick.

What are changes and what do they require. Extreme changes are – youth of integrity require valor. Those who want to transform need to first learn how to accept. Those who want to be definitive need to know how to make decisions. Those who want to improvise need to learn how to adapt. Those who don't want to fall into the regular routine need to know how to be innovative. Now we're going to talk about the experience of the man of extreme change. His biography goes a little something like this. This man would fight for the people. This man was a member of the Sanhedrin. He was a zealous Pharisee. He was from . . . he was a Jew by nationality. And he was a doctor of the law. His characteristics were . . . he was, uh, question, able to answer questions, very curious person, very innovative, he would not conform, and he was very sensitive to the needs of the people. And he was a religious leader. And he was always ready to serve. In John chapter 3 verses 1 through 4. Let us read together. There was a man of the Pharisees named Nicodemus, a ruler of the Jews. The same came to Jesus by night and said to him, "Rabbi, we know that thou art a teacher come from God. For no man can do these miracles that thou does except God be with him if God was not with him." And Jesus said to him, "Verily, verily I say unto thee except a man be born again he cannot see the kingdom of God." [break in clip]

Jessi Youth Sermon Part 2
http://www.youtube.com/watch?v=xU9AZCu2I7Q&NR=1

Nicodemus said to him, "How can a man be born when he is old? Can he enter a second time into his mother's womb and be born again?" The man of extreme change is Nicodemus. He came by night because he wanted to avoid criticism. He wanted to hide from judgment. And in reality he knew compared to Jesus he was in spiritual darkness. Verse number 2 and he said, "We know that thou art a teacher come from God for no man can do these miracles that thou does except God be with him." Here Nicodemus recognizes that Jesus was an extraordinary man. That his miracles and his works had to come from God. Observing Jesus and the way that he talked and walked opened up and woke up the curiosity of Nicodemus and the desire for extreme change. The answer that Jesus gave to Nicodemus confirmed his great need and his great, uh, his great need for salvation. In verse number three says, "Verily I say unto thee except a man be born again he cannot see the kingdom of God." Whoever wants to see the kingdom of God and whoever wants to be there and experience it . . . they need an extreme change. As I mean to say, you need to experience a reform or a new lifestyle.

We're going to analyze a little bit the way man offers extreme change and then the way God offers extreme change. In John 3:4 we read, "Can I enter in the second time into . . . can man enter a second time into his mother and be born again?" Man always looks for his own way to salvation. He thinks that the answer is in him and that he has whatever it takes. But when he realizes what God's way is, he is surprised. In John 3:5 we read, "Verily, verily I say unto thee except a man be born of water and the Spirit, he cannot enter into the kingdom of God." God's way is always free. It is always simple and it's always easy. But even though it's simple, easy, and free, they have conditions that are non-negotiable. He who is not born of the water—the being born of water is a symbol of baptism. It's a commitment realized between God and man. It is the cleansing of a sinful heart. And it's a change for a brand new heart. And when we switch hearts, we change our habits and we change our acts into acts of obedience. Whoever is not born of the Spirit, it's the Holy Spirit that makes sense of our life. And it makes our Christian walk possible. To be born of the Holy Spirit is to receive the help from God so that we can understand and be empowered to do God's will.

In conclusion, extreme change is only possible when our weakness and our will unites with the powerful will of God. It's the extreme change that God does in us that allows us to go into heaven. We all here tonight every one of us need an extreme change. Something that can transform our lives forever. To change our broken promises to fulfilled promises by the power of God. To change our sadness into joy and to turn our tears into gladness. Amen.

Let us pray. Holy father, help all of us make a real change. Not just a change but an extreme change in our lives so that when Jesus comes we can be with you in heaven. We ask all these things in the name of Jesus, Amen.

6.8

JOSHUA LaPERRIERE

Suncoast Youth Group: Joshua LaPerriere: The Swords of David
http://www.youtube.com/watch?v=KvgxOxxEiDM

Baptist
White Male

Many of you already know that this passage tells the story of David and Goliath. David experienced one of his greatest victories of his life in these verses. And tonight, I'm not going to take the time to explain the entire story in detail, but I will give you a brief summary in case you aren't familiar with the story. (sings) Only a boy named David, only a little sling. Only a boy named David, but he could pray and sing. Only a boy named David, only a rippling brook. Only a boy named David, but five little stones he took. And one little stone went into the sling and the sling went round and round. And one little stone went into the sling and the sling went 'round and 'round. And 'round and 'round and 'round and 'round and 'round and 'round and 'round. And one little stone went into the air and the giant came tumbling down. (Audience claps)

I just want you guys to know, Pastor Lee forced me to sing that. Anyways, but, tonight I would just like to uh point out one particular verse in this story which is verse 51. And it says, "Therefore David ran and stood upon the Philistine and took his sword and drew it out its sheath and slew him and cut off his head therewith. And when the Philistines saw that their champion was dead, they fled." So in other words, David walks up to Goliath and hits him with a rock and David falls, I mean, Goliath falls down and David takes Goliath's sword and severs his head from his body. Now a man's sword is generally proportional to his body. Kind of like this one is proportional to me. I know it's not the sword that they used, but hey, it's only story time. Now, I'm like about five feet tall, or so, and Goliath is ten feet tall so twice the size of this sword. David picks this up I mean like "man that's huge!" Anyways, but, often times we would read a story like that and not realize the ripple effect that it has in people's lives. That sword that was a symbol of victory that day is brought up in several different places throughout the

Old Testament. Each time the sword is brought up, which symbolizes the first victory, it's used as an inspiration or a stepping stone if you will to win the next victory.

Now remember back in elementary school you know when you had to take, uh, spelling tests? That good grade that you got became a trophy or to remind you of what you've done and what you can do in the future. In the same way, every time you live through a victory in our spiritual life it can be used as a trophy and as inspiration to win the next victory. So, here's the thing—that trophy isn't only going to encourage me again, but it's going to encourage others as well. So what I want to convey to you guys tonight is pretty much, "We must win spiritual victories for the glory of God." Why you might ask? Because of the effect that it will have on your own life. Turn your Bibles to 1 Samuel chapter 21. Now we see here in these verses that just a short time later, David is about the king's business and when he comes to Ahimelech the priest it says, in verses 8 and 9, "and David said unto Ahimelech and is there not here under my hand a spear or a sword for I have neither brought my sword nor my weapons with me because the king's business required haste. And the priest said, the sword of Goliath the Philistine whom thou slewest in the valley of Elah, behold it is here wrapped in a cloth behind the ephod, if thou will take that, take it for there is no other save that here. And David said, There is none like that; give it me." So, pretty much David's [stumbles] is doing the king's business and requires haste. So like I don't know like maybe he's going to pick fruit I don't know and he needs a sword, whatever. So he goes up to his old buddy Ahimelech and he's like, "Hey, you got a sword or a spear or something?" And he's like, "Well I got this thing, Goliath's sword. You used it to chop his head off before. So, then David's like, "Hey, that right there is an awesome sword. Give it to me." So, when David took the sword, it probably . . . it probably brought back some memories. As he held the handle, touched the blade, it must have reminded him of his day when he fought Goliath, when he stood up and trusted the Lord to give him that victory. Now if he didn't do that, and fought Goliath, he wouldn't have that sword to do the king's business, so what would he have? It's because of that one trophy that he was able to get the job done.

6.9

KATIE

Redeemer Lutheran Youth Sermon
http://www.youtube.com/watch?v=DPunXsiuaMs

Lutheran
White Female

Good morning everyone. Hope you all are enjoying the service so far. Before I start, I want to give a round of applause to Pat (inaudible). She did a good job organizing and encouraging us teenagers, which is not easy to do—and we couldn't have done it without you. Alright. So to start off, I wrote this on the bus ride back from my basketball game on Wednesday, so my intro. is a bit lacking. But everyone bear with me and Andy, don't fall asleep this time.

So to begin, here's a little bit about me. My name is Katie Whiteman and I'm a junior at Bettendorf [High School] and I've been going to Redeemer since I was about seven years old. I love *The Office*. Dwight Schrute is my absolute favorite. I whistle when I feel awkward and I can fold an elephant out of a dollar bill. Some other stuff: I play varsity basketball and varsity soccer. And I just started rowing this fall. I've been taking piano lessons since I was ten and art lessons since I was seven. I'm a part of a lot of different clubs, one of them being German club despite the fact that I've never taken a German class in my life. Now, I bet you all are thinking, "Hm, she's a junior. One more year, I wonder where she's going to college. I wonder what she's going to do with the rest of her life?" I think I get asked the question just about ten times a week. Five of those being my parents. You could be a teacher, I tell myself. You really like kids. And this stint teaching Sunday school has been a good one. Or why not a journalist? You really like to write. Even a doctor? You like helping people. You've been drawing since before you could walk—why not an artist? So, as all of you can see, my future has a big fat question mark at the end of it. In other words, I have absolutely no idea.

I wish it were simple. I wish I could just be handed a scroll with all the plans God has for me. I'd open it up, read it, and instantly know what I was going to do with the rest of my life. But wait, this sounds familiar. It happened to

Jesus in our gospel for today. Let's take another look. "He stood up to read and the scroll of the prophet Isaiah was given to him. He unrolled the scroll and found the place where it was written, 'The Spirit of the Lord is upon me because he has anointed me to bring good news to the poor. He has sent me to proclaim release for the captives and recovery of sight to the blind, to let the oppressed go free, to proclaim the year of the Lord's favor. And he rolled up the scroll, gave it back to the attendant, and sat down. The eyes of all the synagogue were fixed on him." So basically, (inaudible—Jesus threw it down?). Jesus walks into the synagogue where he's supposed to give a sermon. Some random person hands him a piece of paper with basically all the answers these people are looking for on it—who he is, where his powers comes from, and what his job on earth is all about. These people had been listening to this guy named Isaiah talk about this problem for a long time. Jesus walks in and basically says, "Hey, I'm the one you're talking about." He reads a sermon and once again, wows the crowd.

And I know, all of you are going to have the same exact reaction when I'm done with my sermon right now. God, however, did not give me a scroll— not for my sermon or for my future. Instead, God has given me a pen and a blank piece of paper. But he hasn't left me alone to write it myself. In fact, it's the exact opposite. He has given me his word in the Bible and I'm try- ing to use it to guide me. He's also given me his Holy Spirit, which calms me down and keeps me from freaking out when everyone asks me these dreaded "future" questions. And finally, he's given me his son, Jesus Christ, who died on the cross for my sins. And he's also done this with every one of you (inaudible). Because no matter what we do with our lives, no matter whether we succeed or fail, we can know that his love and forgiveness will always be with us.

So figuring out what we are supposed to do with our lives is not going to be as easy as Jesus had it on that day in Galilee. I know I'm going to make mistakes. I think we all do. We're going to have to cross things out on our scrolls, maybe even start a new paragraph. But that's ok, God . . . because God will always be with us. He'll always be over our shoulders, comforting us, guiding us, and helping us every step of the way. Thank you.

6.10

MATTHEW S.

Youth Sunday Sermon, Part 1
http://www.youtube.com/watch?v=HDhKipjeuLU&feature=related

Presbyterian Church (USA)
African American Male

Introduction from an adult

Good morning. I'm glad she said that the word comes from Matthew because I didn't know whether she was talking about me or the Lord. Either
one is accurate. Um, I'm glad you guys came out here on youth Sunday this
morning. Um, I really appreciate you guys coming out here again. As Jessica
said, I am a senior at Decatur High School. And actually as a graduating
senior I've been assigned a good number of books to read. And because of
this, the high school has made the bookstore my second home. And Borders
actually being my favorite. I don't know if you guys spend much time in
Borders but my experience is that everyone in there is so nice and friendly.
Like when you go in there they just run up to you with a smile on their face.
And not only do they point you to the section where the book you're looking for might be in like Barnes and Nobles, like, the go to you to the section,
pick the book and hand it to you, ask you what the next book is on your list
so they can repeat the process over again.

Now it makes me feel bad sometimes when I actually don't want the book
because they actually go through all that trouble. So sometimes I actually
sneak the book back when they're not looking. It works, it works a lot better
when it's busy in there, they don't notice you as much.

Um, I actually went into Borders this past Spring break looking for books
to fill my time and so I had free time and I actually noticed that there were
crates near the front of the store with books marked down to 3.99 a piece.
And now, mind you, these are books that are usually ten, twelve, fourteen
dollars. So, and I was even more excited to find out that the books were
buy two, get the third one free. However, the smile on my face faded a little

when I found out that the books that were on sale were either cook books or children's books. So, I actually still had to kill some time so I rummaged through the piles to hope that something would pop out and to my satisfaction, something did pop out. It was actually a New York Times bestseller um, called *Please Stop Laughing at Me* by Jodee Blanco. Now I'm thinking that New York Times bestsellers shouldn't be on sale for 3.99 but in the same sense, it seems like everything these days is a New York Times bestseller. And, actually Blanco begins the novel in the parking lot of a hotel where a high school reunion is taking place. She is quite hesitant, she is hesitant to go inside to face the faces that she faced in high school. Um, she's hesitant because she remembers the experiences and the suffering she had to go through in high school. She, in her New York Times bestseller, tells how she was bullied and shunned in elementary school, middle school, and high school. This happened not because of how she looked, or who her parents were, or where she lived, but because of her personality and values. Now I'm sure you're asking yourself, how can a person's values result in their being teased by their classmates? She recounts that the bullying starts when she befriended a handicapped girl. Her once then best friend, or her former best friend began to ignore her because of this. She began to call her really ugly names because of this. She later stands up for a group of deaf children who are being teased by the older kids. She received more ridiculing because of this. She tells of how she was shunned because she wouldn't play nasty jokes on her teachers or classmates. Because she wouldn't make fun of the mentally challenged kids in her class. Instead she saw the kids as just people like herself. She engaged them in conversation and made them feel comfortable by volunteering her free time to help them with their lessons. She invited, she invited those who were outcast into her life because she saw that she needed them and they needed her. Because of this, again, she was shunned and excommunicated if you will.

After the Columbine shooting a couple years ago, or a few years ago rather, students who knew the young man, who knew the young men who took their lives and the lives of their classmates were interviewed. The students who happened to be on the wrestling team with the young men stated they were surprised that anyone would plan such a thing. Everyone at Columbine was so nice to each other. However, the students who knew the students really well, the best friends of the two young men said that they had to face humiliation, teasing, and were spat upon—and they had to hide while they were transferring classes through the hallways. Now how can both of these be true you ask.

Jodee also, in her book, also called, or was called names. She had her life threatened, she was spat upon, had her hair pulled out, gum put in her hair. She found articles of her clothing found in toilets, as well as her lunch. She was, she found garbage stuffed in her locker and her back pack. She was held on the ground many times, had snow stuffed down her throat to the result of her choking, and she had rocks pelted at her and was again held down and beaten over and over again until she wouldn't even scream anymore because it would go by faster and she wouldn't feel it as much if she zoned out mentally. One day a teacher witnessed these attacks. The teacher told her that it would be better if she learned to fight her own battles by herself. Her teachers, school administrators, and even psychiatrists dismissed it as kids being kids and blamed Jodee for not trying hard enough to fit in. When this first started happening at her elementary school, her parents made Jodee switch schools. The first few months of the new school would be fine with her making friends, but as soon as she held out a helping hand to those who needed her, as soon as she showed compassion to others who were bullied, who were tormented, she would find herself shunned as well and left out to an even worse extent than before. Her new friends would now see her as the enemy. She would be in the same situation as she once left at the previous school. She would eventually change schools numerous times up until she went to high school. Actually, before class she would pray, please God don't let anyone see what I really look like. She had to put on facades to fit in. She wanted to be accepted and to do so, she couldn't nor didn't show compassion for others. She didn't volunteer her time to those who were deemed unacceptable by society. She didn't want her suffering to continue. She wanted to fit in and she tells of a time when she even went to the length of playing a cruel joke of one of her teachers, on one of her teachers. Afterwards, she confessed that she felt extremely guilty and apologized to that same teacher. And it was on this day that she realized that you cannot run from who you are.

Now many of you can probably imagine why I chose to speak from the book of Matthew this morning. It probably reminds me of an old friend. However, I wanted to speak about suffering and persecution today because it's relevant in the world that we live in. In national news, local news, and even at the lunch tables, everyone is on the subject of suffering. The car companies are suffering, this economy, the stock market is suffering, the divorce rates is on the rise because of this, and children are suffering. The internet has provided new ways for bullies to harass people and youth through cyberspace. Civil wars are going on around the world and nations are also suffering. Everyone is either suffering or knows someone who is suffering.

In fact the suffering and persecution that I want to talk about today and that Jesus spoke about is a persecution for his sake. Suffering for standing up for people what we, for people and what we know is right in the name of Christ. I have listened and watched and it seems that both Christians and non-Christians alike are shocked with how much suffering and persecution is happening and going on in the world today. But however we should not be surprised by this because persecution is not a new problem. Christians in the early church have had to suffer terrible penalties for being followers of Christ. They were jailed, fed to lions, [end of clip]

Youth Sunday Sermon, Part 2

http://www.youtube.com/watch?v=4Xk8TYcl2sY&feature=channel

and even burned alive. Now Matthew 5:10–12 says, "Blessed are those who are persecuted because of righteousness." Then it goes on to say, "blessed are you when people insult you, persecute you falsely, and all kinds of evil against you." But it asks you to, to rejoice and be glad because great is your reward in heaven. These Christians were blessed for their persecution for righteousness in God's name. They lived life and with their eyes firmly (inaudible) on Christ and they died knowing that they lived in him and to the fullest gave him everything. And now they are with him in the heavenly kingdom today. Yes they are blessed. Our time here in this world is hardly anything at all. The real life is the eternal life following. The world is the small picture. Time spent with Jesus here in the eternity is the big picture. A day in his presence is worth everything. And the peace we feel in his presence, the love he freely gives and the forgiveness he shares with us daily are worth the persecution.

Jodee, the author of the book, wasn't burned alive, but she is an example of modern day persecution for righteousness. She tells how her parents raised her Catholic and taught her to follow in Christ's name. She was persecuted for following Jesus' example. And Matthew 5:10–12 goes on, as I said, and asks the persecuted to be rejoiceful. Jodee used her pain and suffering in school to build her literature skills by writing about what she had to deal with and then she went on to NYU to become an author and English major. After graduating, she planned huge events in which she met huge celebrities and heads of state by (inaudible)-ing with them. God has blessed her with these opportunities and has learned to rejoice in suffering and her persecution has become her blessing.

Believe it or not, when we are persecuted, we are brought closer to God. Our eyes are taken off what society deems is important and put on him and his purpose. Our world gets a lot smaller when we realize that it's just us and him. When we walk with Christ, when we live in his example, and build a life in him, the world will reject us and we cannot run from the fact that the teachings of God are contrary to what society deems is important. The teachings of God are contrary to the teachings of society because . . . and because of this to be followers of Christ we will be marked by society.

A little less than a month ago, on April 16th, an eleven-year-old boy who lived in Stone Mountain, like myself, by the name of Jaheem Hererra, came home happy to have his report card in hand. He rushed to show it to his mother and his mother gave him a high-five because of the A's and B's it contained. Afterwards he went upstairs to wait for his mother to finish dinner. When dinner was ready his mother sent his sister upstairs to tell Jaheem that it was time to eat. Moments later, screams came from within his room. Jaheem had hung himself by his belt. It turned out that he was continuously being bullied and being called obscene names at his elementary school. His mother knew of his bullying because he would tell her from day to day. And she complained numerous times not only to the school but the school board. And the day of his death, Jaheem told his best friend that he was tired of telling his mother and other adults what he was experiencing because nothing was being done by the school board or the school at all. Jaheem thought that he was alone in his struggle. He did not know that Jesus was right there with him in his struggle. He didn't have anyone in his class putting their neck on the line with him facing down his persecutors with him and he died thinking that there was no hope.

School grounds are not the only place where persecution can take place. A while back a soccer player in Brazil accidentally scored a goal on his own team's . . . on his own team. He was taunted, bullied, and after the game even killed by the fans because of this. Persecution also takes place in the office or work place. Just because people grow up does not mean that they mature. And you may go to work every day and have to face people who taunt, mock, dis-, or discriminate against you. But no matter whether we are persecuted in the school, on the sports field, or in the place of work, we will not be alone in our struggles. Christ is with us and he will always be. And if we are honest with each other about what we are going through, we can also be with each other. And we shouldn't have to fight our own battles alone. No matter whether we are persecuted in the school or sports field or the work place, we will not be alone in our struggle. Jodee during her senior year of high school won a scholarship to a writing conference at a university. And at this conference she met other students who were going through exactly what she had experienced in her years of schooling. And she was shown that she was not only alone nor neither were the others. Because of this she was able to get through her persecutions. She was able to do what she knew was right without worrying about judgment and how she was treated by others. Again she made her persecution . . . again she made her persecution into . . . and rejoiced and made it her blessing. Because of this she was able to, again, to go to NYU, to become a writer, and to inform others out there who might be going through the exact same experiences that she went through . . . that they are not alone.

I'm here to tell you that no matter what you go through no matter what persecutions you go through that you are not alone. And Christ will be with you. And that the people sitting right next to you will be with you. Thank you.

6.11

MINISTER KEITH J.

"Going Forth In The Beauty of Holiness" 1, 2, and 3
http://www.youtube.com/watch?v=Ksy8btH8JcQ&feature=related

Pentecostal Holiness
African American Male

(Inaudible) but I give you what the Lord has given me and I thank God for removing the fear because we didn't come to tend to Satan's affairs but I come to give you what the Lord has given me. What he says is what you'll receive. In Isaiah the 35th chapter beginning at the 8th verse, "And a highway shall be there and a way and it shall be called the way of holiness. The unclean shall not pass over it but it shall be for those the wayfaring men, though fools shall not err therin. No lion shall be there nor any ravenous beast shall go up thereon. It shall not be found there, but the redeemed shall walk there. And the ransomed of the Lord shall return and come to Zion with songs and everlasting joy upon their heads. They shall obtain joy and gladness and sorrow and sighing shall flee away." And Saint Matthew the 16th chapter and the 18th verse reads, "And I say also unto thee that thou art Peter and upon this rock I will build my church and the gates of hell shall not prevail against it."

And the subject that the Lord gave me on today—he said—going forth in the beauty of holiness. Going forth in the beauty of holiness, now, now, this is not a beautified or some type of special message, but he said, "going forth in the beauty of holiness." Holiness is right, holiness is God's standard it is beautiful and we shall move forth in it and I thank God for it. In the scripture read, "and there shall be a highway and a highway shall be there and a way shall be called holiness." And it said the unclean shall not pass over it so I have come to learn that in the way of holiness there is no unclean thing and I thank God for it. He said the unclean shall not pass thereover. And it said it shall be for those the wayfaring men, those that are willing to pick up the cross and follow the Lord—I thank God for it—he said, "going forth in the beauty of holiness."

And just something he said right quick, he said holiness is not a revelation or a vision that the Lord gives to an individual church. He said holiness is God's standard for every church. So he said at the end of the day when you finished going from this church to that church and this center to that center, he said you're still required to be holy and I thank God for it. He said, we're going forth in the beauty of holiness and there is an attack on holiness because nobody wants to live holy in today's society, in today's world, but God is requiring that every one of us live holy. We shall go forth in the beauty of holiness because anything that the Lord does shall prevail. And he said that the gates of hell, shall not prevail. So whatever God has set forth to do, it shall prevail—and I thank God for it. He said going forth in the beauty of holiness. And the scripture said, the unclean shall not pass over it. And anything that's sin and unrighteousness is unclean, so the adulterer shall not walk in the way of holiness. The fornicator shall not walk in the way of holiness. Nor shall the liar, or the cheater, or whatever sins fall under the category of sin shall not walk in the way of holiness. That is the unclean thing that shall not pass over it.

He said the fools shall not err therein. They shall not. (Inaudible) The unclean shall not go in the way of holiness. Those that are fools or those that may not understand, they still will have some type of understanding of the way of holiness because that's what the word says. The fools shall not err therin, they shall not do wrong in this way. And he said no lion shall be there nor any ravenous beast so as we're walking in the way of holiness and if we're really committed to seeking the Lord and we're walking this walk, we don't have to worry about any lion or any ravenous beast coming before us to hinder us because he said we're going forth in the beauty of holiness.

And he told me just pinpoint the word going forth. Going forth, and I said, "Well, Lord, going forth, what do you mean?" And he said he'll manifest it at the end but it just said pinpoint going forth. Then the scripture goes on to say that the redeemed—but the redeemed—shall walk there, so I've come to learn that as we're walking that if we want to be holy, we have first to be redeemed, we have to be washed in the blood of the lamb, we have to be clothed in righteousness in order to live a holy life before the Lord. And, and as I was before the Lord, before I came to preach, the Lord was just speaking to me then and he said, "This message—he said, I want you to go and preach on the battlefront." So I said, "Lord, what does that mean?" He said, "As I'm preaching, he said, I want—he want me to stay down here for most of the time." So once I've finished with the scriptures you'll see me down here for most of the time because he said, "You cannot intimidate the people of God, so you cannot choke the word of God, so as the preacher is preaching we hope to be able—I could have a chair and sit right here and preach under the anointing of God because whatever he sets forth to do shall be done. He said you cannot hinder his preachers, you cannot intimidate these preachers from preaching the word of God. He said we're going forth in the beauty of holiness.

See, see, nobody, there's so many churches taking down from holiness but we have to live holiness. I was looking online the other day and I came across this church that said New Covenant Christian Church. And, and I said, "OK, what is this about?" And I looked it up and it said there was the pastor, his name was Pastor Randy Morgan and he was married to the assistant pastor whose name was Pastor John Morgan. And I said, "Lord, Randy and John. Randy is bald. John got a short cut, you know, he got his pants on." I said, "Both of them are men, pastoring the church." And the deacons are married. The deacons are women and they're married to each other. And all the other pastors and member of this congregation were homosexuals but that's unclean and it shall not go in the way of holiness.

So we have to go forth in the way of holiness. And the preachers, we have to continue to preach and stand on the word of God because we must be holy. But, see, see nobody wants to live holy because they feel that it's just, "you do this and you do that. And you give this and you give that." But the scripture just goes on to say that, it says that "the ransomed of the Lord shall return and shall come to Zion with songs and joy, everlasting joy upon their heads." So as we're walking this life, clean and holy before the Lord there's also joy and there's songs of praise going up before the Lord because I'm still saved and I'm still living a holy life before the Lord. He said going forth in the beauty of holiness. There's so many people, even though they realize they're not holiness, they're professing to be holiness because, because it brings on some type of—there's an attraction behind that name holiness. But he said don't carry the name if you're not going to live holy. (inaudible) go forth in the beauty of holiness. And he said, he said, in Saint Matthew the 16th chapter and the 18th verse when he said, "Thou art Peter" and, and, and "upon this rock I shall build my church and the gates of hell shall not prevail." Because Jesus wondering, you know, "Peter who do you say that I am?" And he said, "Thou art the Christ, son of the living God." And Jesus said, "Surely flesh and blood has not revealed this to you but it was my spirit. It was the father which is in heaven that revealed this unto you." So just as sure that Jesus Christ is the son of the living God that he came and he bled and he died for the remission of our sins—just as sure as the gates of hell shall not prevail against what God has set for us. He said going forth in the beauty of holiness. So we have to continue to stand on the word of God we have to continue to preach against sin. We have to continue to lift up a standard of holiness. And we cannot bow down and I thank God for it.

There's something else that the Lord shared with me. And the enemy is trying to snatch it from my mind, trying to make me forget it. But, but, the Lord was speaking to me. The Lord was speaking to me. And the enemy, he's trying to take it, he's trying to take it. But it's there, and I thank God for it. Going forth in the beauty of holiness. And he said, holi- and there it is! He said holiness, in holiness, there is structure in holiness. And I looked up the word structure. And the word structure said that it's uh, uh a unique or there's a systematic uh, composure of something. Something that has been composed systematically. And, and what the Lord showed me, he said "Could you imagine that your brain is the center of your nervous system, so every nerve in your body functions through the brain. So he, he showed, this is what the Lord said to me, he said, "Could you imagine your arm one day saying, 'You know what? I think I can do this. I'm going to send signals through the body now.'" Because, because that's what, that's what the conception has been that—what, what, how, how can, you know if I had those same nerves in my arm then I'm gonna, I'm gonna take control of this body. But could you imagine the arm trying to, trying to control the body, when the brain holds every, every function of the nervous system. So what he's saying is the structure will not work because it's not according to the system. So he said the head controls every nerve in the body so therefore the arm cannot control anything because it has not been given the power or the authority to do so through the function of the body.

Now, spiritually we have to apply that because the Lord did not tell me to elaborate on it. He said, but we're going forth in the beauty of holiness. So everything that is unclean and everything that is unholy shall not prevail in the house of God because we are a holy people and we will serve the Lord in the beauty of holiness. He said going forth in the beauty of holiness.

[break in clips]

http://www.youtube.com/watch?v=mPb_YGSmfZg&NR=1

Don't forget the vision. And what that means is, the Lord woke me up one Sunday morning. It was about 4 . . . 4:30 in the morning, and he said, "We're coming out." So I said, "OK, Lord we're coming out." And then he brought my attention to Joshua the 6th chapter when, when the walls of the city of Jericho were shut up because of the children of Israel and he said that we're coming out. And he sent Joshua over the city and over the king and he said, "I want you to gather your men and seven priests." I need, I need seven people, uh, I need seven people to show you what the Lord showed me. Elder Thompson, Elder Middleton, Elder Pendleton, Minister Johnson, Minister. Gifford. We've got two . . . four . . . five . . . Mr. Thompson. Is that six? And I'll be seven because the seventh that the Lord showed me is not here. And he said . . . this is the vision that the Lord showed me, he said, "we're coming out." And he showed me the scripture where Joshua was over the city of Jericho and all the people and the walls of that city were shut up because of sin, because the children of Israel had been sitting and doing wrong, but he said

[break in clips]

http://www.youtube.com/watch?v=CsbeFDSW4n4&NR=1

Oh boy, y'all was supposed to grab y'all Bibles, but that's alright. He said, we're gonna, we're gonna take these seven priests and we're gonna march around the city. We're gonna march around the walls of the city seven, six . . . . seven times. But he said, on the seventh day, I want you to march around the walls on the seventh day seven times. But the Lord intervened and he showed me we're only gonna march around three times: one for the Father, one for the Son, and one for the Holy Ghost. And he said on the 3rd time we're gonna shout "Jesus!" and you were supposed to have your Bibles. Because in the scripture, those men and those priests that were marching around the walls they all had horns. And they were supposed to blow the horns at the time they marched around the walls the seventh time. So as we're marching around the walls with the word in our hand, it's the word of God that's going to tear down every stronghold that's coming up against the standard of holiness because he said we're going forth.

So this is what the Lord showed me. Y'all come on. He said we're going to march around these walls seven times, but we're only going three times. He said I need some power, I need some anointing. He said I need some Holy Ghost because the walls are coming down. He said we're going forth in the beauty of holiness. So we're going around the walls three times. And we're gonna (inaudible) because the Lord said we are coming out in the name of Jesus. He said we're going forth in the beauty of holiness. He said we shall not bow down. Every unclean thing shall be (inaudible). He said we're going forth in the beauty of holiness. He said you cannot (inaudible). He said anything (inaudible). He said it shall prevail. He said it shall prevail. It shall prevail. Somebody tell the Lord thank you. He said we're going forth in the beauty of holiness. Ohhhhh yeah. He said we're going forth in the beauty of holiness. And the gates of hell shall not prevail. Ohhhhh. Somebody tell the Lord thank you. The walls are coming down, the walls are coming down. He said we shall be holy. We shall live righteous. Somebody say yeah. Owwwww. (inaudible) Ohhhhh. (inaudible). He said because holiness is (inaudible). Holiness is God's standard. He said preach the word in season. Out of season. You don't like it? Then tell it anyhow. He said who (inaudible) will not want to know the truth. In order to reign in the end. But we're going forth . . . Holy Ghost . . . oh yahyahyahyahyes. Ohhhhh. He said we're going forth in the beauty of holiness. And he said every . . . every wicked imagination that has exalted itself against the knowledge of God . . . . he said it's coming down. Because he said that the enemy comes in like a flood. The spirit of God will lift up a standard high. A standard. Holiness. Ohhhhh. Thank you Jesus. Ohhhhh. He said the walls are coming down. He said the walls are coming . . . yes. He said the walls are coming down. He said the walls are coming down. (inaudible) The Spirit will lift up a standard of holiness. Ohhhhhh. He said all the walls must come down. He said the walls of deceit (inaudible). Owwwww. Owwwww. Jesus. Jesus. Jesus. Jesus. Jesus. Jesus. Every wall must come down. Jes-, Jes-, Jes-, Jes-, Jes-, Jesu-, oh glory. He said we're coming out. He said the walls are coming down. Ohhhhh. Ohhhhh. The walls are coming down. (inaudible) Jes-, Jes-, the walls will come down. Ohhhhh. Yeah, yeah, yeah, yes. Come on, Jes-, come on, Jes-, come on Jes-. Tear 'em down. Said we're going forth in the beauty of holiness. Woah-ohhhhh. The gates of hell shall not prevail. He said we're going forth in the beauty of holiness. He said if you don't like it, you don't have to (inaudible). Said that we're going forth in the beauty of holiness. Ohhhhh, yeah, yeah. Come on and tell him thank you. Tell him thank you. Tell him thank you that the walls are coming down. Tell him thank you. Ohhhhh. Thank you. Oh.

6.12

SAM N.

Sam N. preaching Vietnamese A/G Charlotte part 1 of 2
http://www.youtube.com/watch?v=FpAdw4pppBs&feature=related

Assembly of God
Asian American, Male

(inaudible) what you have in store for them and what you want to teach them. Because it's not by me that this lesson's being produced, it's by you God. And I pray that you would speak through me because as you can see, I'm very stuttering with words and, uh, I pray that you would help me to become less nervous and less hungry as they all take away from my focus (inaudible) oh God. In your precious name I pray, amen.

Alright, everybody can sit on down. Alright. So how's everybody's week – the first few days of school? Ok, that's great everybody answered. Ok, the topic of my sermon is called, "The Second Inward Struggle." Uh-huh. Good question. So what's the first, right? The first struggle is to live daily with Christ. Right? That's already a struggle in itself. You have to fight the devil to live right. But the second is being able to . . . the second struggle . . . I lost my train of thought there . . . ok . . . the second struggle is the fight for people's heart. Ok, and Mark 16:15, ok . . . yeah, if you could all turn at all . . . up . . . to me . . . with me. Like I said, stuttering my words. Alright, in . . . it says, "He said to them, Jesus, go into all the world and preach the good news to all creation." Sound familiar? We've been learning a lot about "the mission" these past few weeks, correct? So I'm just going to expand on this. We talked a lot about the mission itself, the people involved, and what we have to do. But we haven't talked about the struggle within this mission.

What's the struggle? People aren't always very cooperative. Some people fight you off, some people don't believe you, some people just act like you're stupid. Countless things. I know y'all have experienced those and if you haven't, I know you know what I'm talking about. Now 1 John 3:13, you don't have to open up to me, says that, "Do not be surprised, my brothers, if the world hates you." So once again, assurance that you will be hated, ok?

First John 3:13—that the world will not accept you. That's not saying that everybody in the world—some people will accept you—some people will believe, and that's our point, right? That's our purpose in life, to reach out to those few and to spread the seed to those few who will receive it. But the majority will not receive you, ok? You've heard all these things before, but here's an example of it to clarify more of what it really feels like, ok?

Who here has read the Chronicles of Narnia? Yeah, favorite book! Or books. Well, you're going to have to follow along. Alright, so this party was traveling, right? A party is a group of people. Ok. Alright. A party was traveling. Lucy, who is the youngest sibling of the four which has ruled Narnia, had spoken to the great Lion Aslan, he wished for them to follow him down a road which seemed to take them in the opposite direction of their destination. Others couldn't see Aslan and so didn't believe and went the wrong way. They met the enemy and had to run back to the same spot before, which is twice the work. Later that night, Aslan showed up again and once again wanted them to follow them on account of belief that he knew what he was doing. "Will the others see you too?" asked Lucy. "Certainly not at first," said Aslan. "Later on, it depends." "But they won't believe me. Oh dear, oh dear," said Lucy. "And I was so pleased at finding you again. And I thought you'd let me stay." "It is hard for you, little one," said Aslan. Lucy eventually waked the others and after some surprising support from their brother Edmond, they set off not knowing where they'd end up. Later on, (inaudible) turns to a happy ending. Ok?

So, how do we relate to this story? Um, some of you may have guessed it already. But I'm going to explain so everyone can hear it. Ok, um, ok, who are we like? Lucy, exactly. What are we trying to do in this world? Convince some people of something they can't see. Convince people that there is something there. And he wants something so great for us. He wants what's better for us than we could ever think of ourselves. But people can't see that. And ever heard of that saying, "A picture's worth one thousand words?" So they can't see the picture, there's no use in one thousand words. Ok? That means we have to say two thousand.

Alright, but then, continuing on, so what did Lucy have to do? She had to go to people who were older than her, more mature than her, and definitely people more grumpier than her, because they had to wake up from sleep, right? Cause everyone's grumpy after having been wakened up. So she had to go to them, which was a struggle in itself to wake them. Then she had to convince them that somebody that they all knew, somebody that they all thought they knew, was standing right there and they couldn't see him. How's that feel? Does that sound like you walking up to someone and telling them "Jesus loves you" and then they walk away from you because they said, "Jesus doesn't exist. I don't see Jesus. Where's Jesus at?" Ok?

But then, we see that although he . . . there's actually another quote in here that says, Aslan is talking to Lucy, I didn't want to include this earlier, "and they will not . . . and they will not follow you and you at least must follow me alone." And then later on, Lucy says something to herself to keep her going: "I musn't think about it. I must just do it."

Those exact words, although they might not be from the Bible, relate to us really clearly. Even though people around us don't follow Jesus, we have to follow Jesus. If we can lead them, that's great. But that doesn't mean we stop following Jesus just because people around us don't.

How do you do it? Don't think about it. Don't sit there and think about, "Oh well, what is he going to think of me? Ahh, they're not going to be friends with me anymore." Don't think about that stuff. Do what's right in your heart. Because the Holy Spirit's inside of you convicting you. And nothing that he says can be wrong. What you think of, what you say, "Oh this is going to make me happy. This is going to make me popular. This is going to make me full . . . is what drives you away, right? Am I right in saying that everything that seems to make you happy is in the wrong direction, but everything that makes God happy seems so hard until you really look at it.

This is one of the ways that I, like, cope with struggle at school, most definitely. Because school is one of the most diverse places you can walk into. And that's the best battleground for the Christian faith. John 16:32b to 33 says, ooh that's not it. "You will leave me all alone. Yet I am not alone, my father is with me. I have told you these things so that indeed you may have peace. In this world you will have trouble, but take heart, I have overcome the world." I'm not going to explain that verse because every person has a different perception on that. To me, when I read those verses and when Jesus is talking, I feel that it's saying what my heart thinks because don't I feel alone sometimes? Don't I feel like God's abandoning me? God's left me all alone to fight this long, hard battle . . . this battle that takes a whole life-time. But then, words of reassurance. My father is with you . . . Holy Spirit, remember? So the Holy Spirit is always there even though we can't see him.

Even though sometimes we can't even feel him or hear him. So . . . but the most important verse is "I have overcome the world." So everything that will control you in this world . . . persecution from people such as making fun of you, looking down on you, not being friends with you. You might be the outcast in the school. Everyone knows about those, right? People, people who sort of sit by themselves. You might be the outcast in the school. I'm just warning you right now, you could be that person. Ok, and, you could even die. Everyone's heard of martyrs. I'm not saying each of you is going to die for Jesus, but there's always that calling. If someone pointed, if somone pulled a gun at you right now and said, "Do you believe in Jesus? If you say yes, I'll pull the trigger." Can all of y'all say to me, look me in the eye, and say yes. [break in clip]

Sam Nguyen, Part 2
http://www.youtube.com/watch?v=NZpP7u5oRwQ&NR=1

We face a lot of things from this world, because the world doesn't believe in Jesus. The world is against Jesus. It says in the Bible, "Do not love the world or anything that's in the world for if any man loves the world, the love of the father is not in him." Can't tell you the verse number. Um, but, guys it's gonna be hard. I can tell you that for sure. It's gonna be hard, so don't think, "Alright, I'm gonna live for Jesus. I'm gonna be pumped about this. I just came from a convention. I'm like brimming with the Holy Spirit. I'm going to walk into school like, ah, "Believe in Jesus. Believe in Jesus. God loves you." You can't be like that. It's not going to be a battle like that. You're not going to walk in in full glory and take everybody in the school for Jesus. It's going to be a long, hard, tedious struggle. And you have to work at it. How do you do things? Simple things, such as acts of caring, acts of love. Like sitting with the person that's sitting by themselves. Ok?

But, I know we're growing short on time so these are my main points. Ok? Not what will they think of me and how will they treat me and will I feel after this, but rather we should think about what will they think of him, what would or did they treat him, and how will he feel after this? Because if we keep our attention on God, there's gonna be . . . it takes away from the focus on our own lives and gives us the bigger picture, alright? We can see things through God's eyes and we can see that, ok, we talked to five people about Jesus, none of them believed you. But afterwards, after they've heard you talk and then they see someone else working in their lives for Jesus, they all begin to see Jesus (inaudible). Right? We may not see that, but God sees that, so God rewards us for that.

And, alright, who here likes Christmas? Everyone loves Christmas? Dang. Alright. Laney, you wanna stop writing for a second? Volunteer. Um, Lydia. And . . . Tara. Can you guys come up here since you volunteered so willingly, because you love Christmas? Alright, I'm gonna give each of you a sign, alright? Here's yours. And I personally made these so these look kinda garbage. Hold that out. Alright, stand in a line. Shhhhhhh . . . Alright, you're backwards. So everyone can see this, right? Tim, can you see it? Alright. Alright. This word says "Christmas." And I personally love Christmas. It's the best time of the year. Alright, but we can see in this that, there's the word "Christ." But there's the word "Sam" as well. It's backwards, don't turn it, don't turn it. Alright, "Christ-mas," which is "Sam" backwards. But if you turn Christmas around, you lose sight of Christ and keep your attention on Sam. Sh . . . stop moving. So, if we focus on Christ, flip it back around, we can't see "Sam," alright? It's either one or the other, you can't see both at the same time. Ok? And it would have been better if I could tape it because (inaudible) smart and turn it around right now. But, uh, you can't see Christ and yourself at the same time. These are all the little things which keep you going which keep you remembering that God's in control. You can't control everything in your life. Because (inaudible) do it, then where would God be? Alright, you can give me my signs back. You didn't? I'll show you afterwards.

Alright, so, that's kind of cool, right? And, uh, I did think of that myself, I was laying in bed and it came to me. Big man upstairs. But, um, yeah, so, each and every one of us has these little things which remind us God is still there, but that we have to focus on him. Because if we look down and look at ourselves, we can't see people around us. But if you look at God, he'll show you each person around you that you need to touch.

So the struggle in school becomes easier and harder at the same time because of this, right? You realize the extremity of your fight and the battle it's going to be, but you realize that you have help. Alright, so before anything else, let's pray so we can close this.

Dear heavenly father, I just thank you for this wonderful time that, uh, we've gathered here and, um, both everyone in the teen group and me myself has learned something from this, uh, sermon, o God. And it's all because of you though Lord. Um, I just thank you for this. And I pray that each and every one of us may remember you in our hard struggles and remember that you're still here, you're still walking beside us, you're carrying us O God, and God I pray for each and every one of us, for our struggles at school because it is a hard struggle, it is a hard, long battle, God. Lord help us so that we can overcome this world and we can fight for you and can remember that you're always there. In your precious name I pray, Amen.

6.13

TREVOR

Youth Sunday Preachers at All Saints Pasadena, Part 2
http://www.youtube.com/watch?v=3E0GHpSvQcA&NR=1

Episcopal
White Male

It is my honor to be speaking here before you today sharing with you my journey at All Saints. When I first came to All Saints, three years ago, I had few expectations. I had never heard of the place, I figured it was simply another church I would go to for a couple of months before I phased out on it. Boy was I wrong. Instantly I had connected with the kids, community, and leaders. All Saints was not my first church. I had attended Church of the Valley for as long as I could remember. I thought it was normal to wake up at six in the morning and drive an hour to church every Sunday. Around the time of middle school though, my pastor retired, my parents divorced, and church took a back seat in my life. When I was a freshman in high school, I started going to a youth group on Wednesday nights at a large church in Pasadena. My mom had already stumbled upon All Saints and it was only five minutes away from home. After about a year, she bribed me to try the youth group here one Wednesday. I didn't want to come, but when we got home that night I told her, "I hate it when you're right." I didn't want to like your church. Ever since then I've been coming every Wednesday.

My first year here gave me a place to be myself, share my feelings, and in a sense to get away from home. Not to mention how nice it was to be able to sleep until eleven and still be able to go to church. The divorce wasn't easy and it happened very quickly. I've never been a fan of psychologists so I dealt with it on my own, which wasn't too hard but it was at times stressful. My dad was still there to pick us up after school though and numerous occasions I would sleep over at his house after watching a movie or going to a baseball game. All these things made what would happen next so much harder. One week after my sixteenth birthday, my dad called to say that he was sick and couldn't pick me up. He sounded tired, so I told him to get some rest, feel better, and I could get a ride home. If I had known that that would be the last conversation with my father as I once knew him, I certainly would have thought to say something more important like how much he meant to me and how I've appreciated every moment he has spent on making me a better person. On Wednesday the same thing happened except this time no call. He wasn't picking up at home or on his cell, so my mom got us and we went home. I don't know exactly what happened but we rushed to the ER and learned that my dad had been found unconscious on his kitchen floor. The doctors wouldn't tell us anything more and all I saw was him asleep on his bed. I had no idea on earth what was going on and all I could think of right then and there was how much I wanted to be at All Saints for youth Wednesdays. We went straight from the hospital to the church and it was so great to have All Saints here for comfort when there was no other forms of it around. My dad slipped into a coma for the first two months and we didn't think he was going to come out of it. Shannon Ferguson came to the hospital and performed the sacrament of unction. Amazingly enough, as we were around praying him, he woke up right then and there. He is now living in a facilitated care center which isn't ideal, but it's still nice to have him here even if he isn't the same person he once was. Through the worst times and the ups and downs, I had All Saints to help.

They say Wednesday nights are for youth group, but that meant little to me. There were numerous occasions where I would show up unannounced looking for Dave Erickson and he would always have time for me—something I will never be able to thank him enough for.

All Saints has not been simply a place of consolation for me. It has been a place of many opportunities as well, most importantly my transformational journey trip to Nogales with Borderlinks. I was one of two high school students, the other being (inaudible), to go on this trip which certainly is not one designed for kids. It was a real look at immigration and the reform that is needed. There was not sugar-coating or beating around the bush. I was thrown into a situation where nothing is hidden. We walked the same path that a group of immigrants might use to cross the border and one person got a cactus stuck in his foot. Mind you this was the daytime—I couldn't even imagine navigating a route like this in the freezing cold at night with no real light to guide you. We spoke with people who have made such a trip sometimes nine times in failure and were now beginning to give up hope for a better life for themselves and for their families. It is not typical for a teenager to know so much about a big issue like immigration, but thanks to the opportunity All Saints gave me, I have a firsthand knowledge and can help to cause change in the world. This is just the type of program that makes our youth program so very special. Just this past year my sister went with a group to New Orleans to help rebuild and another group went on the same trip that I did with three kids this time.

The opportunities for our youth are only growing and I've been lucky enough to have been given so many opportunities and taken advantage of so much. Speaking here today I am humbled by what All Saints has offered me so freely only to help me become a better version of myself. In the lyrics of Matisyahu's "Youth," he says "some of them are looking for fun, some of them are looking for a way out of confusion, some of them don't know where to go, some of their teachers squash the flame before it's had a chance to grow." All Saints gives our youth a place to find whatever they are looking for and so much more. No flames are squashed here by the teachers, they're given a chance to grow and glow. We depend on people like you who volunteer to help more flames to be ignited.

All Saints has truly been the greatest example of God and one of his miracles in action. When a home was broken, I was given a new one here with the most welcoming inhabitants I have ever known. When my father fell ill and I had no adult male figure to turn to, I was given Dave, who was always there for me before and after youth group and any other day of the week for hot coffee and a warm hug. Too often have I heard that God is not around anymore, that no one knows if God is there. But I can say with conviction that God is alive and well here and for me and anyone else who enters these grounds. I don't need to see the Virgin Mary in a rock cliff or a misshapen chicken McNugget. I know for a fact that All Saints is the greatest miracle God has ever given me. Thank you.

Bibliography

Abbott, Jacob. *The Young Christian: Or a Familiar Illustration of the Principles of Christian Duty.* Rev. ed. New York: American Tract Society, 1832.

Acland, Charles R. *Youth, Murder, Spectacle: The Cultural Politics Of "Youth in Crisis" Cultural Studies.* Boulder, CO: Westview, 1995.

Allen, Ronald J. *Interpreting the Gospel: An Introduction to Preaching.* St. Louis, MO: Chalice, 1998.

———. "Preaching and the Other." *Worship* 76.3 (2002) 211–25.

———. *Thinking Theologically: The Preacher as Theologian Elements of Preaching.* Minneapolis: Fortress, 2008.

———. *Preaching and the Other: The Other, Deconstruction, Social Location, Transgression, and Pluralism: Themes for the Pulpit in a Postmodern Setting.* St. Louis, MO: Chalice, 2009.

Anderson, Victor. *Beyond Ontological Blackness: An Essay on African American Religious and Cultural Criticism.* New York: Continuum, 1995.

Andrews, Dale P. *Practical Theology for Black Churches: Bridging Black Theology and African American Folk Religion.* Louisville, KY: Westminster John Knox, 2002.

Ariès, Philippe. *Centuries of Childhood: A Social History of Family Life.* New York: Vintage, 1962.

Arthur, Sarah. *The God-Hungry Imagination: The Art of Storytelling for Postmodern Youth Ministry.* Nashville: Upper Room, 2007.

Austin, Joe, and Michael Nevin Willard. *Generations of Youth: Youth Cultures and History in Twentieth-Century America.* New York: New York University Press, 1998.

Baker, Dori Grinenko. *Doing Girlfriend Theology: God-Talk with Young Women.* Cleveland, OH: Pilgrim, 2005.

Barnard, John. *Two Discourses Addressed to Young Persons to Which Is Added, a Sermon Occasioned by the Earthquake, Which Was October 29, 1727.* Boston: S. Gerrish, 1727.

Barrett, Samuel. *Youths Void of Understanding a Discourse Delivered in the Twelfth Congregational Church, Boston, on the First Sunday of March.* Boston: Crosby, Nichols, 1857.

Barth, Karl. *Homiletics*. Translated by Geoffrey W. Bromiley and Donald E. Daniels. Louisville, KY: Westminster John Knox, 1991.

Batstone, David B., et al., eds. *Liberation Theologies, Postmodernity, and the Americas*. New York: Routledge, 1997.

Beales Jr., Ross W. "In Search of the Historical Child: Miniature Adulthood and Youth in Colonial New England." In *Growing Up in America: Historical Experiences*, edited by Harvey J. Graff, 94–109. Detroit: Wayne State University Press, 1987.

Best, Amy L. *Fast Cars, Cool Rides: The Accelerating World of Youth and Their Cars*. New York: New York University Press, 2006.

Black, Kathy. *A Healing Homiletic: Preaching and Disability*. Nashville: Abingdon, 1996.

Blake, John, "Author: More Teens Becoming 'Fake' Christians." *CNN*. August 27, 2010. Online: http://www.cnn.com/2010/LIVING/08/27/almost.christian/index.html?hpt=T2.

Bourdieu, Pierre. *Outline of a Theory of Practice*. New York: Cambridge University Press, 1977.

Boylan, Anne M. *Sunday School: The Formation of an American Institution, 1790–1880*. New Haven, CT: Yale University Press, 1988.

Braxton, Brad Ronnell. *Preaching Paul*. Nashville: Abingdon, 2004.

Brekus, Catherine A. *Strangers and Pilgrims: Female Preaching in America, 1740–1845*. Chapel Hill, NC: University of North Carolina Press, 1999.

Broadus, John Albert, and Vernon L. Stanfield. *On the Preparation and Delivery of Sermons*. 4th ed. San Francisco: Harper & Row, 1979.

Browning, Don S., and Bonnie J. Miller-McLemore. *Children and Childhood in American Religions*. New Brunswick, NJ: Rutgers University Press, 2009.

Brownson, Abraham. *Memento to Youth a Sermon, Delivered at the West Church in Arlington at the Funeral of Miss Polly Miner, Who Departed This Life, June 6th, 1808, in the 21st Year of Her Age*. Bennington, VT.: Anthony Haswell, 1808.

Brueggemann, Walter. *Finally Comes the Poet: Daring Speech for Proclamation*. Minneapolis: Fortress, 1989.

———. *Texts under Negotiation: The Bible and Postmodern Imagination*. Minneapolis: Fortress, 1993.

———. *Cadences of Home: Preaching among Exiles*. Louisville, KY: Westminster John Knox, 1997.

———. *Theology of the Old Testament: Testimony, Dispute, Advocacy*. Minneapolis: Fortress, 2005.

Bunge, Marcia. "The Child, Religion, and the Academy: Developing Robust Theological and Religious Understandings of Children and Childhood." *Journal of Religion* 86.4 (2006) 549–79.

Bunge, Marcia J., ed. *The Child in Christian Thought, Religion, Marriage, and Family Series*. Grand Rapids: Eerdmans, 2001.

Burke, Kenneth. *A Rhetoric of Motives*. Berkeley, CA: University of California Press, 1969.

Buttrick, David. *Homiletic: Moves and Structures*. Philadelphia: Fortress, 1987.

Campbell, Charles L. *Preaching Jesus: New Directions for Homiletics in Hans Frei's Postliberal Theology*. Grand Rapids: Eerdmans, 1997.

———. *The Word before the Powers: An Ethic of Preaching*. Louisville, KY: Westminster John Knox, 2002.

Campbell, Neil, ed. *American Youth Cultures*. Edinburgh: Edinburgh University Press, 2004.

Capps, Donald. "Curing Anxious Adolescents through Fatherlike Performance." *Interpretation* 55.2 (2001) 135–47.

Carbaugh, Donal A. *Situating Selves: The Communication of Social Identities in American Scenes*. Albany, NY: State University of New York Press, 1996.

Carroll, John T. "Children in the Bible." *Interpretation* 55.2 (2001) 121–34.

Cartwright, Peter. *Autobiography of Peter Cartwright*. Nashville: Abingdon, 1956.

Casey, Michael W. Saddlebags. *City Streets, and Cyberspace: A History of Preaching in the Churches of Christ*. Abilene, TX: ACU, 1995.

Chakravorty Spivak, Gayatri. "Can the Subaltern Speak?" In *Colonial Discourse and Post-Colonial Theory: A Reader*, edited by Patrick Williams and Laura Chrisman, 78. New York: Columbia University Press, 1994.

Chauncy, Charles. *Seasonable Thoughts on the State of Religion in New-England, a Treatise in Five Parts*. Boston: Rogers and Fowle, for Samuel Eliot in Cornhill, 1743.

Childers, Jana. *Purposes of Preaching*. St. Louis, MO: Chalice, 2004.

Chopp, Rebecca S. *The Power to Speak: Feminism, Language, God*. New York: Crossroad, 1989.

Clark, Francis E. "An Organized Revival among the Young." *The Andover Review: A Religious and Theological Monthly* 17.102 (1892) 573–580.

Clowes, Timothy, and Associated Instructors of Youth in the City of Albany (NY). *A Sermon Delivered in St. Peter's Church, May 22d, 1816, to the Associated Instructors of Youth in the City of Albany*. Albany, NY: Packard & Van Benthuysen, 1816.

Collier-Thomas, Bettye. *Daughters of Thunder: Black Women Preachers and Their Sermons, 1850–1979*. San Francisco: Jossey-Bass, 1997.

Colman, Benjamin. *A Devout Contemplation on the Meaning of Divine Providence, in the Early Death of Pious and Lovely Children Preached Upon the Sudden and Lamented Death of Mrs. Elizabeth Wainwright. Who Departed This Life, April the 8th. 1714. Having Just Compleated the Fourteenth Year of Her Age*. Boston: Printed by John Allen, for Joanna Perry, 1714.

———. *Early Piety Again Inculcated from Those Famous Words of Solomon, Eccles. Xii. 1. Remember Now Thy Creator in the Days of Thy Youth in a Sermon Preached to a Society of Young Men, in Boston, July 10. 1720*. Boston: Printed by S. Kneeland, for D. Henchman, and J. Edwards, 1720.

Colman, Benjamin, et al., eds. *A Course of Sermons on Early Piety*. Boston: S. Kneeland, for N. Buttolph, B. Eliot, and D. Henchman, 1721.

Conrad, Leslie. "Preaching to Young People." *Lutheran Quarterly* 9.2 (1957) 144–50.

Cooper, Burton Z., and John S. McClure. *Claiming Theology in the Pulpit*. Louisville, KY: Westminster John Knox, 2003.

Craddock, Fred B. *As One Without Authority*. Rev. ed. St. Louis, MO: Chalice, 2001.

Crapullo, George A. *Messages to Modern Youth*. New York: Fleming H. Revell, 1936.

Crosby, Howard. *Social Hints for Young Christians in Three Sermons*. New York: Broughton & Wyman, 1866.

Côté, James E. *Arrested Adulthood: The Changing Nature of Maturity and Identity*. New York: New York University Press, 2000.

Côté, James E., and Anton Allahar. *Generation on Hold: Coming of Age in the Late Twentieth Century*. New York: New York University Press, 1996.

Davis, Ken. *How to Speak to Youth—and Keep Them Awake at the Same Time*. Loveland, CO: Group, 1986.

———. *How to Speak to Youth—and Keep Them Awake at the Same Time*. Rev. ed. Grand Rapids: Zondervan, 1996.

Dean, Kenda Creasy. *Practicing Passion: Youth and the Quest for a Passionate Church*. Grand Rapids: Eerdmans, 2004.

———. *Almost Christian: What the Faith of Our Teenagers Is Telling the American Church*. New York: Oxford University Press, 2010.

Dean, Kenda Creasy, and Ron Foster. *The Godbearing Life: The Art of Soul Tending for Youth Ministry*. Nashville: Upper Room, 1998.

Debusmann, Bernd, "Older People Enjoy Reading Negative Stories About Young." *Reuters* August 31, 2010. Online: http://www.reuters.com/article/idUSTRE67U43Z20100831.

Delgado, Melvin, and Lee Staples. *Youth-Led Community Organizing: Theory and Action*. New York: Oxford University Press, 2008.

DeVries, Dawn. "Toward a Theology of Childhood." *Interpretation* 55.2 (2001) 161–73.

Doddridge, Philip. *Sermons to Young Persons on the Following Subjects, Viz. I. The Importance of the Rising Generation, Ii. Christ Formed in the Soul the Foundation of Hope, Iii. A Dissuasive from Keeping Bad Company, Iv. The Young Christian Invited to an Early Acceptance on the Lord's Table, V. The Orphan's Hope, Vi. The Reflections of a Pious Parent on the Death of a Wicked Child, Vii. Youth Reminded of Approaching Judgement*. Hartford, CT: Oliver D. Cooke, by Lincoln & Gleason, 1803.

Dykstra, Craig R. *Growing in the Life of Faith: Education and Christian Practices*. 2nd ed. Louisville, KY: Westminster John Knox, 2005.

Dykstra, Robert C., Allan Hugh Cole, and Donald Capps. *Losers, Loners, and Rebels: The Spiritual Struggles of Boys*. Louisville, KY: Westminster John Knox, 2007.

Edie, Fred P. *Book, Bath, Table & Time: Christian Worship as Source and Resource for Youth Ministry*. Cleveland, OH: Pilgrim, 2007.

Edwards, O. C. *A History of Preaching*. Nashville: Abingdon, 2004.

Emerson, Joseph. *Early Piety Encouraged a Discourse Occasion'd by the Joyful and Triumphant Death of a Young Woman of Malden, Who Died of the Throat-Distemper, Sept. 6. 1738. Aetat. 21.: With a Dedication to the Children and Youth of Said Town*. Boston: J. Draper, for H. Foster, 1738.

Epstein, Jonathon S., ed. *Youth Culture: Identity in a Postmodern World*. Malden, MA: Blackwell, 1998.

Eubulus. "On the Imperfect State of Holy Affections in Young Converts." *The Western Missionary Magazine, and Repository of Religious Intelligence (1803–1805)* (1804) 72.

Fagerburg, Frank Benjamin. *This Questioning Age, Sermons Preached to Young People*. The Judson Press Sermons. Philadelphia: Judson, 1936.

Farley, Edward. *Theologia: The Fragmentation and Unity of Theological Education*. Philadelphia: Fortress, 1983.

———. *Practicing Gospel: Unconventional Thoughts on the Church's Ministry*. Louisville, KY: Westminster John Knox, 2003.

Farley, Wendy. *Eros for the Other: Retaining Truth in a Pluralistic World*. University Park, PA: Pennsylvania State University Press, 1996.

Fish, Elisha. *The Art of War Lawful, and Necessary for a Christian People, Considered and Enforced in a Discourse, the Substance of Which Was Delivered in Upton, May 26, 1773. To a Company of Youth, Voluntarily Engaged in Acquiring the Use of Arms*. Boston: Printed by Thomas and John Fleet, 1774.

Florence, Anna Carter. "Preaching to the Exiles Who Live at Home: Youth, Testimony, and a Homiletic Of 'True Speech.'" *Journal for Preachers* 24.1 (2000) 23–9.

———. "A Prodigal Preaching Story and Bored-to-Death Youth." *Theology Today* 64.2 (2007) 233–43.

———. *Preaching as Testimony*. Louisville, KY: Westminster John Knox, 2007.

Floyd, Silas Xavier, et al. *Life of Charles T. Walker, D.D. ("The Black Spurgeon") Pastor Mt. Olivet Baptist Church, New York City*. Electronic ed. Chapel Hill, NC: University of North Carolina at Chapel Hill, 2001. Online: http://docsouth.unc.edu/neh/floyd/menu.html.

Fobes, Peres. *A Sermon, Addressed to Youth the Substance of Which Was Delivered at Wrentham, Mass., August 4, 1793, on Lord's Day, P.M.* Hanover, NH: Re-printed by Moses David, for I. Newton, 1808.

Foote, Gaston. *Keys to Conquest; Inspirational Addresses to Young People*. New York: Fleming H. Revell, 1933.

Fornäs, Johan, and Göran Bolin. *Youth Culture in Late Modernity*. Thousand Oaks, CA: Sage, 1995.

Foss, Sonja K. *Rhetorical Criticism: Exploration & Practice*. 3rd ed. Long Grove, IL: Waveland, 2004.

Foss, Sonja K., Karen A. Foss, and Robert Trapp. *Contemporary Perspectives on Rhetoric*. 2nd ed. Prospect Heights, IL: Waveland, 1991.

Foucault, Michel, and Paul Rabinow, eds. *The Foucault Reader*. New York: Pantheon, 1984.

France, Alan. *Understanding Youth in Late Modernity*. Maidenhead: Open University Press, 2007.

Fraser, Nancy. *Justice Interruptus: Critical Reflections on The "Postsocialist" Condition*. New York: Routlege, 1997.

Freire, Paulo. *Pedagogy of the Oppressed*. Translated by Myra Bergman Ramos. New York: Herder and Herder, 1972.

Fulkerson, Mary McClintock. *Changing the Subject: Women's Discourses and Feminist Theology*. Minneapolis: Fortress, 1994.

Giroux, Henry A. *Fugitive Cultures: Race, Violence, and Youth*. New York: Routledge, 1996.

———. *Youth in a Suspect Society: Democracy or Disposability?* New York: Palgrave Macmillan, 2009.

Gladden, Washington. *Myrrh and Cassia Two Discourses to Young Men and Women*. Columbus, OH: A.H. Smythe, 1883.

Graff, Harvey J. *Conflicting Paths: Growing up in America*. Cambridge, MA: Harvard University Press, 1995.

———, ed. *Growing up in America: Historical Experiences*. Detroit: Wayne State University Press, 1987.

Graves, Mike, ed. *What's the Matter with Preaching Today?* Louisville, KY: Westminster John Knox, 2004.

Green, Garrett. *Imagining God: Theology and the Religious Imagination*. San Francisco, CA: Harper & Row, 1989.

Greven, Philip J. "Youth, Maturity, and Religious Conversion: A Note on the Ages of Converts in Andover, Massachusetts, 1711–1749." In *Growing up in America: Historical Experiences*, edited by Harvey J. Graff, 144–155. Detroit: Wayne State University Press, 1987.

Grimes, Ronald L. *Rite out of Place: Ritual, Media, and the Arts*. New York: Oxford University Press, 2006.

Groome, Thomas H. *Christian Religious Education: Sharing Our Story and Vision*. San Francisco, CA: Jossey-Bass, 1999.

Gutierrez, Gustavo. "Renewing the Option for the Poor." In *Liberation Theologies, Postmodernity, and the Americas*, edited by David B. Batstone et al., 71–72. London: Routledge, 1997.

Habermas, Jürgen. *Communication and the Evolution of Society*. Boston: Beacon, 1979.

———. *The Theory of Communicative Action: Lifeworld and System: A Critique of Functionalist Reason*. Translated by Thomas McCarthy. Vol. 2. Boston: Beacon, 1984.

———. *The Theory of Communicative Action: Reason and the Rationalization of Society*. Translated by Thomas McCarthy. Vol. 1. Boston: Beacon, 1984.

———. *Moral Consciousness and Communicative Action Studies in Contemporary German Social Thought*. Cambridge, MA: MIT Press, 1990.

Haenfler, Ross. *Straight Edge: Clean-Living Youth, Hardcore Punk, and Social Change*. New Brunswick, NJ: Rutgers University Press, 2006.

Hall, Stuart, and Tony Jefferson. *Resistance through Rituals: Youth Subcultures in Post-War Britain*. 2nd ed. New York: Routledge, 2006.

Hambrick-Stowe, Charles E., and Institute of Early American History and Culture (Williamsburg). *The Practice of Piety: Puritan Devotional Disciplines in Seventeenth-Century New England*. Chapel Hill, NC: University of North Carolina Press, 1982.

Handelman, Don, and Galina Lindquist. *Ritual in Its Own Right: Exploring the Dynamics of Transformation*. New York: Berghahn, 2005.

Harner, Nevin Cowger. *Youth Work in the Church*. New York: Abingdon-Cokesbury, 1942.

Harris, James H. *Preaching Liberation*. Minneapolis, MN: Fortress, 1995.

Hart, Roderick P., and Suzanne M. Daughton. *Modern Rhetorical Criticism*. 3rd ed. Boston: Pearson/Allyn & Bacon, 2005.

Hauerwas, Stanley, and Samuel Wells, eds. *The Blackwell Companion to Christian Ethics*. Blackwell Companions to Religion. Malden, MA: Blackwell, 2004.

Hauerwas, Stanley, and William H. Willimon. *Resident Aliens: Life in the Christian Colony*. Nashville: Abingdon, 1989.

Haven, Elias. *Youthful Pleasures Must Be Accounted for, at the Day of Judgment a Sermon on Ecclesiastes Xi. 9. Preached (in Part) at the Second Precinct in Wrentham, May 27. 1741*. Boston: Printed and sold by J. Draper, 1742.

Hebard, Ebenezer. *A Sermon Delivered at Brandon, Lord's Day, October 23, A.D. 1814 Designed More Especially for the Benefit of the Youth*. Rutland, VT: Printed by Fay & Davison, 1814.

Heltzel, Peter, ed. *Chalice Introduction to Disciples Theology*. St. Louis, MO: Chalice, 2008.

Hendley, Steve. *From Communicative Action to the Face of the Other: Levinas and Habermas on Language, Obligation, and Community*. Lanham, MD: Lexington, 2000.

Herzog, Kristin. *Children and Our Global Future: Theological and Social Challenges.* Cleveland, OH: Pilgrim, 2005.

Hine, Thomas. *The Rise and Fall of the American Teenager.* New York: Bard, 1999.

Hiner, N. Ray, and Joseph M. Hawes. *Growing up in America: Children in Historical Perspective.* Urbana, IL: University of Illinois Press, 1985.

Holly, Israel, and Isaac Watts. Youth Liable to Sudden Death; Excited Seriously to Consider Thereof, and Speedily to Prepare Therefore the Substance of a Discourse, Delivered on the Day of the Funeral of Three Young Men, Who Were Killed by Lightning, at Suffield, May 20, 1766. 5th ed. Hartford, CT: Printed by Thomas Green, 1767.

Jagodzinski, Jan. *Youth Fantasies: The Perverse Landscape of the Media.* New York: Palgrave Macmillan, 2004.

James, Allison, and Alan Prout, eds. *Constructing and Reconstructing Childhood: Contemporary Issues in the Sociological Study of Childhood.* Washington, DC: Falmer, 1997.

Jenkins, Henry, ed. *The Children's Culture Reader.* New York: New York University Press, 1998.

Jensen, David Hadley. *Graced Vulnerability: A Theology of Childhood.* Cleveland, OH: Pilgrim, 2005.

Jeter, Joseph R., and Ronald J. Allen. *One Gospel, Many Ears: Preaching for Different Listeners in the Congregation.* St. Louis, MO: Chalice, 2002.

Johns, Cheryl Bridges. "What Can the Mainline Learn from Pentecostals About Pentecost?" *Journal for Preachers* 21.4 (1998) 3–7.

Kendal, Samuel. *Seven Sermons to Young Persons.* Boston: Munroe & Francis, 1814.

Kett, Joseph F. *Rites of Passage: Adolescence in America 1790 to the Present.* New York: Basic, 1977.

Kitwana, Bakari. *The Hip Hop Generation: Young Blacks and the Crisis in African American Culture.* New York: Basic Civitas, 2002.

———. *Why White Kids Love Hip-Hop: Wankstas, Wiggers, Wannabes, and the New Reality of Race in America.* New York: Basic Civitas, 2005.

Lakeland, Paul. *Theology and Critical Theory: The Discourse of the Church.* Nashville: Abingdon, 1990.

Lakoff, George, and Mark Johnson. *Metaphors We Live By.* Chicago, IL: University of Chicago Press, 1980.

Laqueur, Thomas Walter. *Religion and Respectability: Sunday Schools and Working Class Culture, 1780–1850.* New Haven, CT: Yale University Press, 1976.

Lash, Nicholas. *Theology on the Way to Emmaus.* London: SCM, 1986.

Lathrop, Gordon. Holy Things: A Liturgical Theology. Minneapolis: Fortress, 1993.

Lesko, Nancy. "Denaturalizing Adolescence: The Politics of Contemporary Representations." *Youth & Society* 28.2 (1996) 139–61.

———. *Act Your Age!: A Cultural Construction of Adolescence Critical Social Thought.* New York: Routledge/Falmer, 2001.

Lindbeck, George A. *The Nature of Doctrine: Religion and Theology in a Postliberal Age.* Philadelphia: Westminster, 1984.

Long, Thomas G. *Preaching and the Literary Forms of the Bible.* Philadelphia: Fortress, 1989.

———. *Testimony: Talking Ourselves into Being Christian.* San Francisco, CA: Jossey-Bass, 2004.

———. *The Witness of Preaching*. 2nd ed. Louisville, KY: Westminster John Knox, 2005.

Loomba, Ania. *Colonialism/Postcolonialism*. 2nd ed. New York: Routledge, 2005.

Lord, Benjamin. *Sober-Mindedness, an Excellent Character of Young Men Considered in a Discourse, Address'd to the Youth: (Being the Substance of Three Sermons) Delivered at Norwich; Chiefly on March 13, 1763*. Providence, RI: Printed and sold by William Godddard, 1763.

Loring, Israel. *The Duty and Interest of Young Persons to Remember Their Creator as It Was Shewn, in a Sermon Preach'd at Lexington, on a Day of Prayer, Set Apart to Implore the Blessing of God on the Rising Generation.: And at the Desire of Some Young Persons in the Town, Now Published*. Boston: Printed for Daniel Henchman, 1718.

Loveland, Anne C., and Otis B. Wheeler. *From Meetinghouse to Megachurch: A Material and Cultural History*. Columbia, MO: University of Missouri Press, 2003.

Luhr, Eileen. *Witnessing Suburbia: Christian Conservatives, "Family Values," And the Cultural Politics of Youth*. Berkeley, CA: University of California Press, 2009.

Lévinas, Emmanuel. *Totality and Infinity: An Essay on Exteriority*. Boston, MA: Martinus Nijhoff, 1979.

Macclintock, Samuel. *The Advantages of Early Piety a Sermon Preach'd at Greenland, in New-Hampshire, and Now Published at the Desire of a Number of Young People, to Whom It Is Inscribed, with Sincere Wishes, That It May Be Profitable for Their Instruction*. Portsmouth, NH: Printed by Daniel and Robert Fowle, 1770.

Mather, Cotton. *Youth under a Good Conduct: A Short Essay to Render Young People Happy, by Engaging Them in the Wayes of Early & Serious Religion: Made, at Boston-Lecture, 2.D. I.M. 1704*. Boston: Printed and sold by Timothy Green, 1704.

———. *Youth in Its Brightest Glory an Essay, Directing Them That Are Young in Age, to Become Strong in Grace, by the Word of God Abiding in Them.: Published by a Religious Society of Young Men, That Were the Hearers of It.: [Three Lines in Latin from Virgil]*. Boston: Printed & sold by T. Green, 1709.

———. *The Young Man Spoken to Another Essay, to Recommend & Inculcate the Maxims of Early Religion, Unto Young Persons; and Especially the Religion of the Closet. In a Sermon Preached Unto Them on a Special Occasion*. Boston: Printed by T. Green, for Samuel Gerrish, 1712.

———. *Vita Brevis an Essay, Upon Withering Flowers. Or, Mankind Considered, as First Flourishing, and Then Withering. In a Sermon, Preached on, the Joyful Death of a Valuable Youth; and the Awful Death of a Desirable Child, in the North Part of Boston*. Boston: Printed by John Allen, for Nicholas Boone, 1714.

———. *The City of Refuge the Gospel of the City Explained; and the Flight of a Distressed Sinner Thereunto, Directed and Quickened; with a Special Aspect on the Intentions of Early Piety.: [Two Lines from Samuel]*. Boston: Printed by T. Fleet and T. Crump, 1716.

———. *Columbanus. Or, the Doves Flying to the Windows of Their Saviour a Sermon to a Religious Society of Young People. June 4th. 1722.: [Five Lines in Latin]*. Boston: Printed by S. Kneeland, for J. Edwards, 1722.

———. *Juga Jucunda a Brief Essay to Obtain from Young People, an Early and Hearty Submission to the Yoke of Their Saviour, and His Religion.: With a Relation of the Glorious Peace and Joy, Which Brightened the Dying Hours of Mrs. Abiel Goodwin; Who Having Born the Yoke in Her Youth, Triumphantly Expired October 3. 1727.:*

A Sermon Preached at the Desire of the Deceased.: [One Line from Deuteronomy]. Boston: Printed for D. Henchman, 1727.

McClure, John S. "Narrative and Preaching: Sorting It All Out." *Journal for Preachers* 15.1 (1991) 24–9.

——. *The Roundtable Pulpit: Where Leadership and Preaching Meet.* Nashville: Abingdon, 1995.

——. *Other-Wise Preaching: A Postmodern Ethic for Homiletics.* St. Louis, MO: Chalice, 2001.

——. *The Four Codes of Preaching: Rhetorical Strategies.* Louisville, KY: Westminster John Knox, 2003.

——. *Listening to Listeners: Homiletical Case Studies.* St. Louis, MO: Chalice, 2004.

McClure, John S., and Nancy J. Ramsay. *Telling the Truth: Preaching About Sexual and Domestic Violence.* Cleveland, OH: United Church, 1998.

McKim, Donald K. *The Bible in Theology & Preaching.* Nashville: Abingdon, 1994.

McNemar, Richard, and Shakers, Presbytery of Springfield (Ohio). *The Kentucky Revival; or, a Short History of the Late Extraordinary Outpouring of the Spirit of God, in the Western States of America, Agreeably to Scripture Promises, and Prophecies Concerning the Latter Day: With a Brief Account of the Entrance and Progress of What the World Calls Shakerism, among the Subjects of the Late Revival in Ohio and Kentucky. Presented to the True Zion-Traveller, as a Memorial of the Wilderness Journey.* Joplin, MO: College Press, 1974.

Mercer, Joyce. *Welcoming Children: A Practical Theology of Childhood.* St. Louis, MO: Chalice, 2005.

Migliore, Daniel L. *Faith Seeking Understanding: An Introduction to Christian Theology.* 2nd ed. Grand Rapids: Eerdmans, 2004.

Miller, Mark. *Experiential Storytelling: (Re)Discovering Narrative to Communicate God's Message.* El Cajon, CA: Zondervan, 2003.

Miller-McLemore, Bonnie J. *Let the Children Come: Reimagining Childhood from a Christian Perspective.* Families and Faith Series. San Francisco, CA: Jossey-Bass, 2003.

——. "Children and Religion in the Public Square: 'Too Dangerous and Too Safe, Too Difficult and Too Silly.'" *Journal of Religion* 86.3 (2006) 385–401.

Min, Anselm Kyongsuk. *The Solidarity of Others in a Divided World: A Postmodern Theology after Postmodernism.* New York: T. & T. Clark International, 2004.

Mintz, Steven. *Huck's Raft: A History of American Childhood.* Cambridge, MA: Belknap Press of Harvard University Press, 2004.

Mitchell, Henry H. *Celebration and Experience in Preaching.* Nashville: Abingdon, 1990.

Moodey, Samuel. *The Vain Youth Summoned to Appear at Christ's Bar. Or, an Essay to Block up the Sinful Wayes of Young People, by Most Solemn Considerations, Relating to That Judgment Unto Which They Are Hastning in a Lecture-Sermon (June 25. 1701) Preached at York, in the Province of Main [Sic].* Boston: Printed and sold by Timothy Green, 1707.

Moore, Mary Elizabeth, and Almeda Wright, eds. *Children, Youth, and Spirituality in a Troubling World.* St. Louis, MO: Chalice, 2008.

Moore, R. Laurence. *Selling God: American Religion in the Marketplace of Culture.* New York: Oxford University Press, 1994.

Morris, Paul Judson. *Winning Youth for Christ.* Philadelphia: Judson, 1930.

Muir, James. *Ten Sermons.* Alexandria, VA: Cottom and Stewart, 1812.

Mulligan, Mary Alice. *Believing in Preaching: What Listeners Hear in Sermons*. St. Louis, MO: Chalice, 2005.

Muuss, Rolf Eduard Helmut, et al. *Theories of Adolescence*. 6th ed. New York: McGraw-Hill, 1996.

Nakayama, Thomas K., and Judith N. Martin, eds. *Whiteness: The Communication of Social Identity*. Thousand Oaks, CA: Sage, 1999.

"The New Year." *The Guardian and Monitor* 7.1 (1825) 3.

Newell, H. *Memoirs of Mrs. H. Newell, Wife of the Rev. S. Newell, American Missionary to India*. London: J.F. Dove, n.d.

Nichols, J. Randall. *The Restoring Word: Preaching as Pastoral Communication*. San Francisco, CA: Harper & Row, 1987.

Nieman, James R., and Thomas G. Rogers. *Preaching to Every Pew: Cross-Cultural Strategies*. Minneapolis: Fortress, 2001.

Palladino, Grace. *Teenagers: An American History*. New York: Basic, 1996.

Palmer, Parker J. *The Company of Strangers: Christians and the Renewal of America's Public Life*. New York: Crossroad, 1981.

Parker, Evelyn L. "Hungry for Honor: Children in Violent Youth Gangs." *Interpretation* 55.2 (2001) 148–60.

———. *Trouble Don't Last Always: Emancipatory Hope among African American Adolescents*. Cleveland, OH: Pilgrim, 2003.

———. *The Sacred Selves of Adolescent Girls: Hard Stories of Race, Class, and Gender*. Cleveland, OH: Pilgrim, 2006.

Pearson, Eliphalet, and American Society for Educating Pious Youth for the Gospel Ministry. *A Sermon Delivered in Boston before the American Society for Educating Pious Youth for the Gospel Ministry, Oct. 26, 1815*. Andover, MA: Printed by Flagg and Gould, 1815.

Perelman, Chaïm, and Lucie Olbrechts-Tyteca. *The New Rhetoric: A Treatise on Argumentation*. Notre Dame, IN: University of Notre Dame Press, 1969.

Poling, Daniel A. *Youth Marches!* Philadelphia: Judson, 1937.

Presbyterian Church in the U.S.A. Synod of Pittsburgh. "A Narrative." *The Western Missionary Magazine, and Repository of Religious Intelligence (1803–1805)* (1803) 99.

———. "A Short Narrative." *The Western Missionary Magazine, and Repository of Religious Intelligence (1803–1805)* (1803) 45.

Prince, Thomas, and Mather Byles. *Morning Health No Security against Sudden Arrest of Death before Night a Sermon Occasioned by the Very Sudden Death of Two Young Gentlemen in Boston, on Saturday January 14th, 1726,7.: Dedicated to the Youth of the Town*. 2nd ed. Boston: Printed for D. Henchman, 1727.

Providence Female Tract Society. *The Second Annual Report of the Providence Female Tract Society*. Providence, RI: Printed at the Rhode-Island American office, 1817.

Pufall, Peter B., and Richard P. Unsworth, eds. *Rethinking Childhood*. New Brunswick, NJ: Rutgers University Press, 2004.

Ramsey, G. Lee. *Care-Full Preaching: From Sermon to Caring Community*. St. Louis, MO: Chalice, 2000.

Rayner, Menzies. *A Dissertation Upon Extraordinary Awakenings or Religious Stirs; Conversion, Regeneration, or Change of Heart; Conference Meetings; Extraordinary Gifts in Extempore Prayer; Evangelical Preaching*. 2nd ed. Hudson, NY: William E. Norman, 1816.

Reid, Robert Stephen, ed. *Slow of Speech and Unclean Lips: Contemporary Images of Preaching Identity*. Eugene, OR: Cascade, 2010.

"Religion: Air Worship." *Time* 17.6 (1931).

Reynolds, David S. "From Doctrine to Narrative: The Rise of Pulpit Storytelling in America." *American Quarterly* 32.5 (1980) 479–98.

Riley, W. B. *Youth's Victory Lies This Way*. Grand Rapids: Zondervan, 1936.

Robbins, Duffy, and Doug Fields. *Speaking to Teenagers: How to Think About, Create, and Deliver Effective Messages*. Grand Rapids: Zondervan, 2007.

Robinson, Haddon W. *Biblical Sermons: How Twelve Preachers Apply the Principles of Biblical Preaching*. Grand Rapids: Baker, 1989.

Rogers, John, et al. *Death the Certain Wages of Sin to the Impenitent: Life the Sure Reward of Grace to the Penitent Together with the Only Way for Youth to Avoid the Former, and Attain the Latter.: Deliver'd in Three Lecture Sermons; Occasioned by the Imprisonment, Condemnation and Execution, of a Young Woman, Who Was Guilty of Murdering Her Infant Begotten in Whoredom.: To Which Is Added, an Account of Her Manner of Life & Death, in Which the Glory of Free Grace Is Displayed*. Boston: Printed by B. Green, and J. Allen, 1701.

Rollin, Betty, "Interfaith Divorce." *PBS* August 27, 2010. Online: http://www.pbs.org/wnet/religionandethics/episodes/august-27-2010/interfaith-divorce/6874/.

Roof, Judith, and Robyn Wiegman, eds. *Who Can Speak?: Authority and Critical Identity*. Urbana, IL: University of Illinois Press, 1995.

Rose, Lucy Atkinson. *Sharing the Word: Preaching in the Roundtable Church*. Louisville, KY: Westminster John Knox, 1997.

Satterlee, Craig Alan. *Ambrose of Milan's Method of Mystagogical Preaching*. Collegeville, MN: Liturgical, 2002.

Scheper-Hughes, Nancy, and Carolyn Fishel Sargent, eds. *Small Wars: The Cultural Politics of Childhood*. Berkeley, CA: University of California Press, 1998.

Schipani, Daniel S. *Religious Education Encounters Liberation Theology*. Birmingham, AL: Religious Education, 1988.

Skott-Myhre, Hans Arthur. *Youth and Subculture as Creative Force: Creating New Spaces for Radical Youth Work*. Toronto: University of Toronto Press, 2008.

Smith, Christian, and Melinda Lundquist Denton. *Soul Searching: The Religious and Spiritual Lives of American Teenagers*. New York: Oxford University Press, 2005.

Smith, Christine M. *Weaving the Sermon: Preaching in a Feminist Perspective*. Louisville, KY: Westminster John Knox, 1989.

———. *Preaching as Weeping, Confession, and Resistance: Radical Responses to Radical Evil*. Louisville, KY: Westminster Knox, 1992.

———. *Preaching Justice: Ethnic and Cultural Perspectives*. Cleveland, OH: United Church, 1998.

Smith, Ted A. *The New Measures: A Theological History of Democratic Practice*. New York: Cambridge University Press, 2007.

Soskice, Janet Martin. *Metaphor and Religious Language*. New York: Oxford University Press, 1985.

Stanford, John, and Charles I. S. Hazzard. *The Goodness of God in the Conversion of Youth a Sermon on the Death of Charles I.S. Hazzard, Son of the Late Alderman Hazzard, Who Died of the Late Epidemic, Aged 18 Years.: In Which Are Introduced, an Account of His Very Early Enjoyment of the Grace of God, and the Exercise of His*

Mind to the Period of His Death. Transcribed from the Diary Written with His Own Hand. New York: Printed by T. & J. Swords, 1799.

Stearns, Josiah, and Simon Peirce. *A Sermon, Preached at Epping, in New-Hampshire. On Lord's-Day, September 19, 1779.* Exeter, NJ: Printed, and sold by Zechariah Fowle, 1780.

Stillman, Samuel. Y*oung People Called Upon to Consider, That for Their Conduct Here, They Must Be Accountable Hereafter, at the Judgment Seat of Christ in a Sermon, Delivered on Wednesday Evening May 8, 1771, in Boston, at the Desire of a Number of Young Men.* Boston: Printed by John Boyles, 1771.

Stock, Harry Thomas. *Church Work with Young People.* Chicago: Pilgrim, 1929.

Stout, Harry S. *The New England Soul: Preaching and Religious Culture in Colonial New England.* New York: Oxford University Press, 1986.

Stout, Harry S., et al., eds. *Sermons and Discourses, 1739–1742, The Works of Jonathan Edwards.* New Haven, CT: Yale University Press, 2003.

Tanner, Kathryn. *Theories of Culture: A New Agenda for Theology Guides to Theological Inquiry.* Minneapolis: Fortress, 1997.

Tracy, David. *Plurality and Ambiguity: Hermeneutics, Religion, Hope.* San Francisco, CA: Harper & Row, 1987.

Trafton, Mark. "The Duties and Responsibilities of Young Men." *The American Pulpit* 1.5 (1845) 101–8.

Troeger, Thomas H., and H. Edward Everding. *So That All Might Know: Preaching That Engages the Whole Congregation.* Nashville: Abingdon, 2008.

Turner, Mary Donovan, and Mary Lin Hudson. *Saved from Silence: Finding Women's Voice in Preaching.* St. Louis, MO: Chalice, 1999.

Vadeboncoeur, Jennifer Andrea, and Lisa Patel Stevens. *Re/Constructing "The Adolescent": Sign, Symbol, and Body.* New York: Peter Lang, 2005.

Voelz, Richard W. "Oh Be Careful Little Eyes What You See: Preaching to Youth and Homiletical Analysis, A Case Study." *Practical Matters* 2 (2009). Online: http://practicalmattersjournal.org/issue/2/practicing-matters/oh-be-careful-little-eyes-what-you-see.

Wall, John. "Childhood Studies, Hermeneutics, and Theological Ethics." *Journal of Religion* 86.4 (2006) 523–48.

Wallach, Glenn. *Obedient Sons: The Discourse of Youth and Generations in American Culture, 1630–1860.* Amherst, MA: University of Massachusetts Press, 1997.

Weiner, Susan. *Enfants Terribles: Youth and Femininity in the Mass Media in France, 1945–1968.* Baltimore, MD: Johns Hopkins University Press, 2001.

Welch, Sharon D. *A Feminist Ethic of Risk.* Minneapolis: Fortress, 1990.

Weston, Sidney A., ed. *Sermons I Have Preached to Young People.* Chicago: Pilgrim, 1931.

Wheelwright, Philip Ellis. *Metaphor & Reality.* Bloomington, IN: Indiana University Press, 1962.

White, David F. *Dreamcare: A Theology of Youth, Spirit, and Vocation.* Eugene, OR: Cascade, 2013.

———. "Illusions of Postmodern Youth Ministry." *Journal of Youth Ministry* 6.1 (2007) 7–26.

———. *Practicing Discernment with Youth: A Transformative Youth Ministry Approach.* Cleveland, OH: Pilgrim, 2005.

Williams, Angie, and Crispin Thurlow. *Talking Adolescence: Perspectives on Communication in the Teenage Years.* New York: Peter Lang, 2005.

Williams, Patrick, and Laura Chrisman, eds. *Colonial Discourse and Post-Colonial Theory: A Reader.* New York: Columbia University Press, 1994.

Willimon, William H. *Peculiar Speech: Preaching to the Baptized.* Grand Rapids: Eerdmans, 1992.

———. *The Intrusive Word: Preaching to the Unbaptized.* Grand Rapids: Eerdmans, 1994.

Willingham, William F. "Religious Conversion in the Second Society of Windham, Connecticut, 1723–43: A Case Study." *Societas* 6.2 (1976) 109–19.

Wilson, Paul Scott. *The Four Pages of the Sermon: A Guide to Biblical Preaching.* Nashville: Abingdon, 1999.

———, ed. *The New Interpreter's Handbook of Preaching.* Nashville: Abingdon, 2008.

Youth's Guide to Happiness Consisting of Poems, Essays, & Sermons. Newark, NJ: John Tuttle, 1814.

Zepho. "The Days of Youth." *The Western Missionary Magazine, and Repository of Religious Intelligence* (1803–1805). (1804) 146.

Index